To Dennis

From Ernie   30/8/88

"Happy Sailing"

SEAMANSHIP HANDBOOK
for basic studies

by George J. Bonwick

Sixth edition revised by

Captain P. H. Adlam

STANFORD MARITIME LONDON

Stanford Maritime Limited
Member Company of the George Philip Group
12–14 Long Acre London WC2E 9LP

First published 1952
Fifth Edition 1971
Reprinted 1974
Sixth Edition 1978
© 1978 Stanford Maritime Limited

MADE AND PRINTED IN GREAT BRITAIN BY
THE GARDEN CITY PRESS LIMITED
LETCHWORTH, HERTFORDSHIRE
SG6 1JS

ISBN 0 540 07376 8

CONTENTS

Preface to the Sixth Edition   *page* v

Syllabus for examination   vi

1   THE SHIP   1

2   MANNING   22

3   ROPE—FIBRE, NYLON AND WIRE   33

4   KNOTS, BENDS, HITCHES AND WHIPPINGS   42

5   SPLICING   60

6   BLOCKS, HOOKS, SHACKLES AND TACKLES   71

7   DERRICK RIGS AND CARGO GEAR   79

8   TYPICAL CARGO SPACES   96

9   ANCHORS AND CABLES   108

10   THE MAGNETIC AND GYRO COMPASSES   119

11   STEERING GEAR   131

12   HELMSMANSHIP   137

13   LOG AND LEAD   141

14   MOORING   152

15   FIRE APPLIANCES   155

16   LINE-THROWING APPLIANCES   168

17   LOAD LINE AND DRAUGHT   174

18   SHIP'S MAINTENANCE AND DECK STORES   179

19   SAFETY ABOARD   192

20   HEAVY WEATHER   197

Glossary   199

Index   229

PREFACE TO FIFTH EDITION

When introducing the first edition of this well-known practical seamanship book, the author wrote:

> In whatever type of ship he may be serving, however, a seaman's job is similar. He is called upon to play a part in the smooth running of the floating community of which he is temporarily a member. If for any reason at all he fails to carry out his duties, someone else will have to carry them out for him, either until the ship reaches port or until the ship has completed her voyage. It therefore devolves upon every seaman to learn his job properly, and the principal object of this book is to assist him in that direction.

The ever-increasing size of cargo ships, particularly bulk carriers, coupled with the decrease in manning scales, has made the individual seaman's job as an integral member of the ship's crew even more important than it was at that time, and it is up to every seaman to learn both his job and the operation of the many new and complex items of equipment as quickly and as efficiently as possible.

To enable him to learn the basic elements of practical seamanship thoroughly, the entire contents of this book—chapter by chapter—have been systematically revised, amplified where necessary and brought into line with present-day requirements. Four comprehensive new chapters on Manning, Deck Stores, Safety and preparing for Heavy Weather have been added, together with many new illustrations. Used either on a pre-sea course or as a self-tutor, the book is a first-class aid to becoming an efficient practical seaman.

A word of warning. 'Seamanship' covers a wide variety of subjects and, like driving a car or a motor cycle, proficiency only comes with experience. Hatches and cargo-handling gear, steering gear and bridge equipment are becoming increasingly complicated, and a basic book of this kind can only show the most common types of equipment. The keen young seaman, anxious to learn his trade thoroughly, would be well advised as he encounters new designs, to find out all he can about them either from available literature or from the ship's officers, and systematically to note down details with operational working and diagrams for future reference. He should then be able either to write or talk fluently when asked such stock questions as 'Describe the steering gear or derrick rigs of your last ship.'

Conditions of service in the Merchant Navy are better now than they have ever been and the ambitious young seaman, whether apprentice or deck hand, must always bear in mind that while he is climbing the promotion ladder, these conditions will improve still further in the future. For those aspiring to officer status and not already studying, by correspondence course from one of the nautical colleges, for their Second Mate's Certificate, the Seafarers' Education Service, Mansbridge House, 207 Balham High Road, London, S.W.17 will be only too pleased to encourage, advise and provide education either by correspondence course or otherwise.

Captain J. P. Bowman

August 1966 Captain F. S. Campbell

PREFACE TO SIXTH EDITION

A critical reading of the 1966 preface leaves me with the feeling that what was said then, is in general terms every bit as relevant in 1978. This edition has of course been further updated, though two problems arise.

Firstly, I would have liked to have revised and extended both drawings and text on basic ship construction, but pressure of time has frustrated this.

Secondly, company technological advances vary considerably. At what point exactly, can one say, that this is now out of use aboard ship and that we should drop it. By the same token, there are so many items of sophisticated equipment in increasing, but not as yet in general use, that it would be easy to give way to the temptation to include them prematurely, this could merely confuse a young seaman.

To try and present everything outgoing, but not yet completely gone, with all the incoming but not yet generally arrived, and without extending the manual to a ridiculous extent, calls for super-human judgement.

I hope that I have achieved a reasonable balance.

P. H. Adlam

SYLLABUS FOR EXAMINATION FOR RATING OF EFFICIENT DECK HAND

NAUTICAL KNOWLEDGE

1. The meaning of common nautical terms.

2. The names and function of various parts of a ship; for example decks, compartments, ballast tanks, bilges, air pipes, strum boxes.

3. Knowledge of the compass card 0° to 360°. Ability to report the approximate bearing of an object in degrees or points on the bow.

4. Reading, streaming and handing a patent log.

5. Markings on a hand lead line, taking a cast of the hand lead and correctly reporting the sounding obtained.

6. Marking of the anchor cable.

7. Understanding helm orders.

8. The use of lifesaving and fire fighting appliances.

PRACTICAL WORK
(To be tested so far as possible by practical demonstration)

9. Knots, hitches and bends in common use:

Reef knot	Bowline and bowline on the bight
Timber hitch	Sheet bend, double and single
Clovehitch	Sheepshank
Figure of eight	Round turn and two half hitches
Wall and crown	Marlinspike hitch

To whip a rope's end using plain or palm and needle whipping. To put a seizing on rope and wire. To put a stopper on a rope or wire hawser, and derrick lift.

10. Splicing plaited and multi-strand manila and synthetic fibre rope, eye splice, short splice and back splice. Splicing wire rope, eye splicing using a locking tuck. Care in use of rope and wire.

11. Slinging a stage, rigging a bosun's chair and pilot ladder.

12. Rigging a derrick, Driving a winch; general precautions to be taken before and during the operation of a winch whether used for working cargo or for warping.

13. The use and operation of a windlass in anchor work and in warping. Safe handling of moorings with particular reference to synthetic-fibre ropes and self-tensioning winches. Precautions to be taken in the stowage of chain cable and securing the anchors for sea.

14. A knowledge of the gear used in cargo work and an understanding of its uses. General maintenance with particular reference to wires, blocks and shackles.

15. The safe handling of hatch covers including mechanical hatch covers, battening down and securing hatches and tank lids.

Chapter 1

THE SHIP

Examiners do not expect able seamen and young officers to be naval architects, but the syllabuses for E.D.H. and Second Mates' Certificates respectively show that they are required to know something about the construction of the ships in which they serve and earn their livelihood—the latter considerably more than the former, of course. Candidates for the certificate of Efficient Deck Hand, for example, are expected to know, among other things, 'the names and functions of various parts of the ship (e.g. decks, compartments, ballast tanks, strum boxes, etc.)', and there is no better way to learn than by observing on shipboard the manner in which the various parts of the structure are connected, and by asking one of the officers or engineers the correct names of the different components.

This chapter is not intended to be highly technical or comprehensive—on the contrary, it merely prepares the ground for further study in the case of those who aspire to senior professional status and serves as an introduction to ship construction generally. It does contain, however, all the information on the subject of construction required for the E.D.H. certificate.

The diagrams on pages 2 and 3 (inclusive) show a modern standard type of cargo ship, the main specifications of which are listed on page 3.

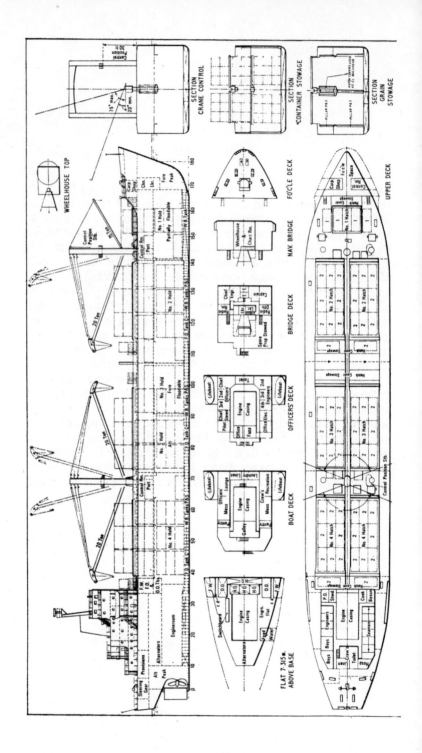

"CLYDE" DESIGN

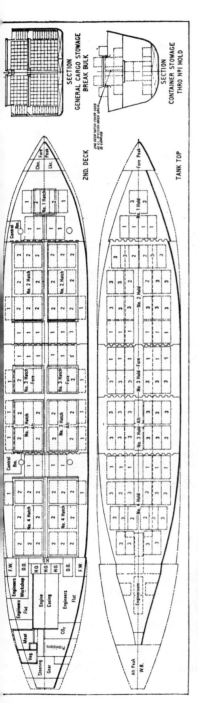

SECTION
GENERAL CARGO STOWAGE
BREAK BULK

2ND. DECK

SECTION
CONTAINER STOWAGE
THRO Nº1 HOLD

TANK TOP

PRINCIPAL PARTICULARS

Length (o.a.)	481ft 9in	(146·80m)
Length (b.p.)	454ft 0in	(138·40m)
Breadth (mld)	75ft 0in	(22·86m)
Depth to M.D.	45ft 0in	(13·72m)
Depth to 2nd deck	31ft 3in	(9·52m)
Normal load (design) draught	28ft 0in	(8·53m)
Corresponding d.w.	14 570 tons	14 800 tonnes
Summer load draught	32ft 10in	(10·00m)
Corresponding d.w.	18 470 tons	18 700 tonnes
Gross register (normal)	12 100 tons	
" " (tonnage mark)	7 800 tons	
Net register (normal)	8 200 tons	
" " (tonnage mark)	4 800 tons	

Capacities (approximate)

General cargo	Grain (with hatch covers forming CL divisions)	940 000ft³ (26 600in³)
General cargo	Bale (with hatches closed)	870 000ft³ (24 600in³)

Reprinted from Shipbuilding and Shipping Record

Containers

On deck		120
In holds and 'tween decks within hatches		270
In holds and 'tweendecks beyond hatches		60
	Total	450

Classification
Lloyd's Register Class ✠100A1 heavy cargoes
1965 Grain cargo regulations for the common loading of holds and 'tweendecks.
British BOT regulations
British, Suez & Panama tonnage

Propulsion (standard version)

Machinery	Sulzer 5RND68
M.C.R.	8 250 b.h.p.
Service rating	7 400 b.h.p.
Speed (trial)	15·4 knots

After peak. The space between the aftermost transverse watertight bulkhead and the stern frame. It is normally used as a trimming or fresh-water tank.

Air pipe. The pipe running from a fuel oil, water tank or double bottom tank to the upper deck to prevent air locks forming when liquid is pumped in or out. Air pipes are fitted at the outboard corners of each tank at the opposite end to the filling pipe.

Alleyway. A narrow corridor in passenger or crew accommodation.

Angle iron. A steel bar of right-angle shape, used for attaching one plate or bar to another. The toe of each flange is its free edge; the heel is where the flanges join to form a right angle; the inside of the angle is known as the fillet, and the whole inner surface, the bosom. Also termed angle bar.

Apron plate. (1) One of the plates fastened on either side of the stemhead and extending a short distance aft for housing the bow chocks or bow mooring pipes; (2) The waist-high plates usually provided on the fore ends of the navigating and lower bridges.

Backstays. Wire ropes forming part of the standing rigging. They stretch from mastheads (except in the case of lower masts) aft from the masts, and assist in supporting them against forward pull.

Balanced frames. Midship frames that are of equal shape and square flanged. There are thirty or more in the average cargo vessel, half the number being on each side.

Balanced rudder. A rudder in which part of the blade surface is forward of the axis. The water pressure on this portion helps to counterbalance that on the after part.

Ballast line. A system of piping installed for filling and emptying ballast tanks.

Ballast tanks. Tanks—double bottom, deep, and peak—for carrying water ballast.

Beam. A transverse member of the ship's framing supporting the deck.

Beam knees. Connections used in tying beams to frames and making the ship more rigid at deck corners.

Beam socket. A steel fitting riveted or welded to the inside of the hatch coaming to support the end of a hatch beam. Also termed beam carrier, or beam shoe.

Bedplate. Foundation framework for a marine engine, main or auxiliary.

Bending shackle. The shackle connecting the anchor cable to the anchor shackle. Always fitted crown aft. Also anchor shackle.

Bilge. In vessels with a double bottom the bilge is the channel formed by the tank margin plate and the outside shell. It runs fore and aft, being subdivided into sections by the ship's watertight bulkheads.

Bilge keel. Flat surfaces projecting from the hull at the turn of the bilge to reduce the ship's roll.

Bilge plating. Shell plating covering the outside of the frames in the bilge.

Bilge suction pipe. One of a system of drain pipes at the after end of each hold or compartment.

Bitts. Cast steel posts on board ship to which mooring lines are belayed. Also termed bollards when on the quay.

Boot-topping. (1) Surface of the outside plating between the light and the load lines. (2) Hard-drying erosion-resisting enamel applied to a ship's boot-topping or top-boot.

Bosom piece. A short piece of angle bar used as a butt strap or connecting piece for the ends of two angle bars, fitted inside the flanges of the bars it joins.

Boss. The central part of the propeller from which the blades protrude.

Bottom plating. Shell plating extending across the bottom or flat of the ship on both sides of the keel.

Bow. Forward part of a ship beginning where the sides trend inward and ending where they unite in the stem.

Bracket. Steel plate used to stiffen or tie beam angles to bulkheads, frames to longitudinals, etc.

Break. The point at which a deck erection or superstructure is discontinued.

Breakwater. Plates fitted forward on a weather deck to form a coaming against water shipped over the bow.

Breasthook. Horizontal plate of triangular shape fitted between the decks or deck stringers abaft the stem to strengthen the bow framing.

Breast plate. Horizontal plate connecting the bow chock plates of the stem.

Bridge. Partial deck extending from side to side of a vessel over a comparatively short length amidships, forming the top of a bridge house or partial superstructure.

Bridge house. Erection or superstructure amidship above the main deck, the top of which forms the bridge deck. Also centre castle.

Bulb angle. An angle with one of two unequal flanges having a bulb or rib at the toe of the longest flange.

Bulkhead. Any vertical partition separating shipboard compartments or spaces.

Bulkhead stiffeners. Bars, angles, bulb angles or channels welded or riveted vertically to a bulkhead to strengthen it.

Bulwark. The plating running along each side of a vessel above the weather deck.

Bulwark stay. A brace extending from the deck to a point near the top of the bulwark, to strengthen and support it. Also known as bulwark stanchion.

Bunker. Coal or fuel oil space below decks.

Butt strap. Strip of plating connecting the plates of a butt joint.

Cable stopper. A stopper provided for relieving the strain on the windlass cable holders when a vessel is riding to an anchor, as well as for holding the cable or 'hanging off' the anchor. Also called bow stopper, chain stopper, riding chock, etc.

Camber. The curvature or 'round up' given to decks, etc. Deck camber—desirable for all weather decks—is usually about one-fiftieth of breadth.

Cant beam. One of the deck beams extending radially abaft the transom beam at the stern.

Cargo battens. Long lengths of wood, about 152mm × 38mm (6 in. × $1\frac{1}{2}$ in.) fitted to the inboard side of frames in the holds of a steel vessel to keep cargo away from the shell plating and frames. Running fore and aft in cleats, which are bolted to the frames about 305mm (1 ft.) apart. Cargo battens are variously known as hold sparring, hold battens, spar ceiling, etc.

Cargo port. An opening in the ship's side for loading into, and discharging from, 'tween decks.

Cat davit. A davit from which the cat-fall was rigged in old-fashioned ships. It was used for lifting the anchor. Nowadays the solitary davit to be seen on the fo'c'sle head of many ships is used only for handling the Suez Canal searchlight.

Ceiling. The planks laid on a ship's tank top either in the square of the hatch only or from bilge to bilge.

Cellular double bottom. A double bottom subdivided into numerous small 'cells' by the vertical floors and intercostal girders.

Centre girder. The continuous fore and aft centreline member of every ship built with a double bottom. On the top of the girder is the centre strake of inner plating; at the bottom is the flat plate keel.

Centreline bulkhead. Longitudinal bulkhead extending between hatchways on the centreline.

Chain locker. The compartment located forward, beneath the windlass, for storing the anchor chain. In all modern ships it is subdivided by a longitudinal bulkhead extending from the bottom of the locker to about 914mm (3 ft.) from the deck above. For attaching the end shackles of the cables an eye with an elongated link is sometimes fitted on each side of the bulkhead.

Cleat. Metal fitting having two projecting arms to which halyards, guys, etc., are belayed. Fitting on frames to take spar ceiling. Fitting on hatch coaming to take battens, wedges and tarpaulins.

Coaming. The raised framework about any deck opening. A hatch coaming is the vertical plating built round a hatchway to prevent water from running below, and to serve as framework for the beams and hatch covers and to secure the tarpaulins. The coaming's purpose is also to restore the strength lost through cutting the deck by stiffening the edges of the hatch openings.

Cofferdam. A vacant and unused space between two bulkheads separating adjacent compartments. In tankers, cargo spaces are always isolated from other parts of the ship by means of cofferdams.

Coffin plate. A shell plate of distinctive shape which is used on the propeller bossing of a twin-screw vessel. It is the last plate in a flat plate keel.

Counter. That part of a ship's stern between the knuckle and the waterline. Underside of the stern which overhangs abaft the rudder.

Countersinking. The operating of cutting the sides of a drilled or punched hole into the shape of the frustum of a cone thereby providing a shoulder for the rivet, and allowing a flush surface to be maintained. Countersinking removes the metal made brittle by punching. The angle varies with the plate thickness.

Counter stern. A form of stern, now out of fashion, in which the upper works extend abaft the rudderpost.

Curtain plate. Vertical fore and aft plate connecting the outboard ends of a deck supported at the side by stanchions or open framework.

Cutwater. Forward edge of the stem at or near the water level.

Deadlight. Round metal plate which fits over a porthole to prevent compartments from being flooded in the event of the port glass breaking, and also to exclude light.

Deck. Principal component of a ship's structure. It consists of a planked or plated surface, roughly horizontal, extending between the ship's sides and resting on a tier of beams. Apart from their more obvious functions decks contribute to the structural strength and rigidity of the hull.

DECKS

After Deck. Part of a deck extending abaft the 'midship portion of a ship.

Awning deck. A deck fitted on a light superstructure from bow to stern. The space below is completely closed in and may be used for passengers or for stowing light cargo. Sometimes referred to as the hurricane deck.

Boat deck. Uppermost deck, of light construction, on which lifeboats are, and other lifesaving appliances may be, stowed.

Bridge deck. A partial deck, extending from side to side over a comparatively short length amidships, forming the top of a bridge space or partial superstructure.

Bulkhead deck. Uppermost continuous deck to which all transverse watertight bulkheads are carried. It is made watertight in order to prevent any compartment accidentally open to the sea from flooding the adjacent one.

Embarkation deck. The upper deck on which arrangements have been made and fittings provided for the embarkation into the lifeboats of passengers and crew.

Fiddley deck. Raised platform over the engine- and boiler-rooms.

Flush deck. An upper deck which has no fo'c'sle, bridge, or poop erection extending from side to side.

Forecastle deck. That which extends from the stem over the fo'c'sle.

Freeboard deck. Uppermost complete deck having permanent means of closing all openings in its weather portions. In flush-deck ships, and ships with detached superstructures, the freeboard deck is the upper deck; in other types, with complete superstructures, it is the deck below the superstructure deck.

Hurricane deck. An upper deck of light scantlings above the superstructures. Used as a promenade deck for passengers.

Lower deck. The lowest deck in two- and three-deck ships. Next to the lowest in ships having four or more decks.

Main deck. Principal deck in a ship with several decks, or to the deck next below a complete upper deck.

Orlop deck. Partial deck below the lower deck. Also, the lowest deck in a ship having four or more decks.

Platform deck. A partial deck built in the hold below the lowest complete deck, usually without camber.

Poop deck. A deck extending from the stern forward over a poop erection. A partial deck over the main deck at the stern.

Promenade deck. An upper superstructure deck, without bulwarks, in passenger ships.

Quarter deck. The after part of the upper deck. If there is a poop, as far aft as the break of the poop.

Raised fore-deck. Forward portion of an upper deck, between bridge and fo'c'sle, raised above main deck level thereby forming a structural discontinuity.

Raised quarter-deck. After portion of a weather or upper deck which is raised a few feet above the forward portion.

Shade deck. A very light deck not enclosed at the sides and supported by stanchions.

Strength deck. Uppermost complete deck providing resistance to longitudinal bending.

Sun deck. Uppermost deck in large passenger ships. Also known as the sports deck, it is frequently used as a boat deck, providing at the same time room for various sports.

Superstructure deck. A continuous deck, of light scantlings, upon which the superstructures (poop, bridge and fo'c'sle) are built. It is usually the first deck above the strength deck and is also known as the awning or shelter deck.

Tonnage deck. The deck from which a ship's tonnage is measured. The tonnage deck in vessels having more than one deck is the second one from the keel. In other vessels it is the upper deck.

'Tween deck. Any deck below the upper deck and above the lowest deck.

Upper deck. The topmost watertight deck extending continuously throughout the entire length of the ship.

Weather deck. An uncovered deck exposed to the weather. The upper, awning, or shelter decks or the uppermost continuous deck, exclusive of fo'c'sle, bridge and poop, which are also exposed to the weather.

Well deck. The open deck between fo'c'sle and bridge-house and bridge-house and poop in a three-island vessel.

Accommodation ladder. This ladder is the usual method of boarding or leaving the ship, particularly when at anchor or moored. An alternative method is the use of a portable gangway from the afterdeck to the quay and is normally used when the ship is not too high out of the water.

Deckhouse. A light structure—which does not extend from side to side—on an upper or weather deck.

Deck stops. Rudder stops secured to the deck in way of the tiller or quadrant to limit the sweep to 35 deg.

Deep floor. Any of the floors in the forward or after end of a vessel. Due to the converging sides of ships in the bow and stern, floors become deeper at the ends.

Deep frame. A frame about 50 per cent. deeper than an ordinary frame.

Deep strake. A strake of shell plating terminating at some distance from the stem or stern frame and abutting against a stealer plate merging two strakes into one.

Deep tanks. Hold compartments specially strengthened and equipped to carry water ballast or liquid cargo.

Depth. Vertical distance measured at the middle of the ship's length from the top of the keel or ceiling to the top of the upper deck at the sides amidships.

Derrick. A swinging boom over or near a hatchway, supported by a topping lift and controlled laterally by guys. Cargo derricks are made of wooden spars, lattice girder or steel tubing.

Derrick band. A steel band fitted at the head of a cargo boom or derrick. It has loose links for the topping lift block (or eye of the derrick span) and head block, and lugs for port and starboard guy pendants.

Derrick guy. A wire pendant, with rope tackle, secured to the derrick band on each side for trimming and steadying purposes.

Dished plate. A plate of 'U' shape used for connecting the stem and stern-post to the keel.

Displacement. The number of tons (1 ton = 2,240 lb.) of water displaced by a vessel. In salt water a ton measures 991 cu. decimetres (35 cu.ft.).

Docking plug. A brass, screwed set pin about 25½mm (1 in.) in diameter. It is fitted in the garboard strake of the shell plating at the bottom of each compartment to drain off water remaining in the ballast tanks when the ship is in dry dock. Also known as the drain plug, bottom plug.

Donkey boiler. A small boiler supplying steam to the auxiliaries when a ship is in port.

Double bottom. The general term for all watertight spaces contained between the outside bottom plating, the tank top and the margin plates.

Dry tank. Part of a ship's double bottom, under the boilers, in which no water is carried, preventing any possible effects of corrosion brought about by the combined action of dampness and heat.

Duct keel. A keel built of plates and angles in box form extending in the fore part of ships with a double bottom. It is used to house ballast and other piping which would otherwise have to pass through the double bottom.

End coaming. Athwartship coaming of a hatchway.

Engine-room. A compartment in which the main propulsion machinery is located.

Ensign staff. A flagstaff at the stern from which the national flag is usually flown.

Escape hatch. A small hatch cut in a 'tween or weather deck for the exit of workers engaged in trimming coal or grain. Also trimming hatch.

Escape trunk. Emergency exit—from the lower part of a vessel to the weather deck—generally to be found at the after end of a shaft tunnel.

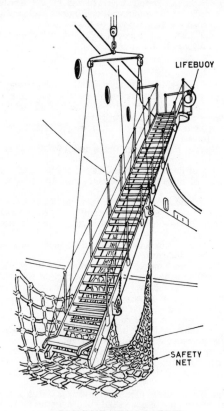

ACCOMMODATION LADDER

Eyebolt. A bolt having either a head looped to form a worked eye, or a solid head with a hole drilled through it forming a shackle eye.

Eye plate. A plate or casting with an eye formed solid with the plate.

Eyes. That part of a ship's bows near the hawse holes.

Fairlead. A term applied to fittings or devices guiding a rope or chain in the required direction.

Fiddley. An opening or trunkway through which the boiler uptakes, stokehold ventilators, etc., are led. At the top deck, or just above, it is decked over with light plating. Small hatchways with gratings and steel covers are provided.

Fire and bilge pump. A general service pump with independent sea suction and overboard delivery. It is used for keeping the bilges free of water, washing decks, and as an auxiliary fire pump.

Flange. Turned edge of a plate, shape, girder or section which acts to resist a bending moment.

Flare. The outward spread from the waterline to the rail at the bow.

Flat plate keel. The heavy central bottom strake of shell plating to which the bottom angles of the centre girder or vertical keel are riveted, or to which the bottom of the vertical keel is welded. Flat plate keels have superseded bar keels in most types of commercial vessels.

Flat plate keelson. Horizontal plate laid on top of the floors and riveted to them and to the vertical keel plate.

Floor. Structural member in the bottom of a ship, usually at every frame, and running athwartships from bilge to bilge.

Floor ceiling. Planking fitted on the tank top in the cargo holds either in the square of the hatch only or from bilge to bilge.

Forecastle rail. Bars extending between stanchions around the fo'c'sle.

Forefoot. Intersection of the curved portion of the stem with the keel.

Forepeak. Space between the collision bulkhead and the stem. When made watertight, as it usually is, it is used as a trimming or domestic water tank.

Frame. One of the transverse girders forming the ribs of the hull and extending from the keel to the highest continuous deck. Frames act as stiffeners holding the outside plating in shape and maintaining the transverse form of the ship.

Freeboard. Vertical distance measured on the ship's side amidships from the load waterline to the upper side of the freeboard deck or a point corresponding to it.

Freeing port. A large opening in the bulwarks just above the deck. It is normally fitted with a flap cover which opens outward to allow water shipped on deck to run freely overboard. Also called wash port, clearing port.

Gangway port. An opening in the ship's side, or a hinged section of the bulwarks, for providing access for people or to facilitate the handling of cargo.

Garboard strake. Strake of plating next to the keel on each side.

Goalpost mast. A type of mast consisting of two vertical steel posts placed athwartships equidistant from the centre-line.

Grated hatch. Wood or steel open cover used for closing the hatchway whilst permitting ventilation.

Guard chain. Short link galvanised chain used with portable stanchions around hatchway openings, etc.

Guard rail. Uppermost of a series of rails around an upper deck made of wood. It must be at least 1·67m (3 ft. 6 in.) above the deck.

Gudgeon. One of several lugs projecting from the after side of the stern or rudder post to support the rudder. Gudgeons are cast with, forged on, bolted or welded to the sternpost.

Gunwale. Upper edge of a ship's or boat's side.

Hatchway. Rectangular opening in a ship's deck affording access to the compartment below.

Hawse. That part of a ship's bow in which are the hawse holes for the anchor chains.

Hawse hole. One of the cylindrical holes in the bows of a vessel on each side of the stem, into which the hawse pipes are fitted.

Hawse pipe. A cylindrical or elliptical pipe through which the anchor cable runs.

Hold pillar. A stanchion which extends from the tank top to the lowest tier of deck beams.

Hold stringer. Fore-and-aft girders on the vessel's side above the turn of the bilge.

Inner bottom. The tank top.

Intercostal. Longitudinal parts of the hull's structure which, on account of obstructions, cannot be worked continuous and must be cut in comparatively short lengths between the vertical floors.

Intermediate frame. A frame in the double bottom which has no floor plate, in ships with floor plates fitted to alternate frames.

Jack staff. A small flagstaff at the stem head on which merchant ships hoist their owner's house-flag or Pilot Jack and warships the Union Jack.

Keel. The main centreline structural member running fore and aft along the bottom of a ship.

Keelson. Fore-and-aft centre line girder extending from stem to sternpost. It is located either above or between the floor plates. In a ship with a double bottom it is usually termed a centre girder or vertical keel.

Lazarette. Space used as a store-room above the after peak.

Length between perpendiculars. Distance between the forward and after perpendiculars of the stem bar and stern post.

Lifting pad. One of the eye plates attached to the outside shell plating aft for hooking tackles used in lifting the rudder or propeller.

Lightening hole. One of the numerous large apertures in floor plates, side girders, tank bracket plates, etc. In double bottom ships they provide access to the different cells, but this is incidental, as their name implies, to their function of reducing the ship's weight and thereby increasing its earning capacity.

Lower hold. Interior below the lowest deck.

Mail room. Compartment where mail is stowed.

Manhole. Round or oval-shaped opening in tank tops, tanks, boilers, etc., fitted with watertight or steamtight cover.

Manhole cover. Watertight, steamtight, or oiltight cover used for closing a manhole. Also called manhole door.

Manhole dog. A drop forging used to hold a manhole cover in place.

Margin clip. Angle clip which connects the bilge bracket to the margin plate. Also called margin lug.

Margin plate. A longitudinal plate which bounds the double bottom at the turn of the bilge. The lower edge is fitted normal to the shell to which it is attached by a continuous angle bar; the top edge is flanged over horizontally and is riveted or welded to the tank top.

Mast. Masts of steamers and motorships are used for navigational purposes and to provide attachments for derricks. They are supported in a fore-and-aft direction by stays, which are named according to the mast they support, and the sides by shrouds. The first mast from the stem is the foremast, the second the mainmast, and the third the mizzenmast. It is now rare for power-driven ships to have more than two masts.

Mast band. A steel band fitted with a number of lugs for taking the blocks of various purchases.

Mast carling. A carling placed on each side of a mast hole between the beams to support the partners.

Mast coat. A conical-shaped canvas cover lashed around the lower part of the topmast and the top of the lowermast over the securing wedges to prevent the entry of water.

Mast collar. An angle bar fitted around the mast hole in a steel deck, the horizontal flange being riveted to the deck and the vertical flange to the mast plating.

Mast house. A small deckhouse built around a mast, serving as a support for the derricks and as a store for deck gear. Wire reels and hold ventilators are usually to be seen on top of a mast house.

Mast ladder. A steel ladder attached to a mast by clips. It extends from just above the upper deck or mast house to the navigation light bracket, or to the crosstrees.

Mast partner. Frames or pieces of planking fitted in apertures of the deck for the support of the masts and rabbeted in the mast carlings.

Mast truck. A small circular piece of wood capping the top of a mast, and fitted with sheave or sheaves for the flag halyards.

MAST TRUCK

Messroom. A room in which crew members have their meals.

Midship section. A plan of a ship's transverse section on which is indicated the arrangement of the structural parts of the hull.

Mizzenmast. The aftermost mast of a three-masted ship and the third mast from forward in ships with more than three masts.

Mooring bitts. Cast-iron standards placed in pairs for belaying mooring lines. Also termed mooring bollards, they are secured to the deck at an angle affording the best lead to the mooring pipes and close enough to the windlass winch or capstan to facilitate transferring the lines speedily.

Mooring pipe. Elliptical openings in the bulwarks with rounded edges to take the mooring lines.

Mushroom ventilator. A deck ventilator serving hold or cabin spaces. The draught is regulated by screwing or unscrewing the hood.

Oxter plate. A shell plate moulded into shape and riveted to the stern frame in way of rudderpost head.

Paint locker. A compartment usually under the fo'c'sle head used for storing paints, paintbrushes, oils, etc.

Panting. Vibratory motion of the frames and plating of a vessel caused by the force of the waves against bows and stern when the vessel labours in a heavy sea.

Panting beam. One of the additional beams at the forward and after ends of screw-propelled ships. Its function is to stiffen the shell plating against panting.

Panting frame. One of the heavy frames fitted to withstand panting.

Panting stringer. One of the fore-and-aft girders in the bow and stern framing between the side stringers to counteract panting of frames and plating.

Partner plate. A strong deck plate through which the mast hole is pierced. It is generally stiffened by a bulb angle coaming.

Peak. Name given to the lower space forward of No. 1 bulkhead and abaft the aftermost watertight bulkhead. Peaks are invariably used as trimming tanks.

Pillar. A column supporting a deck beam or any other part of the structure in a vessel.

Pintle. One of the heavy pins on the forward edge of the rudder frame, by which the rudder is hinged to the gudgeons of the stern- or rudder-post, around which it pivots.

Pintle bearing. A steel disc fitted into the bottom gudgeon of a rudder frame to minimise the friction of the rudder about its axis.

Plated mast. A hollow steel cylinder made of riveted or welded plating and strengthened inside by angle bars.

Plug hatch. A thick airtight hatch with tapered edges and lined with insulating material. It is fitted over a refrigerator compartment to prevent the escape of cold air.

Port hole. A circular opening provided in the sides of a vessel or super-structure to give light and ventilation to passenger and crew accommodation. It consists of a fixed frame riveted to the outside plating, with a brass frame hinged to it. The latter is fitted with thick and strong clear glass. When closed it is watertight. Also called side scuttle.

Propeller aperture. Space provided between the propeller post and sternpost for the propeller.

Propeller boss. Central part of a ship's propeller from which the blades stand out.

Propeller frame. The framing around a propeller. It includes the rudder post, propeller post, bridge piece and sole piece.

Propeller lock nut. Large nut by which a screw propeller is secured on its shaft.

Propeller post. Forward post of the stern frame, on vessels having a centre-line propeller providing a support for the stern tube and propeller shaft as well as a joining frame for the converging sides of the ship at the stern.

Propeller shaft. Aftermost section of shafting carrying propeller. Also called tail shaft, screw shaft.

Pump room. Compartment in tankers where the pumping equipment for the cargo is fitted.

Quadrant tiller. A rudder tiller in the form of an arc of a circle, a half circle, or a complete circle. It consists of a casting or a forged hub with arms.

Rake. Inclination from the perpendicular of a mast, funnel, stem or stern-post.

Raking stem. A stem having a forward rake or extending beyond the forward perpendicular. It assists towards minimising underwater damage in case of collision, apart from improving a ship's appearance.

Reverse frame. A bar riveted to the upper edge of the floor plate on the side opposite to the frame bar, and back to back to the latter above the head of the floor.

Rider plate. A horizontal fore-and-aft plate riveted to the top angles of a centreline keelson running above the floors.

Ringbolt. An eyebolt with a ring worked through the eye. Used on hatch coamings for securing derrick guys, and elsewhere.

Roller chock. A warping chock for mooring lines, fitted with one or more vertical rollers. It is also known as a roller fairlead.

Rudder. A device used for steering and manoeuvring. The most common type consists of a flat surface of steel hinged at its forward end to the stern- or rudder post and rounded at its after end.

Rudder angle indicator. A mechanical appliance indicating the angle the rudder makes with the fore-and-aft line of the ship. Also called helm indicator.

Rudder arm. One of the forgings projecting radially from the rudderstock to which the rudder plate is fastened.

Rudder blade. The main flat portion of the rudder. Narrow and deep rudder blades develop more pressure and require a smaller force to operate than shallow ones.

Rudder brake. A locking device fitted to the rudderhead to keep the rudder steady in case of damage or when changing from one gear (power) to the other (hand). Lloyd's Register of Shipping requires that all vessels 76·2m (250 ft.) long or over shall have power-operated steering gear and makes compulsory the provision of a rudder brake.

Rudder carrier. A fitting placed inboard, either where the rudder stock traverses the shell plating or directly under the tiller. In addition to taking the radial thrust of the rudderstock it carries the whole weight of the rudder, the stock, and the tiller.

Rudder crosshead. An athwartship metal piece bolted and keyed to the top of the rudderhead to which the links of the steering gear are secured.

Rudder eye. Eyebolt fitted at the top of the rudder stock. Used for taking the weight of the stock when shipped or unshipped.

Rudder frame. The framing of a rudder to which the plating forming the rudder blade is attached.

Rudderhead. Continuation of the stock, above the blade, on which the quadrant or tiller is fitted.

Rudder quadrant. A casting or forging by means of which the turning power is transmitted to the rudderhead. Although termed a quadrant it does not necessarily form the quarter of a circle.

Rudder stops. Small projections fitted on the rudder stock and/or on the sternpost the faces of which make contact when the rudder has reached its maximum permissible angle.

Rudder trunk. A casing built around the rudderhead to prevent water entering the hull.

Saddle hatch. Small bunker hatchway situated over the boilers or between them and the engines. It consists of a trunk or shaft the sides of which open into the upper or lower side bunkers, and the bottom being shaped like an inverted V or saddle.

Samson post. A short tubular mast from which a derrick is supported and stayed. Also termed derrick post.

Scupper. One of the drains set in decks to drain away water. Scuppers are fitted in the gutters of waterways on open decks and in the corners of enclosed decks, and connect to pipes leading overboard.

Scupper hole. A drain hole cut through the gunwale angle bar and adjoining shell plate to allow water to run directly overboard from the deck.

Scupper pipe. One of the pipes by which the water from a deck scupper is drained over the ship's side. Those in the weather portions of the decks are led overboard. Those in fully enclosed superstructures on the freeboard deck and on decks below the freeboard or bulkhead deck are led to the bilges. They may also be led overboard if fitted with non-return (or storm) valves as required for the sanitary discharges.

Sea cock. A cock fitted to the ship's side plating. Used in flooding ballast tanks, supplying water to sanitary and fire pumps, and for blowing down boilers.

Self-closing door. An installation used on passenger vessels in which water-tight doors are remotely operated by a hydraulic pressure system, enabling them to be closed simultaneously from the bridge by the officer in charge or separately at the door from either side of the bulkhead.

Semi-balanced rudder. A balanced rudder in which the blade forward of the stock does not extend vertically to the full height of the blade situated abaft the stock. The forward blade area is about 10 per cent less in surface than with the fully balanced rudder.

Shafting. The medium by which the motion of the engines is transmitted to the propeller screws. The after section carrying the propeller is called the propeller or tail shaft, the section fitted to work in the thrust bearing to transmit the thrust of the propeller to the ship is called the thrust shaft; the section in the stern tube, the stern tube shaft, and the intermediate sections are known as line shafting.

Sheer. The fore-and-aft curvature of the deck at side between stem and sternpost.

Sheer strake. Strake of shell plating running next to the main, or strength, deck, its upper edge having the curvature or sheer of the vessel. The sheer strake is always of greatest thickness.

Shell plating. Outer plating of a vessel, comprising bottom plating, bilge plating and side plating. Shell plates are numbered and lettered, each strake corresponding to a letter, the garboard strake, i.e. the one next to the keel, being known as 'A' strake. The numbers of plates may run from forward to aft or from aft to forward.

Shoe plate. A plate connecting the keel and sternpost. Its after end extends right under and around the stern frame.'

Shroud. One of a number of wires extending on each side of a masthead to the sides of the ship to provide lateral support for a mast.

Side plating. Shell plating extending upwards from the curve of the bilge.

Side stringer. A longitudinal girder running along a ship's side above the bilge.

Skylight. A wood or metal structure built over a weather-deck opening to afford light and ventilation to the spaces below.

Sole piece. In single-screw ships, this is the fore-and-aft piece forming the lower part of the stern frame extending from the propeller post to the rudderpost. Also known as the heel piece.

Solid floor. A floor consisting of a continuous plate or of a range of intercostal plates extending from centreline to bilges.

Solid frame. A frame consisting of a single bar such as an angle bar, bulb angle or channel, as distinguished from a built-up frame.

Sounding pipe. A pipe running vertically from an upper deck to the ship's bottom so that the height of water or liquid in any compartment or tank can be measured by means of a sounding rod attached to a line and lowered in the pipe. At the deck they are fitted with a brass screw plug.

Spare bunker. Coal bunker in cargo ships which may be used for either coal or cargo. Also called reserve bunker.

Stanchion. A vertical structural member between decks.

Standing rigging. Semi-permanent wire rigging—shrouds, stays and backstays—which acts chiefly to support the masts.

Stealer. A shell plate of about double width at one end, located near the stem or stern. It takes the combined butts of a through strake and of a drop strake.

Steering column. A pedestal of non-magnetic metal supporting the steering wheel. An indicator is usually fitted on the top or at the side of the column to show the rudder angle, and there is frequently a similar indicator to show the angle transmitted by the steering wheel.

Steering engine. A steam, electric or hydraulic-power engine used for operating the rudder.

Steering gear. The steering wheel, leads, steering engine, and fittings by which the rudder is turned. Steering gear comprises three distinct items:

1. The tiller or quadrant fixed on the rudderhead.
2. The engine or hand wheel giving the necessary power for moving the tiller which may be placed close to the steering apparatus or at a distance.
3. The controlling or transmission gear for the engine.

Steering rod. A length of straight rod connected to the steering wheel chains.

Steering wheel. A wheel which controls the movements of a ship's rudder, and so constructed that the spokes are continued through the rim for a distance sufficient to provide a good grip for the helmsman.

Stem. The upright post or bar of the bow. Usually a casting or forging.

Stern. The after part.

Stiffener. Sections or shapes used for increasing the rigidity of plating, as bulkhead stiffeners.

Strake. A range of plates abutting against each other and extending the whole length of the ship.

Stream anchor. An anchor stowed at the stern and employed with a bower anchor in narrow waterways where there is no room for the vessel to swing with the tide. Stream anchors in modern vessels are frequently of the stockless type. Also called stern anchor.

Stringer. Fore-and-aft strength member girder. There are two sets of these girders in the framing of the usual cargo ship, the keelsons or longitudinals at the bottom, and the side stringers on the sides above the bilges.

Stringer plate. The outer strake of plating on a deck or the plates attached to the top flanges of any tier of beams at the sides of a vessel. Also called deck stringer.

Sunken manhole. A manhole in which the cover is below deck or tank-top level.

Taffrail. The railing about a ship's stern.

Tank top. Plating forming the top part of a double bottom. In cargo holds it is the flooring on which the cargo rests. Also called inner bottom.

Tie beam. A wood or steel batten fitted over each range of hatch covers, for extra security, after the tarpaulins have been battened down. It is held by a strong screw bolt at each end. Usually called a hatch locking bar.

Tonnage hatch. A small hatchway fitted aft on the shelter deck in accordance with Tonnage Rules so that the space below deck may be exempt from tonnage measurement.

Tonnage opening. A well in the uppermost deck of a shelter-deck vessel which has only temporary means of closing. This arrangement is designed to secure exemption from tonnage measurement of the space included between the main and upper decks.

Transom. The framework of the stern at the sternpost. The floor, frame and beam which form the aftermost transverse member are named transom floor, transom frame and transom beam.

Transom beam. A deck beam at the after end situated over the sternpost and bracketed at each end to the transom frame.

Transom floor. A floor connected amidships to the top of the sternpost.

Transom frame. The aftermost frame. It is riveted to the head of the sternpost and from it the cant frames radiate.

Trimming hatch. Small hatch pierced in the 'tween decks of a vessel loading grain in bulk, through which grain is poured so as to bring it close up to the deck at the sides, and also to permit cargo workers to escape from the lower holds after trimming the grain.

Tripod mast. A mast made of three legs. Tripod masts obviate the necessity for lower rigging.

Tubular derrick. A steel derrick consisting of large sections of tubing joined together, or made of one single, solid-drawn tube.

Tumble home. Inward inclination of a ship's sides near the upper deck.

Uptake. Conduit made of light plating connecting the smoke-box with the lower funnel. It conveys the smoke and hot gases of combustion from the boilers to the funnel.

Ventilator coaming. That part of a ventilator trunk which extends above a weather deck and to which the ventilator cowl is fitted.

Waist. The central part of a ship. The portion of the upper deck between poop and forecastle.

Waist plate. Shell plate or bulwark plate which sweeps down at the break of the poop, bridge house, or forecastle deck to the next deck below.

Watertight bulkhead. One of the main vertical partitions in a ship. The minimum number of main transverse watertight bulkheads is four for vessels with the machinery amidships and three when the machinery is aft. Watertight bulkheads also contribute to the structural strength of the ship, and act as safeguards against the spread of fire.

Watertight door. A door in a watertight bulkhead so constructed that when closed it will prevent water under pressure from passing through.

Watertight floor. A solid floor placed at the end of a ballast tank, or well, also under transverse bulkheads, forming one of the sub-divisions of the double bottom.

Waterway. The gutter formed along the sides of a steel weather deck by the waterway angle bar and the gunwale bar.

Web frame. A frame composed of a web plate with bars riveted or welded to each other. Web frames are fitted at every fourth, fifth or sixth ordinary frame when there are no hold beams or in spaces such as engine- or boiler-rooms where there is a great depth of side unsupported between the bottom and the lowest deck.

Web plate. A wide girder plate, as in a web frame or hatch beam, usually reinforced by angle bars on both sides.

Wheelhouse. A house built of wood or steel over the steering wheel as a protection for the helmsman.

OIL TANKERS

There is a tendency nowadays for ships to become more and more specialised for particular trades and the bulk carrier is an increasingly common type. By far the most numerous type of bulk carrier is the oil tanker which is highly specialised and easily recognisable. Tankers range in size from small coasters to ships capable of carrying over 100,000 tons. With the exception of the very largest passenger liners the latter are, in fact, the biggest ships afloat.

Characteristically the engine and boiler rooms of a tanker are placed aft. This arrangement avoids the risk of having machinery and boiler spaces in the middle of the range of compartments which have to carry flammable liquid cargo. Furthermore, the cargo-carrying part of the ship is not divided into two separate sections and no oil-tight propeller shaft tunnel, passing through the cargo spaces, is necessary. The crew accommodation is located aft with some officers' accommodation in the bridge house, or centre castle structure, commonly located amidships. Nowadays it is becoming accepted practice to build the bridge of the tanker aft too, so that there is no 'midships house above the cargo tanks. There are many advantages in this design and and it seems likely to become universal practice in the future, not only for oil tankers but for most bulk carriers. The poop, the 'midships house where fitted and the forecastle head are linked by a fenced gangway called the flying bridge in British ships (or the catwalk in American). This provides ready access for the crew between one part of the ship and another, and also carries steam and water pipes, electric cables and other necessary services between the various parts of the ship.

Tankers are immensely strong. They have to be because of the great uninterrupted length of cargo space. So that they will not bend unduly or break in two when full of cargo and working in a seaway, their internal structure is so designed that the required strength lengthwise is achieved. The hull, which carries the liquid cargo as if it were itself a huge tank, is very closely sub-divided, by a number of longitudinal and transverse bulkheads, into an egg-box pattern. Commonly two bulkheads (but sometimes even three or four) run the length of the ship, and any number between six and fifteen run transversely. Thus the ship is divided into a number of centre tanks with a port and starboard wing tank alongside each. Several purposes are served by such complex subdivision. Much of the strength of the ships depends upon it and the presence of the bulkheads is necessary to keep her stable when she is carrying cargo or ballast. If they did not exist the liquid would surge about them when the ship was working in a seaway and would eventually reach a momentum sufficient to capsize her. This is known as 'free-surface effect' and is much reduced by bulkheads or washplates. The egg-box pattern of tanks, of course, enables the

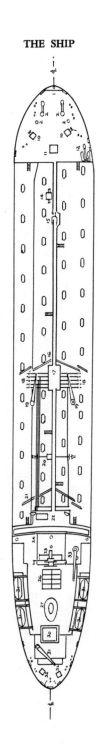

PLAN OF SUPER-TANKER

(1) Jackstaff
(2) Warping capstans and cable lifters
(3) Chain locker
(4) Forecastle space
(5) Forepeak storerooms
(6) Cargo 'tweendecks
(7) Forepeak (water ballast)
(8) Fore Deep (oil bunkers)
(9) Transfer pumproom
(10) Tension winches, fo'c'slehead
(11) Access to 'tweendecks
(12) Spare bower anchor
(13) Forward cofferdam
(14) Foredeck tension winch
(15) Foremast
(16) Forward breakwater
(17) Manifold platform
(18) Pipeline manifold
(19) 5-ton pipeline cranes
(20) Warping winch with extended spindles
(21) After breakwater
(22) Main cargo pumproom
(23) Signal mast with aerial array and radar scanners
(24) Navigating bridge
(25) Master's and officers' accommodation

(26) Engine-room skylight
(27) Funnel casing
(28) Petty officers' accommodation, galley and crew messrooms
(29) Crew accommodation
(30) Swimming pool
(31) Lifeboats
(32) Poop tension winches
(33) Ensign staff
(34) No. 1 cargo tank—port, centre, starboard
(35) No. 2 cargo tank—port, centre, starboard
(36) No. 3 cargo tank—port, centre, starboard
(37) No. 4 cargo tank—port, centre, starboard
(38) No. 5 cargo tank—centre
(38a) No. 5 permanent ballast tanks—port, starboard
(39) No. 6 cargo tank—centre
(39a) No. 6 permanent ballast tanks—port, starboard
(40) No. 7 cargo tank—centre
(40a) No. 7 permanent ballast tanks—port, starboard

(41) No. 8 cargo tank—port, centre, starboard
(42) No. 9 cargo tank—port, centre, starboard
(43) No. 10 cargo tank—port, centre, starboard
(44) No. 11 cargo tank—port, centre, starboard
(45) No. 12 cargo tank—port, centre, starboard
(46) Bunker settling tanks
(47) Side bunkers
(48) Engine-room cofferdam
(49) Forward double bottom (fuel oil)
(50) Aft double bottom (fuel oil)
(51) Engine-room water feed
(52) Lubricating oil
(53) Distilled water
(54) Domestic fresh water
(56) After peak (water ballast or fresh water)
(57) Boiler room
(58) Engine-room
(59) Rope store
(60) Steering flat
(61) Propeller
(62) Rudder

tanker to carry several different grades of oil fully segregated so that they do not contaminate each other.

Liquid cargo is more easily handled than the complicated packages, crates and bales of the dry cargo ship. To deal with its oil the tanker is fitted with an extensive piping layout in the bottom of the tanks, linked to piping on the upper deck and to the pumps in one or several pumprooms. On deck the piping culminates in a manifold of transverse pipes, usually near the 'midships point, to which the shore hoses for loading or discharging are connected. The cargo is delivered into the ship at the loading port either by shore pumps or by gravity flow. At the discharging port the ship pumps it ashore using her own pumps which may be either of the reciprocating or the centrifugal type. Control of the oil flow within the ship is effected by valves located in each tank and at various points in the pipeline. These are operated from deck by means of valve wheels which are usually coloured according to a simple code system and are an easily recognisable feature of a tanker's main deck fittings. The valve system enables the tank pattern to be used for carrying several different grades at once, but ships are fairly rigidly divided into two distinct groups according to the type of cargo which they are expected to carry.

'Clean' oil ships carry the most highly refined products such as aviation fuel, motor spirit and kerosene; 'black' oil ships carry crude oil or the heavier, dirtier refinery products such as diesel fuel and furnace oil. The carrying of several grades at once is more common in the clean trade and the greatest number of 'black' oil ships are in fact large crude carriers which normally carry nothing else but this raw material. An important aspect of the tanker trade of course is that usually freight can only be carried on one part of a round trip, the ship being in ballast for the passage to her loading port. This is not altogether the serious loss it first appears since the ballast voyage enables the tanks to be prepared for the next cargo.

REFRIGERATED SHIPS

These vessels are fast cargo liners, normally running on fixed routes, which carry general cargo outwards and meat or fruit homewards. Their holds and hatches are specially insulated for the carriage of frozen and chilled meat and fruit. Cooling of the insulated chambers (holds and 'tween decks) is either by brine pipes or by cold air.

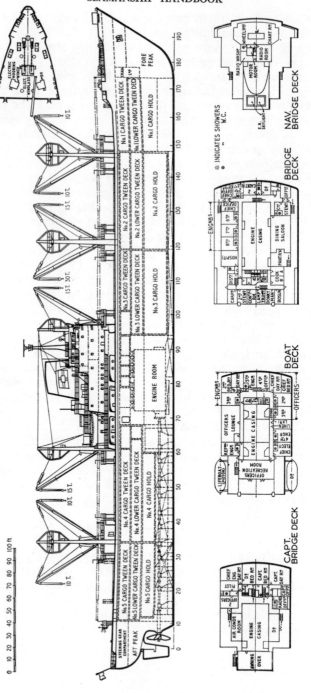

PLAN OF A REFRIGERATED SHIP

The refrigerated cargo vessel *Westmorland* (reprinted from 'Shipbuilding and Shipping Record')

PLAN OF A BULK-CARRIER

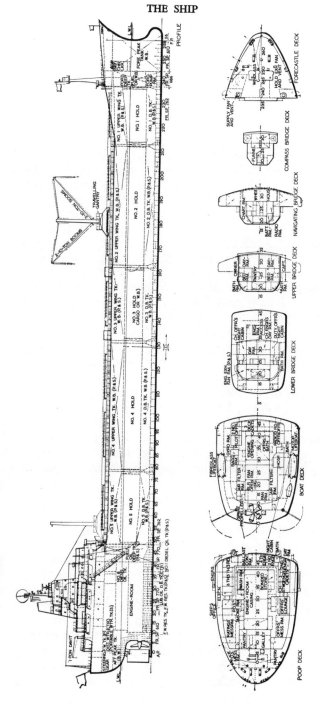

The bulk carrier *Achilleus* (reprinted from 'Shipbuilding and Shipping Record')

Chapter 2

MANNING

The Captain is the owner's or company's representative and he is primarily responsible for the safe navigation of the ship, care and delivery of the cargo and the life and safety of all on board. He must also attend to the many legal points and other complex matters which arise during the voyage. To run the vessel efficiently it is essential that he maintains strict discipline and this must be appreciated by members of the crew, particularly when they are called out to perform additional duties and tasks which circumstances make necessary and especially when life and the safety of the ship are concerned. Although usually formally addressed as the Captain, his correct title is the Master and this designation is used on all documents.

Manning of a cargo ship. The ship's complement is divided into three departments: Deck, Engine and Catering. Each has its own chief assisted by junior officers, petty officers and ratings. At sea continuous watches are maintained by the deck and engine departments and also (to some extent) in port, but the catering is normally a day-work occupation.

Obviously the manning of a cargo vessel will vary slightly from company to company, but the table on page 23 shows the usual complement of an average vessel:

The Deck Department is responsible for the navigation of the ship when at sea and this includes keeping a continuous look-out in all weathers. During this period, the never-ending tasks of rust prevention, painting down, washing, preparing cargo spaces and the maintenance of both cargo and life-saving gear are carried out. All the operations necessary for mooring and unmooring as well as the preparation and stowage of all cargo-handling gear are also the responsibility of this department.

The department is manned as follows:

Master, in command of the ship. He must possess a Master's Certificate of Competency.

1st Mate (*Chief Officer*), who must possess, as the minimum requirement, a First Mate's Certificate of Competency. He is responsible for stowage of cargo, stability, deck equipment and maintenance, as well as the day-to-day management of the officers and personnel in the deck department. At sea, he keeps the morning and dog watches. Several companies, however, now carry both a Chief and a First Officer, and where this

MASTER

DECK	ENGINE	CATERING	RADIO
Chief Officer (1st Mate)	Chief Engineer	Chief Steward	Radio Officer
2nd Officer (2nd Mate)	2nd Engineer		
3rd Officer (3rd Mate)	3rd Engineer		
Cadet(s) or	4th Engineer		
Apprentice(s)	Junior Engineer(s)		
	Electrician(s)		
	Cadets		

PETTY OFFICERS

Boatswain (Bosun)	Engine Storekeeper	Ship's Cook
Carpenter	Donkeyman	2nd Steward

RATINGS

Lamptrimmer	Greasers	Assistant Stewards
Able Seamen (A.B.)	Firemen	2nd Cook and Baker
Efficient Deck Hands		Galley/Pantry Boy
(E.D.H.)		
Deck Hands Uncertificated		
(D.H.U.)		
Senior Ordinary Seamen		
(S.O.S.)		
Junior Ordinary Seamen		
(J.O.S.)		
Deck Boy(s)		

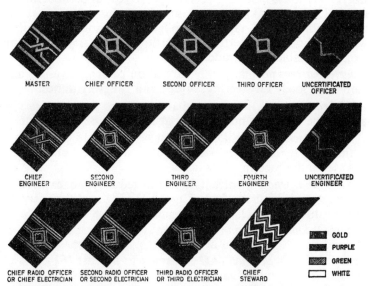

Note. Standard cuff bands for Third Officer, Fourth Engineer and Third Radio Officer have the diamond centred on the band, i.e., like the centre band for Chief Officer or Second Engineer. On most cargo ships, the Chief Steward has the gold band only.

applies, the Chief Officer is always on day work and the First Officer is the watchkeeper.

2nd Mate (*Second Officer*), whose minimum qualification must be a Second Mate's Certificate of Competency. He is usually the navigating officer and assists the Chief Officer with cargo work. He is also responsible for the navigation and bridge equipment and, at sea, keeps the middle and afternoon watches.

3rd Mate (*Third Officer*), who requires no qualification but usually holds a Second Mate's Certificate of Competency. He keeps the forenoon and first watch at sea under the watchful eye of the Master. He is responsible for the upkeep of the Life Saving Appliances and, in port, supervises cargo work when and as required, under the Chief Officer.

Navigating Cadets/Apprentices, who are seafarers under training to become deck officers. They are either indentured for their period of training or are under agreement to the Shipping Company.

Boatswain (*Bosun*): responsible for working the crew under orders from the Chief or Deck Officer. He ranks as a petty officer, must be at least 20 years of age with a minimum of four years' sea service and must hold an A.B.'s certificate.

Carpenter: must first have served a four-year apprenticeship as a shipwright. Ranking as a petty officer, his main duties are the sounding of all tanks and bilges, operating the windlass when anchoring or berthing/unberthing and carrying out all work applicable to his trade.

Quartermaster: normally only carried on passenger vessels and employed solely on steering, bridge and gangway duties.

Able Seaman (A.B.): must have at least three years' sea service and be the holder of both a lifeboat and an A.B.'s certificate.

Efficient Deck Hand (E.D.H.): must be at least 18 years of age with, at least, one years' sea service and be the holder of an E.D.H. and a Steering Certificate.

Deck Hand Uncertificated (*D.H.U.*): requires no experience but must be at least 18 years of age; a D.H.U., with sea service, can substitute as an O.S. in the manning.

Senior Ordinary Seaman (*S.O.S.*): must be at least $17\frac{1}{2}$ years of age and have a minimum of 18 months' sea service.

Junior Ordinary Seaman (*J.O.S.*): must be at least $16\frac{1}{2}$ years of age and have a minimum of nine months' sea service.

Deck Boy: has served less than nine months at sea.

The Engine Department. The propelling machinery may be either steam or diesel and a constant watch has to be kept at sea on the engines, lubrication, pressures, fuel supply, auxiliaries, pumps and generators. In port, power is required for driving winches, lighting, heating, refrigeration, etc.

The manning of this department depends largely on the type of ship, engines and age. Oil fires, diesels and automation have considerably reduced the manning requirements.

Chief Engineer, who must be the holder of a steam or motor first-class certificate or a combined certificate. He supervises all the work appertaining to the engine room and auxiliaries.

2nd Engineer: must hold a second-class certificate, keeps the morning and dog watches and is responsible for the maintenance of the engine-room, deck and other machinery.

3rd Engineer: requires no qualifications and is a watchkeeping engineer keeping the middle and afternoon watches.

4th Engineer: keeps the forenoon and first watches where he is under the direct supervision of the Chief Engineer.

Junior Engineers are recruited from shipyards and assist the watchkeepers and in the repairing and maintenance of deck and other machinery.

Engineering Cadets, who are training to become engineer officers and are under agreement to the Shipping Company.

Electrician(s): for the upkeep, maintenance and repair of all the electrical equipment.

Refrigeration Engineer(s): maintain and run the refrigeration plant on meat and fruit vessels.

Pumpman: engaged only on tankers for operating the discharging/loading/ballasting and attending to pumps and valves. An engine-room P.O. who comes under the instruction of the Chief Officer during cargo operations.

Engine Storekeeper: a P.O. in charge of the store room who is also an experienced fitter.

Donkeyman: A P.O. whose duties are to assist the watchkeeping engineer and to attend to lubrication.

Greaser: for general oiling and cleaning duties.

Fireman whose duties are to attend to the boiler fires ignited and heated by oil fuel.

The Catering Department. On cargo vessels this is a small but busy department under the Chief Steward and is responsible for preparing and serving meals, and for the cleaning of saloons, accommodation and alleyways.

On liners, the Catering Department employs the largest percentage of the vessel's crew as it has to cater for a wide range of passenger's needs and comforts. These include the reception of passengers as they come on board and attendance to their baggage; and the management of cabins, lounges, restaurants, bars, entertainment, shops and hairdressing salons. In addition, specialised galley and pantry staff are required for cooking and preparation of meals, etc.

The Purser is head of the Purser's and Catering Department and is responsible for catering, passengers, and wage accounts.

The Chief Steward is chief of the Catering Department but under the Purser on a passenger vessel. On cargo vessels he is expected to have had some previous galley experience and to possess a Cook's certificate, although the holding of such a certificate is not essential. From the 1st August 1978 an industrial agreement in the U.K. shipping industry will require that Chief Stewards have satisfactorily completed an approved course for Catering Officers and received the M.N.T.B. Catering Officers' Certificate. This would include the Cooks' Certificate. It should be noted that there is no statutory provision within this agreement and recommendation.

The Second Steward ranks as a petty officer and his duties depend on the type of vessel. On cargo vessels he is usually on saloon duties and may be the Captain's steward (Captain's Tiger).

Assistant Stewards should be 18 years of age and have two years' experience. They are employed on general cabin, saloon and pantry duties and some may be assigned for special officer duties.

The Ship's Cook must have a Cook's certificate and is responsible for preparing the meals, but the daily menus are arranged by the Chief Steward. On ships under 1,000 tons, a certificate is not necessary.

The Assistant Cook or Second Cook and Baker assists the cook in galley duties and bread baking.

The Pantry and Galley Boy is the junior catering rating who obtains promotion to Assistant Steward or Assistant Cook on merit or on attaining the age of 18 years.

The Utility Steward/Messman is employed for general messing, pantry and cleaning duties.

The Radio Department. All foreign-going vessels carry at least one Radio Officer who is directly responsible to the Captain. On vessels where continuous radio watches are kept, there will be three Radio Officers, i.e. Chief, Second and Third. The duty of the Radio Officer is to keep radio communication with the shore and other vessels, listen for distress and navigational warnings, and assist, when and as required, with the many other radio navigational aids with which his vessel is equipped.

The preceeding manning notes are still relevant but many companies now operate a G.P. or general purpose rating scheme. No arbitrary pattern can be laid down as companies operating such schemes vary in their approach. Broadly speaking, someone, possibly trained as a deck rating would be re-trained by the company to its own scheme in the other fields of shipboard work. Thus a deck rating could be trained in engine room duties and catering duties. This allows an interchange between departments although generally it is rare for the catering staff to be included. The advantages for the company are less manning requirements, ability to use labour more productively in the consideration of weather conditions, voyage routes and port stays. The advantages to the rating are generally, additional pay, overtime opportunities, superior accommodation, ex-. tended leave and a Company Service Contract, job satisfaction through a feeling of wider knowledge and change of work and working routines.

BELLS

Watch bells. Ashore, life revolves round the clock and you have to keep a constant eye on watch or clock to see that you are on time for work or an appointment. At sea, punctuality is just as important and, to assist you in this, all the hours and half-hours are indicated by strokes on the bridge bell. These bells are struck by the duty helmsman and are repeated by the lookout and in the engine-room. The hour strokes are always made in pairs, the odd stroke indicating the half hour. The New Year is heralded by 16 strokes.

Lookout Warning Bell is struck by the lookout when he sights anything. One stroke denotes a light or object on the starboard side; two single strokes denote the port side; and three single strokes, right ahead. Four single strokes indicate that he wants a relief.

Anchor bells are struck on the fo'c'sle head when anchoring or weighing anchor. A single stroke is struck for each cable shackle indicated. Anchor aweigh, i.e. off the bottom, is indicated by a rapid ringing of the bell.

Fog bells are the audible indication of a vessel at anchor in fog. Ships under 45½m (150 feet) in length ring the bell rapidly for a period of five seconds every minute. Ships over this length make the same signal and also sound a gong aft for a period of five seconds every minute. The sounding of the gong must not be confused with the sound and tone of the bell.

Fire bells are electric bells placed at selected positions throughout the ship calling the crew to fire stations.

WATCHKEEPING

In the majority of vessels the modern practice is to have only one rating on watch. His duties are standing-by on the bridge ready to take the wheel if required to steer by hand, and for steering when entering or leaving port. The watch is doubled up in fog or when coasting to provide a look-out in addition to the Stand-By helmsman.

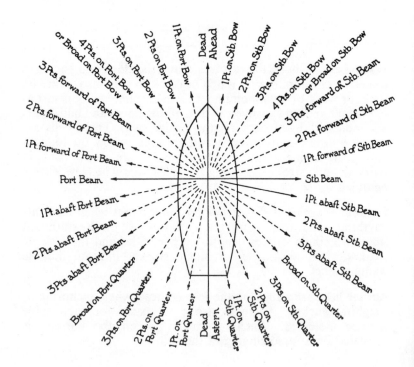

The lookout watchman may be assigned to the fo'c'sle head, the weather side of the bridge, or the crow's nest. His duties are to report all passing ships, lights, ice, land and any other object or navigational hazard sighted. Signals to the bridge, unless he is keeping his watch there, are by strokes on the fo'c'sle or crow's-nest bell, one stroke denoting objects or lights to starboard, two strokes to port, and three strokes denote dead ahead. Four strokes are sounded if he requires a relief. The striking of the bell should be acknowledged by a hail from the Officer of the Watch and, if there is any doubt, the bells should again be struck. On ships where telephones are fitted at the lookout positions, the striking of the bell is followed by a telephone report to the bridge.

Whilst points on the bow are still used for reporting vessels, lights or land, the practice of using the three figure compass notation to indicate objects as so many degrees on the bow, is becoming common practice.

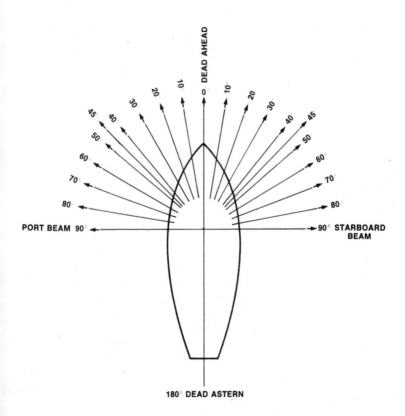

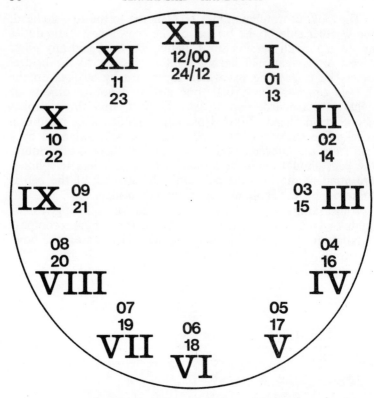

Time at sea is expressed in the 24 hour notation thus: 9 a.m. = 0900 hrs. 11.15 a.m. = 1115 hrs. 12.30 p.m. = 1230 hrs. 5.45 p.m. = 1745 hrs. midnight = 2400 hrs. See sketch diagram

Nightwatch in port. The nightwatchman should report to the duty officer immediately his duties commence in order to obtain any additional duties required for the night. If at a tidal berth, he should have knowledge of the times of high and low water and also hold the keys to the deck stores and lamp room. Moorings, rat-guards, gangways, gangway stanchions, lights and floodlights must be periodically checked. The ship's side-rails should also be checked to see that they are all in position and properly secured. Particular attention must be paid to the gangway when the crew are leaving or returning and no unauthorised persons must be allowed on board. He must also see that the gangway is well lighted and a lifebuoy with lifeline is always handy. If cargo is being worked, cargo clusters should also be checked and kept ready for any replacement required. In frosty conditions steam winches will have to be run slowly or properly drained. A close watch must be kept on the moorings particularly at high water or when other ships are passing. If a mooring rope parts the duty officer should be immediately notified and a replacement rope passed ashore and secured.

A diligent watchman can prevent much pilferage of ship and personal property, and any shore labour working on board should be turned away from crew and officer accommodation. Bum boats should not be allowed to make fast to the ship. All ventilators should be trimmed back to wind and any smoke from cargo or crew spaces should be immediately investigated.

Bridge and ship etiquette. No more is expected of a seaman than would be in any other industry or shore employment. Most of this subject is taught in all pre-sea training establishments, but for those who have had no pre-sea training or have allowed it to lapse, a few points are listed here:

1. In the presence of officers, stand upright and address the officer as 'Sir'. When given an order, reply in a seamanlike manner.
2. When ordered to report to the Captain, present yourself suitably attired.
3. Watchkeepers and helmsmen should wear clean working clothes on bridge duties, and always a shirt even in the tropics. Unnecessary conversations on the bridge should be avoided and the chartroom should not be entered unless your duties compel you to do so.
4. Do not smoke on the bridge, on lookout or on deck duties.
5. Always enter the wheelhouse by the lee door.
6. Always use the appropriate bridge ladder so that the Captain is not disturbed.
7. Close or leave all doors on the hook so that they do not bang.
8. Do not litter decks or empty waste on the weather side.
9. Avoid unnecessary noise during the hours of silence (afternoon and night watches).

Clothing. The accepted working rig is the dungaree trouser, dungaree shirt and dungaree jacket, older clothes being used for working and best for watchkeeping and the watch below. In cold weather a sea jersey and dungaree jacket is worn, and headgear usually consists of a woollen hat or dungaree cap. Heavy half-coats, duffle coats or donkey jackets are suitable for bridge and lookout duties. For heavy weather, oilskins, seaboots and sou'westers are essential, as are seaboot stockings for wearing inside the boots. A belt with sheath knife and spike are essential, but both knife and spike should not be worn when at the wheel in case they affect the magnetic compass needle. Saturday afternoons are traditionally washing (dhobi) days when both day workers and watchkeepers wash and dry their gear. Clean linen is issued and accommodation has to be scrubbed and cleaned ready for the Captain's Sunday morning inspection. Seamen have always been noted for their implicit loyalty and trust in each other. Precautions are naturally taken in port when cabin ports and doors are closed and watched but, at sea, doors are never locked and petty thieving is the most hated crime which can occur. Any seaman found guilty of this during a voyage is usually 'Sent to Coventry' for the remainder of the trip.

Chapter 3

ROPE—FIBRE, NYLON AND WIRE

All rope made from vegetable fibres—manila, hemp, sisal, coir, cotton or flax—is impregnated with oil when it is being manufactured. Manila fibre comes from the abaca plant, a large tree-like herb $4\frac{1}{2}$ to 9m (15 to 30 ft.) high, which is indigenous to the Philippine Islands in the Pacific; it is shipped from the port of Manila, hence its name. Strips of fibre which cover the stalk are removed, cleaned and dried before being shipped to a factory for processing. In appearance, manila is glossy and smooth; in use it is pliable, light, easy to work, durable and strong, and is impervious to salt water.

Hemp and sisal are derived from the leaves of large plants which grow in Italy, Russia, America, East Africa, Mexico and other countries. White in colour, they are not as good as the highest grades of manila. Both sisal and manila ropes can be treated chemically to waterproof the fibre and render it more resistant to rot and mildew.

Coir (sometimes known as grass) rope is made from the fibre of coconut husks. Coarse and light, it is very buoyant, and possesses great elasticity. It is not used much aboard ship, though it is handy for mooring and towing purposes when fitted with a wire pennant. Coir rope is usually laid left-handed.

Cotton and flax ropes are, of course, made from cotton and flax respectively, but their use aboard ship is limited.

Manufacture of rope. Rope is made by first twisting fibres into yarns, and yarns into strands; then the strands are twisted together to form the finished article. The usual degree of twist produces a rope from three-quarters to two-thirds the length of the yarn from which it is made.

Lays of rope. The term 'lay' is employed to describe the degree and nature of twist. Hawser-laid rope consists of three, four or six strands twisted together in the opposite direction to the twists in the strands. Yarns right-handed, strands left-handed, rope right-handed is the usual order of things.

Cable-laid rope consists of three hawser-laid three-stranded ropes laid together left-handed or in the opposite direction to the lay of the three constituent ropes. Cable-laid construction provides more elasticity than a hawser-laid rope. Because of its particular characteristics cable-laid construction is usually confined to ropes of large size.

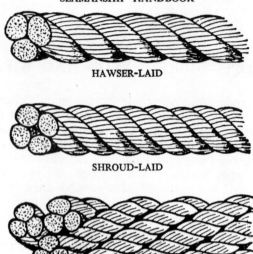

HAWSER-LAID

SHROUD-LAID

CABLE-LAID

A shroud-laid rope is a four-stranded rope laid right-handed around a heart. Ropes are also designated as Soft-laid, Standard-laid, or Hard-laid, according to the amount of twist given to the strands during their manufacture. Standard-laid rope is the most common as it possesses pliability, strength and durability. It is not as strong or as flexible as soft-laid rope, however, or as weather-resisting and durable as hard-laid rope, but it will stand more wear than soft-laid, and is more flexible than hard-laid. What it loses on the roundabouts it gains on the swings.

Eight-stranded plaited rope is now in common use on board ship particularly as mooring ropes. Of plaited construction, each rope is comprised of eight strands laid up in pairs, two pairs being laid up left-handed and the other two pairs right-handed. The eight strands provide increased flexibility and the rope does not kink.

Splicing. Since this type of rope is laid up both right- and left-handed and the strands are in pairs, the procedure for splicing will differ from the usual method.

Eye splice. To make an eye splice in this kind of rope proceed as follows:

1. Unlay the rope as far as required and whip the ends of each pair of strands.

2. Bend the rope round to the size of eye required and lay the

two pairs of left-hand laid strands over the rope and the two pairs of right-hand laid strands on the clear side.

3. Tuck the first pair of left-hand laid strands under the nearest pair of left-hand laid strands and pull tight.

4. Tuck the first pair of right-hand laid strands under their nearest pair of right-hand laid strands and pull tight.

5. Turn the rope over and tuck the two pairs of left and right-hand laid strands in the same way.

6. This will now complete the first tuck.

7. Put in two tucks for natural fibre, three for polypropylene, and four for nylon.

8. Using only one strand, repeat the number of tucks required.

9. The finished splice, if made in nylon rope, would therefore have four tucks with double strands followed by four tucks with single strands.

10. Dog the four pairs of strands with a strong whipping and cut off the surplus ends.

Short splice. Unlay as for a normal rope and whip the ends of each pair of strands. Marry the ropes together in the usual way and then splice as for the eye splice making four tucks for man-made fibres (three for natural fibres). Dog the ends in the usual way. For this splice no additional single strand tucks are required.

Care of Fibre and Nylon Rope. See page 40.

SMALL STUFF

Spun Yarn. Always tarred and usually used for seizing and serving, spun yarn is two-, three-, or four-stranded and is loosely laid, left-handed.

Marline. Two-stranded and used for worming, serving and numerous other shipboard jobs, marline may be either tarred or untarred.

Houseline. The same as marline except that it is three-stranded.

Roundline. Similar to houseline but made of larger strands.

Hambroline. Right-hand laid, and three-stranded, it is made of fine, untarred left-handed yarns.

Codline. Small stuff made of untarred soft hemp.

Ratline. Rarely used nowadays for its original purpose— the 'ratlines' or rungs of ladders of which the shrouds were the sides. Ratline is made from tarred soft hemp and is three-stranded. It is now used extensively for heaving lines, or when a strong lashing is required; lashing down coiled mooring lines on a coastal passage, for example.

Seizing stuff. Three-stranded with two, three or four threads to each strand, and made of tarred hemp, this is used when a strong, neat job is required.

Signal halyards. Made of four-stranded, plain-laid, untarred hemp and ranging in size from 19 to $28\frac{1}{2}$mm ($\frac{3}{4}$ in. to $1\frac{1}{8}$ in.). Braided cord is sometimes used for halyards on account of its freedom from kinks and turns.

Log line. Very strong, pliable and durable, it is made of kink-proof braided cord and is specially manufactured for towing through the water. It is supplied in coils of various lengths and ranges in size from 19 to 35mm ($\frac{3}{4}$ in. to $1\frac{3}{8}$ in.).

Hand lead lines. Three-stranded hemp line of $28\frac{1}{2}$mm ($1\frac{1}{8}$ in.). Supplied in 30-fathom coils, it is invariably left-hand laid.

Deep-sea lead line. Three-stranded hemp line of 38mm ($1\frac{1}{2}$ in.) circumference, supplied in 120-fathom coils. Also laid left-handed.

Point line. Three-stranded manila always measured according to the number of threads, i.e., 12-thread, 15-thread, etc.

Boat lacing. Three-stranded, good quality hemp available in various sizes. It is used for lacing boat covers, securing awnings to spars, and similar purposes.

NYLON CORDAGE

To understand the advantages possessed by nylon cordage over other materials it is necessary to know how this product is made. Primarily the raw materials from which the diamine and acid for making the polymer are obtained are phenol from coal, oxygen and nitrogen from the air, and hydrogen from water. The manufacturing processes are complicated and have to be carefully controlled.

To produce nylon yarn the polymer, in flake or chip form, is fed into a closed, heated vessel, where it is melted and then forced through a spinneret by a pump. The spinneret is a metal disc containing many fine holes from which the individual filaments are extruded, and as they emerge in molten form from the spinneret they are cooled and solidified by a current of air. These filaments are treated with steam, wound on to a bobbin, and then twisted a few turns to form a yarn suitable for further processing.

This yarn is next subjected to a process known as cold drawing, in which it is passed between a system of rollers and drawn out to several times its original length. During this stretching operation the long, chain-like molecules which cor stitute the filament, and which are initially arranged hap hazardly, take up a more orderly arrangement, lying parallel and closer to one another. This drawing action gives nylon the properties of a textile fibre; before this operation it consists of no more than extruded polymer.

Due to the fact that nylon filaments are produced by a carefully controlled chemical process, they are uniform in thickness and reliable in tensile strength, so that variations in rope diameter and tensile are reduced to the absolute minimum. Vegetable fibres such as cotton, hemp and manila are subject to climatic and seasonal variations which affect their properties and even the most carefully selected grades vary with region and season.

A nylon rope of any size contains exactly the same number of filaments in its cross-section throughout its length. In this respect nylon ropes are different from ropes made from vegetable fibres, which, consisting of numerous short filaments twisted together, are unavoidably more variable. Nylon possesses many other attributes which have established it as a pre-eminent cordage material. Flexible and easy to handle it is also attractive in appearance, being white and lustrous, and can be dyed in fast colours.

Summing up, nylon rope has high tensile strength, toughness, flexibility, a high degree of extensibility under load, great elasticity, resistance to rot, water and mildew, remarkable ability to withstand shock loads, and to all intents and purposes may be considered non-inflammable.

Splicing nylon cordage. Like other cordage, nylon ropes can be satisfactorily spliced, but, owing to the large number of filaments in each yarn and their smooth surface, care must be taken to avoid loss of twist and to maintain the form and lay of yarns and strands. The normal long, short and eye splices can be made, but it is advisable to insert extra tucks to maintain full efficiency and prevent slippage. The makers have found that an ordinary short or eye splice requires three full tucks, tapered to finish with one-half and one-quarter tuck. To withstand heavy or rapidly fluctuating loads, five full tucks plus one-half and one-quarter, are desirable.

Knotting. Due to the tendency of nylon ropes to stretch under tension the cross-sectional area may be reduced, to compensate for which knots should be made more carefully and 'pulled home'. Knots are always weaker than the rope from which they are made, and nylon is similar to other cordage in this respect, but because nylon does not swell in water, knots are more readily released when the rope is wet.

WIRE ROPES

Aboard ship wire rope fulfils numerous important functions for standing rigging, cargo runners, mooring and towing lines, boat falls, sounding, radio aerials, etc., and it is desirable for seamen to know something about its manufacture and much about its handling and maintenance. Because its make-up varies according to the role it is designed to play, wire rope made for one shipboard purpose will not necessarily be suitable for another.

Consider wire rope made specifically for standing rigging, for example. This is galvanized, heavy and inflexible. It would be no use whatever for cargo work where lightness and flexibility in particular are essential, even assuming it was small enough to pass through a cargo gin block. On the other hand, wire cargo runners have often been used as standing rigging in emergencies.

First, then, wire rope used for standing rigging usually contains six strands, seven wires to a strand, and a hemp core. It is heavily galvanized to protect it from rust and corrosion. Wire rope cargo runners and hawsers necessarily need to be flexible and strong. Strength and flexibility are attained by employing a higher-grade steel and increasing the number of wires to each strand to between twelve and thirty-seven, each strand having its own fibre core as well as the main core around which the strands are laid.

As a general rule wire ropes are made either *ordinary* (or *regular*) *lay* or *Lang's lay*. In the former the wires are twisted in one direction to form the strands, and the strands are twisted in the opposite direction, about a hemp heart, to make the rope. With Lang's Lay the strands are twisted to make the rope in the same direction as the wires are twisted to form the strands. Lang's Lay is seldom used on board ship. Some wire ropes are laid left-handed, but for all shipboard work right-handed wire rope is employed.

During manufacture the fibre cores (hearts) of all wire ropes, forming as they do a cushion on which the strands rest, are well lubricated before the closing operation, also the strands themselves and the completed rope are further impregnated with lubricant. Regular applications of a good rope oil should, however, be made during the rope's working life, and most ropemakers have their own brands of preparation.

Preformed wire rope is that in which the strands and wires have been given the exact helix they take up in the completed

Heavy, galvanised six-stranded wire rope, seven wires to each strand, as used for standing rigging

Left-hand laid wire, with six strands each having nineteen wires. This rope is of similar construction but of opposite lay to wires used as cargo runners

rope. In the manufacture of ordinary rope the wires are held forcibly in position throughout the life of the rope. This can be seen by cutting such a rope at any point, when the strands and wires will immediately fly apart. Preforming the wires and strands, however, prevents this, as they all lie naturally in their true position free from internal stress. Preformed wire rope has the following advantages:

(1) Easy to handle.
(2) Longer life.
(3) Balanced load on strands.
(4) No high strands.
(5) Broken wires lie flat. When outer wires break in preformed rope after long wear, there is no tendency for them to fray out of the body of the rope. They continue to lie in their proper places, thus preventing damage to adjacent wires, sheaves, drums—and hands.
(6) More easily spliced. There is no need to seize the ends for splicing.
(7) Preformed rope resists kinking better than any other rope of like grade or construction.

Combined steel and fibre rope. After the steel wire strands have been spun, they are covered with fibre so that only fibre appears on the outside of the rope. It is a type of rope easier to grip and handle than rope made entirely from wire, and for this reason is used extensively in fishing craft as ground cables, fishing lines, bag beckets, halfing beckets, snortlers, wind lines and belly lines. Combined rope is usually made in sizes from $31\frac{1}{2}$ to $101\frac{1}{2}$mm ($1\frac{1}{4}$ in. to 4 in.) circumference. In the construction there may be from three to six wire strands, each strand containing six to eighteen wires.

Seizing wire, as its name implies, is mainly used for seizing purposes, but it is also used for mousing hooks and shackles and serving splices. It is usually seven-stranded, six single wires being laid around a seventh of the same size and construction.

Man-made fibre rope. The following recommendations on the use and care of man-made fibre ropes in Marine applications has been issued by the British Standards Institution.

Safety Precautions

1. Do not surge ropes on the drum-ends if it can be avoided. Do not pay out slack or slack away by rendering. Always try to walk back the rope.

2. See that the surface condition of drum-ends is good and that they are free from rust and paint.

3. Do not use more turns of the rope on the drum-end than are necessary for the particular type of rope.

4. On whelped drum-ends, one or two extra turns should be taken to ensure a good grip.

5. Always make certain that the end of the rope is fast to the bitts and not just to the drum-end.

6. Avoid sharp angles in the rope, i.e. at the fairleads when heaving alongside or along the quay or jetty.

7. See that fairleads are in good condition and, if of the roller type, ensure that they rotate freely.

8. Never allow a wire rope to cross a fibre rope on a bollard.

9. Have as few men as possible in the vicinity of a rope under strain, particularly in the path of the rope.

10. Rope stoppers should be of man-made fibre.

Care of Rope

1. Do not leave ropes unduly exposed to sunlight when at sea; keep covered by tarpaulins or store below deck.

2. Keep ropes clear of contamination by chemicals.

3. Do not store ropes in the vicinity of boilers or heaters.

4. When joining a wire rope to a fibre rope a thimble should

always be inserted in the eye of the fibre rope. At all times both ropes should have the same direction of lay.

5. Check splices and ensure that all tucks recommended by the makers have been made.

6. When taking new ropes out of their coil always do so in an anti-clockwise direction to avoid disturbing the lay of the rope. It is best to set the coil on a base which can be rotated by a swivel so that the rope can be taken from the outside of the coil as the coil rotates.

CARE OF FIBRE AND NYLON ROPE

Measuring rope and chain. The size of a fibre, synthetic or wire rope is given in mm and this measurement denotes the circumference of the rope. The size of chain is taken from the diameter of the link. A rope gauge is used for measuring both circumference and diameter as required. The scale on the sliding arm gives circumference in mm, and the scale on the fixed side gives the diameter in mm.

Metric formula for breaking stresses of natural and synthetic fibre rope, steel wire rope and chain.

MATERIAL		Factor
Fibre rope, three strand hawser laid		
Grade 1 Manila	(7mm to 144mm)	
High Grade Manila	(7mm to 144mm)	$2D^2/300$
Polythene	(4mm to 72mm)	
Polypropylene	(7mm to 80mm)	$3D^2/300$
Polyester (Terylene)	(4mm to 96mm)	$4D^2/300$
Polyamide (Nylon)	(4mm to 96mm)	$5D^2/300$
Flexible Steel Wire Rope		
6 × 12	(4mm to 48mm)	$15D^2/500$
6 × 24	(8mm to 56mm)	$20D^2/500$
6 × 37	(8mm to 56mm)	$21D^2/500$
Stud Link Chain		
Grade 1	(12·5mm to 120mm)	$20D^2/600$
Grade 2	(12·5mm to 120mm)	$30D^2/600$
Grade 3	(12·5mm to 120mm)	$43D^2/600$
Open Link Chain		
Grade 1	(12·5mm to 50mm)	$20D^2/600$
Grade 2	(12·5mm to 50mm)	$30D^2/600$

The Diameter D is expressed in mms, the breaking stress in tonnes.

Chapter 4

KNOTS, BENDS, HITCHES AND WHIPPINGS

Although rope does not play the same vital part aboard a ship now as it did aboard a sailing ship, it is nevertheless important that seamen should be able quickly to make the correct knot for any particular purpose. It would be an exaggeration to state, perhaps, that the safety of a vessel may depend upon the ability of seamen to make a knot that will not give, but it is no exaggeration to state that the life of one or more of his shipmates may depend upon a seaman's ability correctly to make one or other of the orthodox knots. So study well the following diagrams and explanations, and if you cannot follow them—and I appreciate this may be difficult in some cases—*ask a shipmate to show you.* Certainly candidates for the E.D.H. or Second Mate's Certificate will be unceremoniously failed by the examiner if he finds out that they are deficient in this respect.

Overhand knot, with the **Figure of eight** or **Flemish knot,** is frequently resorted to to keep the ends of ropes from fraying until time permits a back splice to be made, or whipping put on and also to prevent the end of a fall from running through a block.

Reef knot. Used to join two ropes of equal size. Care should be taken to avoid making a 'Granny' knot (an incorrectly made reef knot). Whilst making a reef remember the phrase 'Left over right and right over left'.

Sheet bend. Used to bend two ropes of unequal sizes together or a rope to a soft eye, for example, a halyard to a flag where hook is not provided, or the sheet to the clew of a sail. It will not slip and is easily released.

Double sheet bend. A more secure method of accomplishing the same purpose as a single sheet bend. It is the only hitch accepted to secure a gantline to a bosun's chair.

Two half hitches. A quick way to secure a line temporarily to a spar or ring bolt. It is often made on a bight when a long end remains.

Round turn and two half hitches. Used to secure gantlines and stage ropes to eyes and stanchions on deck. The half hitches are removed and lowering done on the round turns. It is a more secure method than the two half hitches alone.

OVERHAND KNOT

FIGURE OF EIGHT

REEF KNOT

SHEET BEND

DOUBLE SHEET BEND

SHEEPSHANK
(Bights seized)

TWO HALF HITCHES

ROUND TURN AND
TWO HALF HITCHES

Sheepshank. Used to shorten a rope temporarily rather than cut or waste a length. It will remain secure as long as there is some strain on the rope. If not it will come adrift, but to prevent this the two bights should be seized. The sheepshank is also used for a lifeboat's keel grabline. There are many variations of the sheepshank—knotted sheepshank, toggle sheepshank, sheepshank with reef, for instance—but they are rarely resorted to aboard ship, nor, in fact, is the sheepshank proper except for grablines.

Clove hitch. A simple and secure knot used to make a line fast to a spar, etc. A slip hitch is a variation of the clove hitch, but in this case instead of the end being passed through, a bight is made and tucked under. A jerk on the end instantly releases the hitch.

Timber hitch. Is used a great deal aboard ship for hauling or lifting timber, for it is quickly made and secure, though it is liable to slip. To prevent slippage a half turn can be taken with the standing part.

Rolling hitch. It is used to bend a rope to a spar, or a larger rope or the tail of a handy billy to the hauling part of another purchase when used 'luff to luff'. It is made by passing the end of the rope twice round a spar or rope, riding the second turn over the first, and finishing up with a half hitch. Hauling is in the direction of the riding turns. The two riding turns are also the initial hitch of a rope stopper.

Heaving line bend. As its name suggests, this is used mainly to make a heaving line fast to a hawser, but also to make any small rope fast to a large one.

Bowline. The most useful knot for making temporary 'eyes' in ropes of all sizes. It is quickly made by forming a loop in the rope and passing the end through the loop under the standing part and down through the loop. This knot is used for a variety of purposes in everyday shipboard tasks. It is more popular, indeed, than the *heaving line bend* for making a heaving line fast to a hawser which is to be run ashore. *Nothing can jam it, and it will not slip.* If a hawser, steel or fibre, parts when a ship is being berthed alongside and there is not another line handy, or not one as good available, a bowline can be put in the end with confidence, and the hawser passed over a bollard and hove upon. The four stages in making a bowline are shown on the following page.

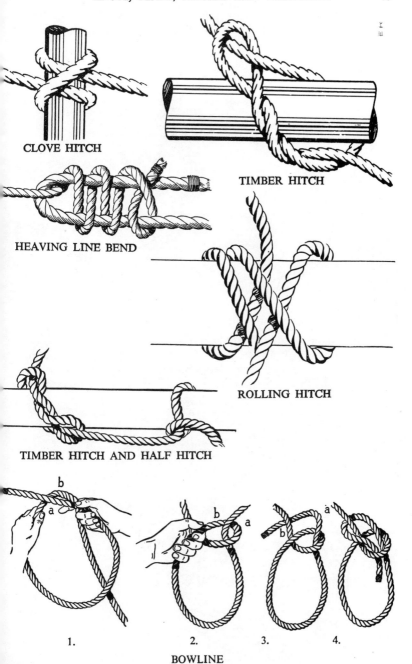

CLOVE HITCH

TIMBER HITCH

HEAVING LINE BEND

ROLLING HITCH

TIMBER HITCH AND HALF HITCH

b

a

1.   2.   3.   4.

BOWLINE

Running bowline. An ordinary bowline with the large loop made round the standing part of a rope, forming a running noose.

Bowline on a bight. A method of making an eye in a rope, the two ends of which are secured. It is made in the usual way but employing the bight instead of the end. When the bight has been passed through the loop it is passed around the standing part by dipping it down and lifting the loop through it.

Marline spike hitch is formed by crossing the bight over the point of the spike and sticking through the point of the spike.

Heaving line knot. This is a handy, easily made knot for weighting the ends of heaving lines, Whip the end of the line and double; $228\frac{1}{2}$mm (9 in.) or so from the bend commence wrapping the end around both parts. Make ten turns in the manner shown in the accompanying sketches, tuck through the end and pull on the standing part, jamming it.

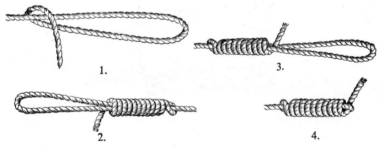

Reeving line bend. Is often employed to unite two large hawsers. Its virtue lies in the fact that it is not bulky and will therefore offer less resistance when the ropes it joins are to be hove through a Panama lead or round a warping chock. The short nips at the loops are a big disadvantage, however, for they are liable to damage the strands.

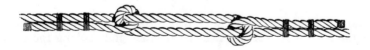

Fisherman's bend. A handy and secure method of securing a line to a bucket, shackle, eye or ring, or even a hawser to a buoy ring. Two round turns are taken, and the end is backed in the form of a half hitch under the standing part and the second round turn; the end is then lashed to the standing part. as in the left-hand drawing, or a half hitch can be taken for extra security, as in the right, before lashing the end.

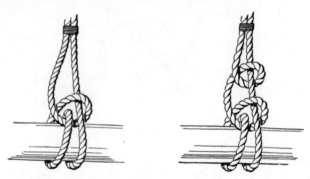

Cat's paw. Made by forming two bights in a rope, one with each hand. The bights are then twisted on themselves for slipping over a hook. Used for shortening a strop.

Crown. Used to commence a **Back splice,** and as a base for

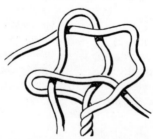

more complicated end knots, it is formed by bending the three strands of a rope's end over each other and tucking the third one down. To complete a back splice after making a crown, pull taut each strand and then splice 'over one and under one' three times.

Blackwall hitch. A quick and secure means of attaching a rope to a hook—provided there is a constant strain on the standing part so that it will jam the loose end. A single blackwall hitch is best used when the rope and hook are of similar size. If they are not, a **Double blackwall** should be used.

SINGLE BLACKWALL   DOUBLE BLACKWALL

RIGGING A STAGE

There are three or four methods in common use of rigging a stage, the two most popular being illustrated below. The first method merely involves making a marline-spike hitch in the

FIRST METHOD

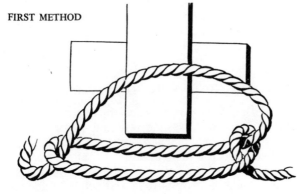

bight of the stage rope and slipping it over the horns (i.e. cross-pieces) of the stage; the second is the true stage knot. Lay the bight of the gantline over the stage inside the horns and then take parts A and B across underneath the stage, and lay them over the stage, outside the horns. Pull the bight C up towards you and then over the stage end. Now pull the two parts of the

SECOND METHOD

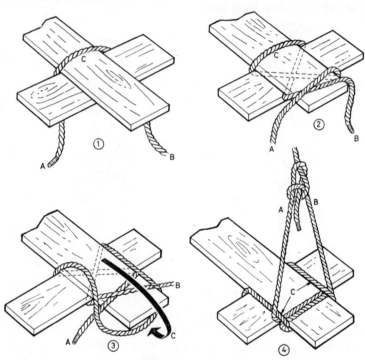

gantline taut and secure the free end to the standing part by means of a bowline. Before tightening the bowline see that A and B are of equal length otherwise the stage will not be level when in use.

RIGGING A BOSUN'S CHAIR

A bosun's chair is used for a variety of purposes aboard ship. From one a hand will wash down and paint the mast and yards, paint the funnel, blacken down the shrouds and stays, etc. The chair itself is a piece of wood about 457mm × 127mm × 25½mm (18 in × 5 in. × 1 in.), having two holes at each end through which a strop is rove and spliced underneath. A gantline is rove through a convenient sheave aloft, one end being made fast to the strop of the chair with a double sheet bend, and seized below the bend. When using the chair aloft a sufficient length of free end should be left on completion of the double sheet bend so that the user can bouse to the mast and ride out to the yard.

The lowering hitch. The hand in the chair is lowered and attended from the deck whilst working on the topmast and yards. On reaching the lower mast, he will now lower himself using a lowering hitch.

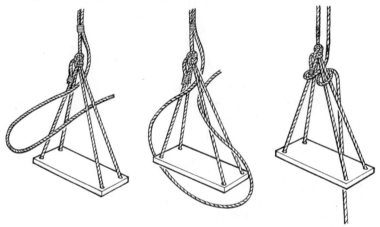

While still held from the deck, the two parts of the gantline are seized together with a good seizing before attempting to make the lowering hitch. This hitch is made by passing the bight of the gantline through the bridle of the chair, over your head, behind you and then down over the chair and underneath to clear your legs. When all clear, haul the gantline taut and release the seizing. You can now lower yourself as required safely on this hitch.

To paint a signal yard. A long tail should be left to the double sheet bend. Pass this tail round the head of the yard-lift and back to the chair, making it fast to the chair strop just below the double sheet bend. The hand on deck will now lower you down until the end of the yard can be reached. By easing the bousing you can now paint the yard inboard towards the mast and, on completion of one side, release the bousing and carry out the same procedure on the other side.

To ride the stays. A tail block, gantline, shackle and bosun's chair are required for this work. Secure the tail block to the

head of the stay and reeve off the gantline. Pass the shackle
over the stay and the pin through the eye at the chair. Bend on
the gantline and haul the hand aloft, who will then treat the
rigging as he is being lowered. Make sure that the bow of the
shackle rides the stay and that the pin is moused.

SLINGING A CASK

First method. Here again there are a few equally reliable ways
of achieving the same objective, but the two most common
methods of slinging a cask are given here. First method: Lay

the rope on deck and place the cask squarely on it. Lift the
two parts on either side and make an overhand knot above the

cask, as in fig. 1. Open out the knot (fig. 2), slide the two bights down, pull taut, and complete with a reef knot (fig. 3).

3.

Second method. Lay the rope strop on deck and, as in the first method (fig. 1 on page 51), place the cask squarely on it.

1.   2.

Lift one part of the strop only and make a half hitch (fig. 2) and slide it down around the cask. Do the same with the second part of the strop and pull taut, when the cask will be ready for lifting (fig. 3).

3.

SHORTENING A STROP

There are several equally effective and efficient ways of shortening strops or slings. Of the two most common methods one is by making two bights and forming an overhand knot (this is illustrated below), and the other by forming two bights and twisting each one separately, like a cat's paw. In each case the two loops formed are taken by the cargo hook.

MOUSING A HOOK

This is done to prevent a hook jumping out of an eyebolt or a fall out of a hook. Double the seizing wire, pass the bight around the hook and dip the two ends through the bight, pulling taut (fig. 1). Then pass each end, one from left to right and the other from right to left across the jaws of the hook for three or four turns (fig. 2), finally knotting the ends around all the turns (fig. 3).

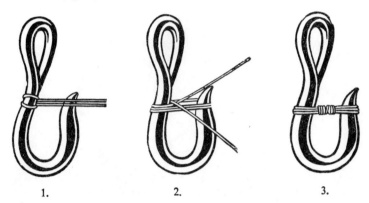

1.   2.   3.

MOUSING A SHACKLE

This is done to prevent the pin from working back, and is carried out in a similar way to mousing a hook, the bight of the seizing wire being passed through the hole in the shackle pin and pulled taut. The ends are then taken round the shackle itself in alternate directions, for a few turns, then being knotted around them.

WHIPPING A ROPE'S END

Plain whipping. Lay the end of a length of sail twine along the end of the rope to be whipped, and take a few tight turns,

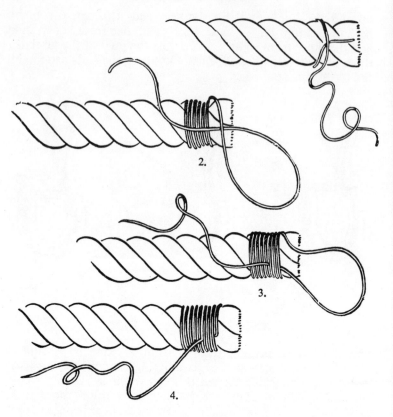

commencing from the part farthest from the rope's end, then make a few loose turns, passing the end of the twine with which you are working under them and in the direction away from end of the rope. Tighten up the loose turns, and pull the end of the twine through, cutting off surplus twine.

Palm and Needle Whipping. This whipping is more serviceable than a plain one. Thread the sail twine through the needle and insert it between two strands, leaving the end of the twine to project about an inch or so. Make several round turns in the same way as in a plain whipping, and insert the needle again exactly under two strands. Now the thread is placed obliquely over the round turns, in the lay of the rope, and inserted again at the other end of the whipping between the same two strands. In this way the thread is guided over the round turns into the spaces between the strands until they are completed. Finish by hitching the thread round its own standing part. If two parts of twine are used, a stronger whipping will result.

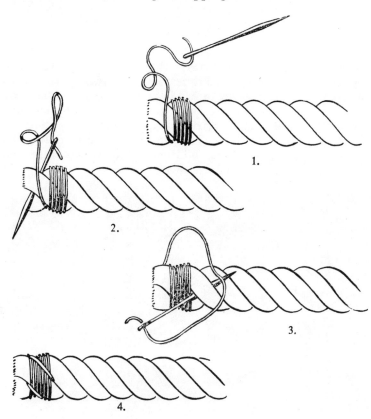

SEIZINGS

Seizings. These are simply small lashings used to hold together two parts of a rope, or two separate ropes, and they are named according to the role they play. If a rope is passed around a thimble, and the end secured to the standing part by means of seizings, that nearest the thimble is known as the eye seizing, the next one to it is the quarter seizing, the next the middle seizing, the next the upper seizing, and the last—the farthest away from the thimble—the end seizing. As regards the construction of seizings there are four kinds, the round, racking, flat and throat, though the last two are merely variations of the first.

Round seizing. Splice a small eye in one end of the marline, spun yarn or whatever material is to be used, pass the other end around the rope and through the eye, drawing the two parts of the rope to be seized as shown in sketch No. 1, below. Take several round turns, heaving each one taut if necessary with a marline spike, and take the working end through the last one, as shown in sketch No. 2. Then lay on a second series of turns (riding turns), but do not heave them so taut that they will separate the turns of the first series; now take two crossing turns between the two ropes, as shown in sketch No. 3, pull taut and hitch as in sketch No. 4. There are several equally effective ways of finishing a round seizing, and it is a matter of personal choice for the individual. Two half-hitches around the two cross turns is a popular method; making the two cross turns in the form of a clove hitch is another.

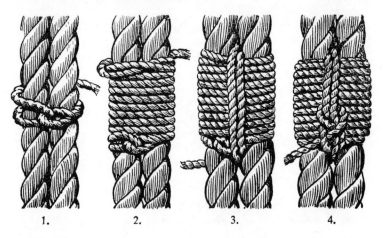

1.   2.   3.   4.

Flat seizing. This is not such a strong or secure method as the round seizing. It is started the same and finished the same, the only difference being that there are no riding turns.

Throat seizing. This, too, is a variation of the round seizing, and is used to turn in hearts, thimbles and blocks. It has riding turns but not cross turns.

Racking seizing. Splice an eye in one end of the seizing stuff, take a round turn around the two ropes and pass the working end through the eye. Then take ten or twelve turns in figure-of-eight fashion in the manner shown in sketch No. 1 below. Next pass a series of riding turns between the first series of turns and around both ropes (No. 2 sketch), add cross or frapping turns between the two ropes and finish off either in the same way as a round seizing or by passing the working end through the racking and riding turns, and the two cross turns, making one or other of the end knots and cutting off surplus seizing stuff (as in sketch No. 3 below).

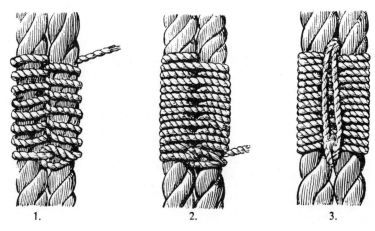

1.   2.   3.

Chapter 5

SPLICING

All sailors worth their salt—and worth an E.D.H.'s certificate —are able to splice. Put another way, any seaman who cannot splice deserves neither to be considered a sailor, nor merits to be qualified as such. There is nothing difficult about this art—but a sailor who 'uses his head' will save his hands, his temper, and some energy, too. Practice makes perfect, and young seamen should practise until they are perfect as far as this side of their job is concerned. They should practise until they do not have to think which way to hold their spike or fid, or where to tuck a strand—until, in fact, they do the right thing automatically.

The principal splices made in rope are the eye splice, the short splice, the long splice, the cut splice, the chain splice, and the back splice. Closely allied to splicing is the grommet—made a lot aboard ships in which deck quoits are played and for stropping wooden blocks of small size.

The only tools needed for rope splicing are a fid, which is a pointed wooden spike made of lignum vitæ or other hardwood, and a sharp knife. A short and thin (though thicker than a marline spike) fid is used for ropes with circumferences up to, say 101mm (4 in.) and a larger one for mooring and tow ropes.

Eye splice. The strands of the rope's end are unlaid three or four turns, care being taken to preserve, as far as possible, their original shape and see that they do not become kinked; they are then whipped. The size of the eye, of course, depends upon the purpose for which it is to be used. The unlaid end of the rope is placed on the standing part in the manner shown in the accompanying illustrations. No. 1 strand lies to the left of the standing part, No. 2 above it and No. 3 to the right of it. The middle strand, No. 2, must be selected so that it lies between strands No. 1 and No. 3 *above* the rope, which is held in the left hand. The fid (assuming it is necessary to use one as it will be with hard-laid rope) is inserted between two strands of the rope at the point below where the middle strand, No. 2, is lying. The fid is inserted exactly between these strands and forced under the strand lying at the top until the opening is large enough to take the strand. The left thumb is then pressed on the bight of the raised strand. The strand is then pulled through until the unlaid end of the rope lies against the standing part. No. 1 strand is then spliced, a half turn being taken in it against the

lay before it is tucked; this loosens the yarns and allows the
strand to lie snugly over that raised when No. 2 strand was
tucked under it. The back of the eye is now turned up and
strand No. 3 is spliced under the only strand of the standing
part now undisturbed. (Fig. 6 on page 61 shows the reverse side
of the splice after No. 3 strand has been tucked.) This com-
pletes the first part of the splice and all that remains to be done
is to tuck each strand 'over one and under one' against the lay
for the requisite number of tucks—say three to five—but after
the third tuck the splice should be tapered by cutting out half
the yarns from each strand, see fig. 7, page 61.

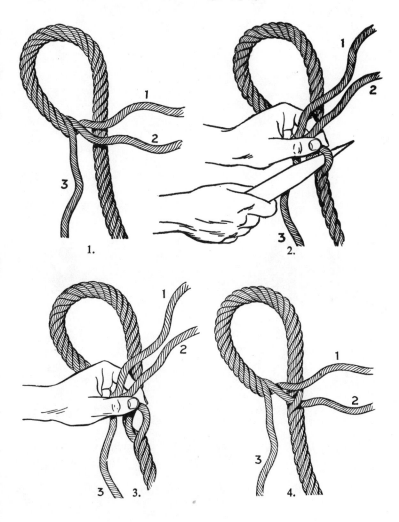

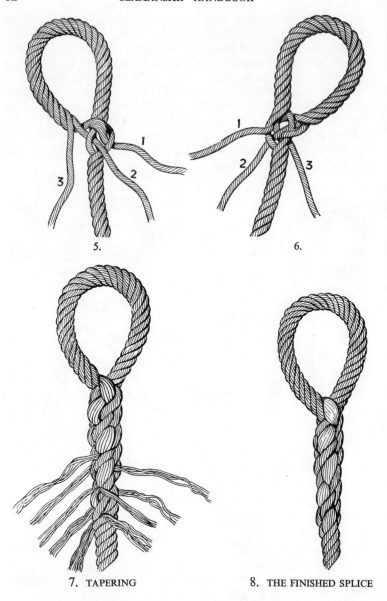

5.

6.

7. TAPERING

8. THE FINISHED SPLICE

Dogging the ends. In cases where the appearance of a splice is of secondary importance, and where utmost strength is required (as in the case of an eye in a mooring rope) it is better to take three full tucks, and then dog the ends by halving each of the three strands. Overhand knot each half to its neighbour over the adjacent strand of the main rope and whip together.

Short splice. Each end of the rope is unlaid from three to four turns and the strands are whipped. They are then placed against each other, crotched in the manner shown in Fig. 1, commencing with the inside strand on the left. The opposing strands are pulled together closely until both rope ends are lying against each other; they are firmly held in this position with the left hand. The middle strand of the three lying to the right is spliced first against the lay, under one strand, the other two strands being spliced next in the same manner. When the three strands lying to the right have been inserted the splice is turned round so that the left side now lies to the right, and the three strands are spliced in the same manner. The strands of each end are then tucked three or four times in this way. An alternative, and for beginners easier, method is to unite the strands of the two ends by means of an overhand knot, the middle strand of each being knotted together first.

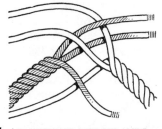 

1. CROTCHING THE STRANDS   2. FIRST TUCKS MADE

3.   READY FOR THE LAST SERIES OF TUCKS

Cut splice. This splice is made by placing two ropes side to side and splicing the ends into each other's standing parts following the same method as in the eye splice. It is important to ensure that the two sides of the eye are the same length.

Cut splices are only made in rope which does not have to pass through a block. Even when expertly made it is unavoidably bulky.

SPLICING WIRE

Wire splicing is an art, and 'bull at a gate' methods are rarely successful in practising it. The bosun should put the 'all brawn and no brain' boys on to some other job and leave wire splicing to a crew member who has some gumption. Candidates for D.T.I. certificates will certainly be required to prove their ability to make an eye splice.

Because of the great tension under which single wires are twisted into strands, and the strands into a hawser, every wire rope except the preformed variety will unlay if it is not held together by a whipping. Before unlaying a wire rope, therefore, both the strand ends and the wire rope itself must be securely whipped. It is only when this characteristic of wire is taken into account, and advantage of, that a large hawser can be readily spliced. The tucks are made throughout with the lay of the rope. When splicing, the point of the marline spike is inserted obliquely between the appropriate strands and if necessary driven in by lightly tapping with a hammer, but care must be taken to ensure that the wires of the strands and the heart of the rope are not pierced and damaged.

As soon as the spike has got a good grip it is forced to the right until it is roughly at right angles to the hawser, thus lifting the strand sufficiently. The strand to be tucked is now bent with both hands until the whipping is in line with the opening on the right close to the point of the spike. If the strand is bent too much it will kink and will not lie flat. It is therefore better for the opening made with the spike to be rather too wide than too narrow, just as it is better for the strands to be made too long than too short. On the other hand, if the opening is made too wide it may kink the lifted strand.

Splicing an eye. A strong whipping is put on the wire about 457mm (18 in.) from its end. The strands are carefully unlaid and the end of each one is plain-whipped with seaming twine. The 457mm (18 in.) of heart now exposed is cut off close to the whipping on the rope. An eye of the required size is then made and the end of the wire is whipped to the standing part. The six strands are then divided into two, three adjacent strands are placed over the rope in the direction of the lay and the other three under the rope in the same direction. The spike is then forced through the middle of the wire and No. 1 strand is inserted so that it lies with the lay of the rope between three fixed strands. Strand No. 2 is put in the same opening but under two fixed strands. Strand No. 3 is then placed in the same opening, but only under one strand. After the three upper strands have been tucked in this way under three, two and one fixed strand respectively, the six strands, that is to say, the three that have been tucked and the three which have not, are grasped with the left hand and with the right hand the wire is hammered down until they are close to the seizing. The lower side of the eye is now turned up and strands numbers four, five and six are spliced

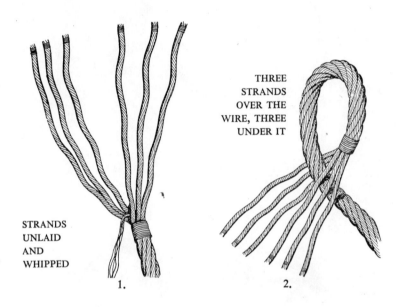

THREE
STRANDS
OVER THE
WIRE, THREE
UNDER IT

STRANDS
UNLAID
AND
WHIPPED

1.

2.

one after the other each under one strand with the lay of the rope, but when doing this each one must be inserted a little to the right of the preceding one. After this first complete tuck of the six strands, start again with strand No. 1, splicing it with the lay of the rope around and under the strand from under which it emerged when first tucked, other strands being spliced one by one in the same fashion. After each strand has been tucked three times the splice should be tapered by removing the whipping from each strand, cutting out the heart and half the wires, replacing the whipping and giving one or two additional tucks. Finally the splice should be parcelled with greased burlap or canvas strips, and served with spun yarn.

3.

OBLIQUELY AND AGAINST THE
LAY ENTERING THE SPIKE

4.

TUCKING THE FIRST
STRAND

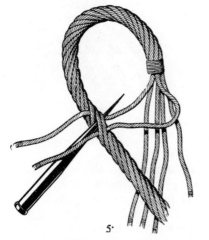

5.

TUCKING THE SECOND STRAND

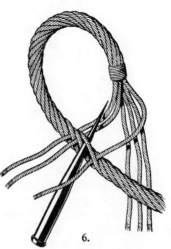

6.

TUCKING THE THIRD STRAND

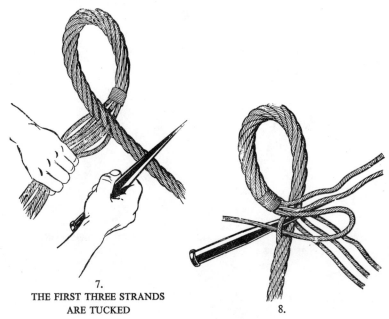

7.
THE FIRST THREE STRANDS
ARE TUCKED

8.

THE EYE TURNED OVER, THE FOURTH
STRAND IS TUCKED

9.
TUCKING IN THE FIFTH
STRAND

10.
THE LAST STRAND
GOES 'HOME'

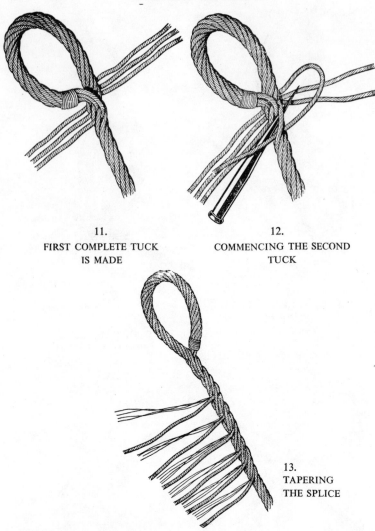

11.
FIRST COMPLETE TUCK
IS MADE

12.
COMMENCING THE SECOND
TUCK

13.
TAPERING
THE SPLICE

Boulevant or five tuck splice. This splice is suitable for use on all flexible wire and is particularly suitable for cargo runners, 'spinning' wires and springs. It has a good lock as the majority of the tucks are laid against the lay of the wire rope. To make this splice prepare as described on pages 63 and 64. Then:

1st end   Under the first and most convenient strand, *with* the lay.

6th end   Under the second strand, *with* the lay. *Do not draw out the spike.*

TAIL **MAIN**

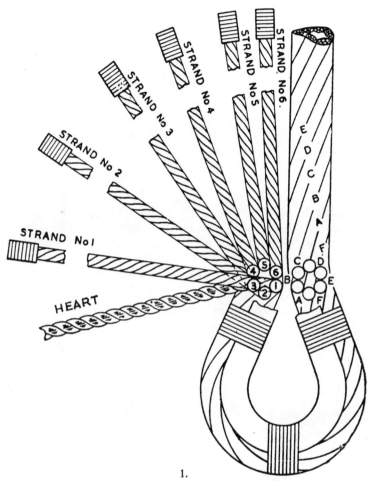

1.

2nd end   Also under the second strand, *against* the lay. It lies
           above the 6th end and locks the splice.
Note   This is the locking tuck which is required by the
           Factory Act to be made in any wire splice on a wire
           which, when free, such as a cargo runner, is liable to
           spin and so cause the wire strands to open out.
3rd end   Under the third strand, *against* the lay.
5th end   Under the fourth and fifth strands, *against* the lay.
4th end   Under the fourth strand only, *against* the lay.
    This completes the first series of tucks. After hammering

down, the second and third series are all tucked *against* the lay with each end over one strand and under the next.

Worming. Filling up the lay of a rope with a smaller one before parcelling to present an even surface for serving.

Parcelling. Winding strips of canvas, burlap or other material round a rope or over the splice in a wire to protect it from the weather. This, like worming, is always done with the lay of the rope.

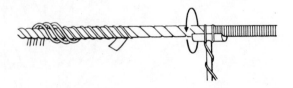

Serving. Covering the parcelling over a splice with marline, etc., not only to keep the parcelling in position, and to make a neater, more permanent job, but also further to protect hands from jagged ends (of wire) and the splice from corrosion. The marline, or whatever small stuff is employed, is hove close and taut by means of a serving mallet or serving board.

Worm and parcel with the lay
Turn and serve the other way

is the rhyme which has long helped young sailors to remember the rule.

Chapter 6

BLOCKS, HOOKS, SHACKLES AND TACKLES

Blocks are made of metal or wood, the various parts being the shell, sheave or sheaves, cheeks, swallow, pin, bush, becket and tail. The sheaves revolve on a pin which lies between the cheeks of the block. The sheaves are made of hardwood (usually lignum vitæ) or metal. In the case of wooden sheaves the bolt hole is punched out, but patent sheaves are provided with ball bearings. The sheaves must be kept well lubricated and all blocks should be frequently overhauled. For this purpose the pin must be knocked out, after the split pin or nut, if any, has been removed, and it is then cleaned with paraffin and coated with grease. The metal bushes are also cleaned with paraffin and likewise greased, the sides of the sheaves, the inside of steel shells being coated with blacklead. In the case of steel cargo blocks the practice nowadays is for sheaves to be made of grey cast iron and to be of the self-oiling type with an oil chamber, the boss being raised slightly above the sides of the sheave so that the latter, when in operation, does not rub the side plates. Phosphor-bronze bushes, with a felt strip fitted horizontally so that the whole bearing surface of the pin is constantly lubricated, are another feature of modern cargo blocks. The oil in the chamber of the sheave percolates through the felt. Alternatively the sheave pin may be fitted with a lubricator for use with a grease gun. In this case the pin is drilled for grease lubrication, the phosphor-bronze bush still being retained. It should be emphasized, however, that no matter how many the refinements with which block sheaves and bushes are fitted, *regular and frequent overhauling is essential.*

To secure the blocks, rings, single hooks, double hooks, swivel hooks, single chain links, swivel links, etc., are attached by one method or another. The function of all purchases is to reduce the power required to lift or shift a given load. In general the more sheaves there are the greater is the power gained. Snatch blocks are used to guide hauling parts in the required direction. When snatch blocks or guide blocks of any kind are employed care must be taken that they are able to be turned in the true direction of the hauling part, otherwise the fall can easily be forced between the sheave of the block and the cheek, thereby damaging the rope as well as the block. To enable a snatch block, or any type of block for that matter, to turn, a swivel link or swivel hook is fitted to it. On the following pages some typical merchant ships' blocks are shown; readers should become familiar with the names of the blocks themselves and their various fittings.

A WOODEN BLOCK AND ITS PARTS

The sketch on the right shows an Admiralty pattern double block complete. Below, the same block is shown taken adrift for purposes of illustration. On the brass description plate are stamped the number of the pattern, the size of the rope to be rove through the block, and the block's safe working load.

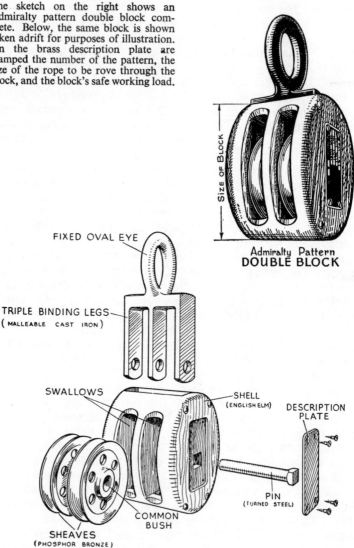

Admiralty Pattern
DOUBLE BLOCK

FIXED OVAL EYE

TRIPLE BINDING LEGS
(MALLEABLE CAST IRON)

SWALLOWS

SHELL
(ENGLISH ELM)

DESCRIPTION PLATE

PIN
(TURNED STEEL)

COMMON BUSH

SHEAVES
(PHOSPHOR BRONZE)

SIZE OF BLOCK

SOME WOODEN BLOCK TYPES AND FITTINGS

| SOLID TURNED CLUMP | BUILT CLUMP | BUILT, DOUBLE |

BLOCKS FOR ROPE STROPS

DOUBLE WITH
STAPLE EYE

SINGLE WITH
BOW EYE

SNATCH BLOCK WITH
SWIVEL HOOK

BLOCKS FOR DERRICK PURCHASES

Left—Double block with removable
shackle and triple binding legs

Right—Treble block, removable shackle
quadruple binding legs. The pins, being
supported between the sheaves, cannot
bend as can happen with double
binding legs.

BOW EYE AND
LOOSE HOOK

EXTERNAL IRON-BOUND
WITH SWIVEL HOOK

BOW EYE AND CLIP
(OR SISTER) HOOKS

TYPES OF SHEAVES
FOR USE WITH WOODEN BLOCKS

LIGNUM VITAE WITH
PATENT ROLLER BUSH

LIGNUM VITAE WITH
PLAIN BUSH

GALVANISED WITH
PLAIN BUSH

GALVANISED WITH
PATENT ROLLER BUSH

STEEL BLOCKS

CARGO BLOCK FOR DERRICK HEAD

HEEL BLOCKS DIFFER ONLY IN SO FAR AS THEY ARE FITTED WITH A DUCK BILL OR LIP EYE

SNATCH BLOCK WITH OVAL EYE

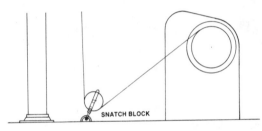

SNATCH BLOCK

Parts of a Metal Cargo Block. A, steel side plate; B, cast-iron sheave (with bush); C, oval eye; D, forged steel binding; E, phosphor bronze bush; F, collar; G, sheave pin and nut; H, distance piece (between side plates); J, bolt (in distance piece); K, cotter pin (through sheave pin).

SOME SHACKLE TYPES

OVAL PIN EYE SCREW FLUSH HEAD SCREW HEART

TYPES OF CARGO HOOKS

  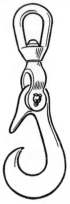 

WESTERN SEATTLE NEW YORK LIVERPOOL

REVERSE EYE HATCH PLAIN CARGO HOOK
WITH SAFETY TONGUE

TACKLES

A combination of ropes and blocks working together affording a mechanical advantage to assist in lifting, shifting or controlling a weight or applying tension is known as a tackle or purchase.

Tackles vary in rig according to their different functions, but most have their own traditional name. The theoretical power of a tackle is equal to the number of parts of rope entering the moving block or blocks, but in practice an allowance has to be made for friction according to the type of tackle, the weight of the block or blocks and the rope itself. The greater the number of sheaves the greater the frictional resistance. An allowance for friction of 10 per cent. of the weight to be lifted for every sheave in the purchase is usually made.

Single whip. A rope rove through a single block.

Double whip. A rope rove through two single blocks, the upper being a tail block, the lower a hooked moving block.

Handy Billy. A small tackle which is 'handy' for a variety of shipboard purposes. It consists of a double block with tail, and a single block with a hook.

Luff tackle. This is similar to a handy billy except that it has two hooked blocks.

Double luff consists of two double hook blocks.

Threefold purchase is one having two threefold blocks. It is customary to reeve the tackle so that the hauling part comes out of the middle sheave of the upper block.

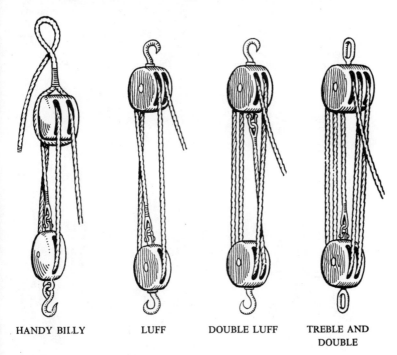

HANDY BILLY   LUFF   DOUBLE LUFF   TREBLE AND
                                                        DOUBLE

HOW TO REEVE A THREEFOLD PURCHASE WITH HAULING AND STANDING PARTS THROUGH MIDDLE SHEAVES

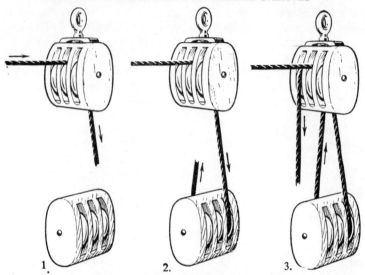

1.   2.   3.

Lay the two blocks on deck, tail to tail, upper block with sheaves upright, lower block with sheaves horizontal. Reeve the end of the fall down through the middle sheave to the upper block (fig. 1) and from right to left through the lowest sheave on the lower block (fig. 2), then up through the left-hand sheave of the upper block (fig. 3), through the upper sheave from left to right on the lower block (fig. 4), down through the right-hand sheave in the upper block (fig. 5), and from right to left through the middle sheave of the lower block (fig. 6), securing the end to the upper block.

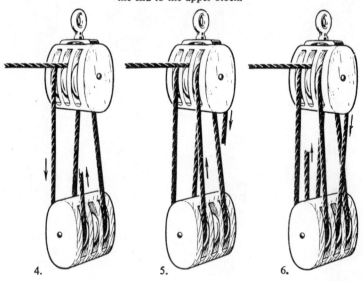

4.   5.   6.

Chapter 7

DERRICK RIGS AND CARGO GEAR

So many different ships are now being constructed specifically for special trades and cargoes that cargo gear is annually becoming more complex. In view of this it might be as well to enumerate the various vessels and the cargo lifting gear which you are likely to encounter on each class of vessel.

Bulk carriers are large vessels engaged in carrying large quantities of bulk products from port to port. The loading/discharging of dry cargoes such as ore, grain, coal, etc., is carried out by mechanical equipment and, for liquid cargoes, by means of pipelines. Obviously such vessels do not require derricks for handling their cargo and the usual equipment found on these vessels consists of a pair of ordinary tubular derricks mounted on samson posts, port and starboard, and used for lifting hoses, stores, etc.

Cargo liners, operating on fast scheduled services, must spend a minimum time in port and have to be equipped with many derricks for the rapid handling of cargo. They should also be able to work both sides of the ship together when necessary. The usual derrick rig at each hatch is either two or four tubular derricks supported either on the masts or on samson posts, port and starboard, and stayed by guys in the required positions. On the latest vessels the cargo gear consists of either cranes or the new 'Hallen' derricks. Cranes are fitted either two or four to a hatch and are worked by the driver who manipulates hoisting, lowering and swinging operations from his cab on the crane. The Hallen derrick is operated by the winchman who controls lowering and hoisting in the usual way and swinging by means of a system of guys operated from winches. Although new in its present design, this system has been in operation on two of Coast Lines vessels since 1948.

Tramps, operating on what might be called roving commissions, where time is not such an important feature, are usually equipped with two tubular derricks at each hatch.

Side loaders have only recently come into operation. These vessels are usually employed on short runs and, although equipped with either derricks or cranes in the usual way, have cargo doors fitted in their sides in the way of the hatches so that cargo can be loaded/unloaded from quay to hold or v.v., using fork-lift trucks both on the quay and in the vessel.

Roll-on, roll-off and Container vessels. The former are employed on very short passages such as Harwich to the Hook of Holland. By means of bow and stern doors, loaded vehicles are driven direct on board, secured for the passage, and driven off through the doors at the other end to their destination. Container vessels carry goods in large specially constructed metal containers which are loaded/discharged by means of special lifting apparatus. Both these methods have produced the biggest advance for many years in certain kinds of cargo handling by cutting down considerably on transit costs and in the protection of goods carried.

DERRICK RIGS

The diagrams on page 81 show the typical derrick rig of a general trader (tramp) and the two normal methods of raising and securing the span.

Sometimes, whilst the derrick is tested to a sufficient safe working load, the safe working load of the gear is insufficient. In this case a system of doubling-up gear is utilised. See doubling-up diagram.

PREPARING AND RAISING DERRICKS

The derricks are usually hoisted by means of a single wire pennant attached to the derrick span or by heaving on the hauling part of a purchase, which is often employed instead of a span. After being 'topped' the derrick is held in position by a span chain, whilst the guys give lateral support.

Topping lifts and guys can be hove upon or slacked away in such a way that the derrick head can be placed above practically any position over the hatchway, adjacent deck and quay. A simple derrick span is shackled to a spider band on the head of the derrick and passes through a block on the mast. To the eye of the span a smaller wire or tackle is connected, and this leads either direct to the winch drum or through a snatch block on deck and thence to the winch barrel.

The span chain has long loose links. It is shackled to the end of the span and to a ringbolt in the deck when the derrick has been hoisted to the desired height. The spider band, to which the guy pennants (two), derrick span and head block are shackled, is forged on to the derrick head. The underside of the spider band is fitted with a chain link in order to facilitate the free movement of the block. The block itself is fitted with a swivel so that it is free to rotate.

The wire cargo runners are rove through the head block before the derrick is hoisted. When the derrick is in position the

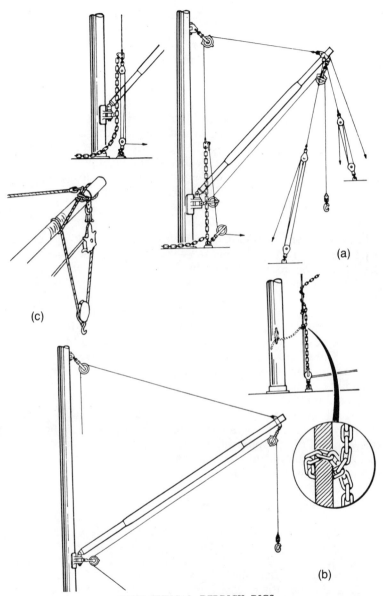

(a)

(c)

(b)

SOME TYPICAL DERRICK RIGS

(a) Derrick rigged with a single span and winch-end whip led through a snatch block to the drum end. The inset (right) shows the rig but using a tackle.

(b) Derrick rigged with single span, the insets (right) show how the wire is held by the chain stopper for transfer to the cleat on the samson post.

(c) Doubling-up gear.

end of the runner is rove through the heel block and thence is passed to the winch, where it is lashed to an eye on the drum. At sea—or for that matter in port when there is no cargo work to be done—the derricks are laid fore and aft above the hatches, the head resting on, and being lashed to, crutches, or else vertically, parallel to the mast, in which case the head is secured by steel clamps.

Before hoisting a derrick the rigging belonging to it is examined, the upper blocks are oiled and the cargo runner is rove through the head block. The guy pennants and the span are shackled to the spider band, the derrick lashing is removed and the topping lift is led to the winch drum, where its end is lashed to the eye thereon. The lower guy blocks are shackled to convenient ringbolts on deck on either side near the bulwarks.

Four men are normally employed in hoisting a derrick— one for each guy, one driving the winch and one standing by to shackle on the span chain when the derrick is in the desired position—though the job can be done by fewer. The links of the span chain are not studded and are large enough for the shackle to fit into each link. The length of the span chain in use varies with the inclination of the boom, so the shackle has to be shifted accordingly and placed into the appropriate link of the chain. Care must be taken when putting the shackle into the link that its bow is clear of the link below it to avoid the possibility of it jamming when the weight is transferred from the topping lift to the span chain.

The pin of the shackle passes through the deck ringbolt and is firmly screwed in. After the preventer has been secured in this manner the topping lift is eased until it bears no weight, run off the winch drum and coiled down handy ready for use again. The guys are set up and the cargo runners can be hove on to the drum ready for lifting the hatch beams.

The union purchase. Where rapid handling of cargo from hold to quay or v.v. is required, the derricks are rigged as in the diagram. One derrick plumbs the hatch and the other the quay (or barge) and the two cargo runners are shackled to the same hook. The cargo is lifted by one derrick to the necessary height and then, by slackening on one runner and hauling on the other, eased over until it is under the other derrick when it can be lowered to the hold or quay. There is a heavy cross-pull on the derricks when the weight is being transferred and the port and starboard ship's side guys must be fitted with strong preventer guys. On many ships the inboard guys are replaced by a wire tackle each end of which

UNION PURCHASE

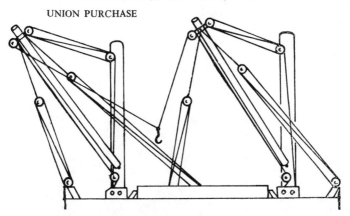

is shackled to the spider band at each derrick head and made fast near one of the derrick heels on the mast or samson post.

Swinging derrick with deadman. When a swinging derrick is required, the offshore derrick is guyed in the required position and the swinging derrick is rigged as follows. A runner is attached to a weight (deadman) and then led through the gin block and secured to the spider band of the swinging derrick. The runner of this derrick is secured to the barrel of the offshore winch and the shore side guy rope led to the shore side winch

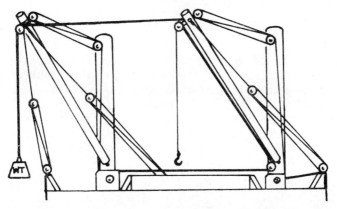

barrel. When the lift to be raised is clear of the hatch coaming, heave on the shore side guy and the derrick will swing overboard, the weight under the standing derrick rising towards the gin block. To bring the derrick back over the hatch, slack on the guy rope and the weight descending from the standing derrick will bring the swinging derrick back to plumb the hatch.

The Hallen derrick. This new type of derrick is operated like a crane in that one man, from a control consol, operates both topping and slewing of the derrick and the raising and lowering of the load. The topping and slewing guys are connected by specially constructed heavy-duty pennants to the port and starboard extremities of the mast table and to the derrick head, and the hauling parts lead down from the derrick head through lead blocks on the bipod masts to separate winches. A third

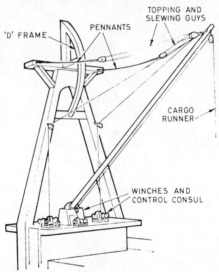

winch is used for the cargo runner. The operator at the control consol controls slewing and raising of the derrick by means of a 'joystick', and raising and lowering of the runner by means of a second lever. Unlike the ordinary rig, the pennants are secured well above the heel of the derrick and this gives great control and stability at wide angles of swing. The large 'D' frame always ensures that there is a sufficiently large angle between the guys when the derrick is swung overside.

The Stuelcken Derricks. The heavy lift equipment shown overleaf consists of two Stuelcken Derricks with a safe working load on the hook of 275 T. each.

The aft Stuelcken derrick is of the swinging type and serves the large hatch between the two heavy derricks and hatch No. 5. The forward Stuelcken derrick arranged immediately aft of the bridge serves the large hatch between the two heavy derricks only.

The posts are made of high tensile steel with a breaking strength of minimum 60 Kg/sq. mm.

As has been the standard of all 200 Stuelcken heavy derricks so far delivered, all bearings, rope sheaves, gooseneck pin sockets and span swivels are equipped with anti-friction bearings thus ensuring a maintenance-free operation for four years or more. To each of these Stuelcken derricks there are more than 100 anti-friction bearings of various types with diameters ranging from 190mm to 1340mm.

In order to ensure the safe functioning of the derrick under all operating conditions, the winches are additionally equipped with safety switches responding to irregularities. Furthermore, the posts have portholes for inspection of the winches from the main deck. Each Stuelcken derrick requires four heavy cargo winches.

These winches (one cargo and one span winch) are arranged in each post in pairs, one above the other.

The maximum rope pull on the span winch drums is 30·5 t., the diameter of the rope is 40mm and the length of the span tackle is 550m. The winches have two ratios which allow operation with half load at the double hook speed.

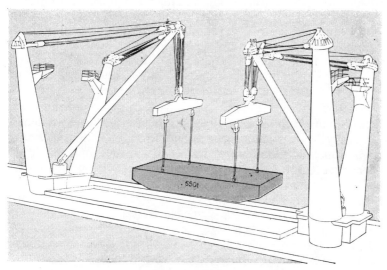

Diagram by courtesy of Constantine & Co. Ltd., British agents for Stuelcken Derricks.

WINCHES

Winches, either steam or electric, are sited near the hatchways and usually there is one to each derrick. The cargo runner end is led through the heel block and secured to the lug on the winch barrel by rope yarns. The winch is slowly rotated and the first turns wound diagonally across the barrel from right to left and then across from left to right. This ensures that the second set of turns jam the first set against the surface of the barrel and provide a good grip for the remaining turns when the weight comes on the wire. If allowed to coil directly on the barrel which is usually oily the wire could slip and the weight break the seizing. Should this happen and the wire run back through the heel and gin blocks, the derrick would have to be lowered for the wire to be re-rove.

Steam winches should not be operated until the drain cocks have been opened and any water in the cylinders drained off. Then, with the cocks open, the winch is run a little, slowly, first forward and then in reverse; the drain cocks are closed and the working parts of the winch are oiled before it is subjected to much heavy usage such as that involved in working cargo.

Driving a winch can only be learnt by practice. The direction of rotation of the drum is adjusted for forward and reverse motion by the reversing lever. The lever is pushed forward, away from the driver, when hauling, and pulled backwards, towards the driver, when reversing. The winch is set in motion by turning the steam control valve in an anti-clockwise direction and is stopped by turning it as far as possible to the right. When heavy weights are being lowered by the cargo runner the control valve of the winch must be closed and the gear lever and foot brake used to control the lowering speed.

Actually reversing with heavy loads presents difficulties as these loads can only be brought to a standstill by quickly pushing the gear lever forward and admitting sufficient steam —by opening the control valve—until the upward thrust generated through the winch is equal to the downward thrust of the load on the runner.

If the winch is to be employed for heavy lifts it should be put into double gear by means of the clutch lever, but care must be taken that the lever is always secured by the securing pins. A winch is in double gear when the two large and two small drums are turning in *opposite* directions. When they are turning in the same direction the winch is said to be in whipping gear.

Electric winches are in common use and, since the basic machinery of a winch (or windlass) is the same whether steam or electric powered, only the controls of an electric winch are shown in the diagram. The control lever or wheel is used for raising or lowering and the speed of operation depends on the amount that the lever is turned to port or starboard. To stop

CLARKE CHAPMAN DOUBLE CYLINDER HORIZONTAL STEAM WINCH

1, Drum; 2, bearing; 3, steam pipe; 4, barrel; 5, reversing counter weight; 6, brake band; 7, guard; 8, stop valve; 9, reversing lever; 10, drum; 11, big end; 12, connecting rod; 13, cross head; 14, piston rod; 15, cross head slides; 16, holding down bolt; 17, drain cocks; 18, cylinder; 19, frame; 20, exhaust; 21, tie rods; 22, bedplate; 23, foot brake; 24, valve chest; 25, frame; 26, cylinder.

1, Drum; 2, reversing lever; 3, gear wheel; 4, guard; 5, barrel; 6, bearing cap; 7, drum; 8, cylinder; 9, drain cocks; 10, fly drum; 11, connecting rod; 12, bottom end; 13, disc; 14, holding down bolt; 15, frame; 16, bedplate; 17, gear levers (note securing pins above); 18, guard; 19, disc; 20, guard; 21, whipping drum.

the winch, the lever is turned to the neutral position thus cutting off the power. When the power is switched off the magnetic disc-brake comes into operation so that the weight on the runner does not run back as is the case with steam operated winches.

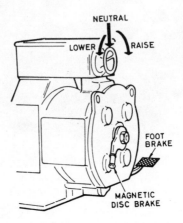

Automatic Mooring Winch (or self-tensioning winch). Loading and unloading rates of modern types of vessels are becoming extremely rapid, particularly in the case of bulk carriers. As a result, the elevation of the vessel in relation to the dock is constantly changing even in non-tidal harbours and by using automatic mooring winches line adjustments are taken care of automatically by the winches without attendance by the crew.

Tidal waters also create problems relative to mooring of vessels. Again adjustments for rise and fall of tide can be taken care of automatically, the winch heaving, stalling or rendering to suit change of conditions.

Automatic mooring winches can be safely left unattended and a periodic inspection by one of the crew is all that is necessary.

The automatic mooring winch is arranged with both "hand" and "automatic mooring" control and once the "automatic mooring" control is selected, the action of the winch will be entirely automatic. The value at which the winch will haul in, stall and render will be dependent on the size of the winch and the particular step of automatic control to which the controller is set. Normally there are three steps of "automatic mooring" control and five steps for "hand" control.

HATCHWAYS

Hatchways are large openings cut in the decks to provide access to the holds and an average hatchway might measure 12 metres × 7½ metres (40 ft. × 25 ft.). To provide compensation for cutting the beams and decks in way of the hatches and also to provide protection against the sea, deep vertical plates, specially strengthened, are fitted along the sides and ends. These plates are called 'coamings'.

The proposals of the 1966 International Load Line Convention are that ships fitted with steel hatchcovers will be able to load to deeper draughts. This will eventually lead to all ships being equipped with this type of hatchcover. Since many ships are still fitted with wooden covers, it will be several years before this design finally disappears.

Wooden hatch covers. Many ships are also fitted with sliding beams. They are identical in shape to the ordinary beams, but each end is fitted with rollers which move along a trackway inside the coaming and are held in their respective positions by snugs which fit into apertures in the coaming. When the wooden hatchboards are removed, the snugs are freed from the apertures and the beams pulled to one end of the hatch. The rollers should be periodically cleaned and greased and the runways kept clean.

Wooden hatches are laid between steel beams. Hatchways closed with wooden covers are the most vulnerable parts of the ship. According to their length, hatchways are divided into a number of sections by the beams which have to be lifted clear of the hatchway before cargo work can commence. To facilitate being shipped their (and there is often a hurry to get hatches battened down before the ship proceeds to sea) beams and hatch covers are marked. The beams are marked on their lower flanges with a centre punch. The marks indicate the deck, hatch number and beam number. 'Different ships, different long splices,' and, it may be said, different ways of marking beams and hatches. It behoves all seamen to familiarise themselves on joining a ship with the method adopted. Hatch covers usually have their numbers cut in and are also generally marked with a broad diagonal stripe painted over the hatch covers when they are in position. Much time can be lost if, through imperfect or inadequate marking and numbering, beams or hatch covers have to be changed around until their proper places are found.

LAYOUT AND EQUIPMENT OF A CARGO SHIP'S HATCHWAY

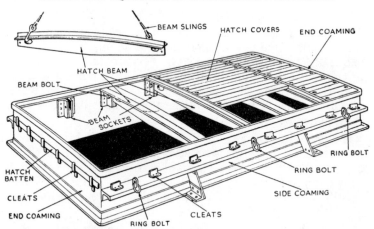

When 'stripping' a hatchway the covers should be removed in sections, starting from the middle of the hatchway and working towards both sides. The covers and beams should be neatly stacked alongside the hatch, allowing a sufficient space to walk round (see photograph). Care must be taken that the piles of covers are firm and will not readily topple over—perhaps on to someone's foot. In no circumstances should the piles of hatch covers exceed in height the level of the coamings.

After the tarpaulins and the hatch covers have been removed the beams are either pulled to the end of the hatch, or lifted out

with wire or chain slings especially made and kept for the purpose. When lifting beams the securing bolts are taken out and the ends of the slings are shackled or hooked into each end of the beam. The height of the derrick should be adjusted for each beam. It is customary to top the derrick initially so that the derrick head block is directly above the beam nearest to the winch, then to lower the derrick to plumb each beam to be removed. In any case the derrick head should be plumbed as near as possible to a position vertically above the beam to be removed and in the centre-line of the ship.

Covering a hatchway, of course, is done in the reverse order. The beams are placed in position and beam bolts inserted. Then the covers are shipped, commencing from the coamings on each side and working towards the middle of the hatchway. It is usual to fit three tarpaulins on top of the hatch covers to keep out the water, the best tarpaulin being put on first, the second-best on second, and the worst on last.

The tarpaulins extend over the hatchway coamings as far as the cleats, which are riveted or welded to the outside edge of the coaming. The edges and corners of each tarpaulin are turned in evenly and tucked between the cleats and the coaming, the steel hatch battens are placed between the tarpaulin edges and the cleats are secured by hardwood wedges. In some ships hatch cleats on either side and at either end of hatch coamings are parallel to each other, and in this case the wedges on the side coamings should be placed in the cleats from forward to aft in the case of forward hatchways and from aft to forward in the case of after ones, the idea being that when seas are breaking aboard, forward or aft, respectively, they will tend to knock the side wedges in rather than out. With parallel cleats on end coamings wedges are put in sharp end inwards, i.e. starboard wedges *from* starboard, and port wedges *from* port. In many ships, however, hatch cleats on both the side and end coamings point towards the middle of the coaming concerned, and in this case wedges must, of course, be placed to suit the cleats' direction. Actually in heavy weather, with seas being shipped fore and aft, it is not often that wedges become loose since the water tends to swell wood. Even so, it is always sound practice—considering that the safety of the ship may, and the safety of the cargo does, depend on hatchways being weather-proof—to have them examined and, if necessary, hammered home at regular and frequent intervals. This is usually 'chippy's' job by day and that of the first stand-by man in each watch by night.

Locking or tie bars are frequently employed across the entire hatchway, or, alternatively, rope lashings overall may be used, but in the latter event burlap or old canvas should be used to prevent the rope chafing the tarpaulins at the sides of the hatchway.

During spells between cargo operations all precautions should be taken to make the hatchways safe. From the safety viewpoint it is better not to cover a hatchway at all than to cover it improperly. *In no case should a tarpaulin be spread over an open hatchway*, because, especially in the dark, the impression is created that the hatchway is closed. The danger of open hatchways is increased in the 'tween decks, which are all too frequently inadequately illuminated. Approach hatchways with caution. Watch your step.

STEEL HATCH COVERS

The portable hatch beam, wooden hatch board and tarpaulin

represent the last characteristic reminders of the sailing ship. Today the long and tedious operation of covering and securing hatches has been reduced considerably by the introduction of the steel hatch cover.

The research and development of the steel cover by the MacGregor organisation who pioneered this field has resulted in a great saving of time during loading and discharging operations, afforded a clear working deck when hatches are open in obviating the placing of hatch boards and beams on deck, and given the mariner added security on the weather deck at deep draughts in heavy weather.

A further advantage of the steel cover is that of more efficient isolation of compartments in event of fire. When 'tween decks are fitted with steel covers, especially watertight covers as in the case of open shelter decks, there is little or no chance of fire spreading vertically from one compartment to another, thus rendering the work of modern methods of steam or gas smothering systems more effective.

In the case of steel 'tween deck covers which fit flush with the deck plating a further advantage is gained in the stowage of cargo and the use of fork lift trucks within the deck, in so far as the $228\frac{1}{2}$mm (9 in.) open shelter deck coaming demanded by Classification Societies for the purpose of battening down is no longer necessary.

There are various types of steel covers perfected by Mac-Gregor & Co. Ltd. but the two most commonly used are the Single Pull and Folding types.

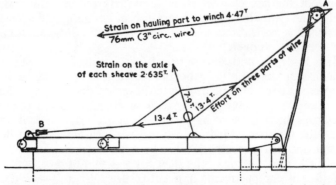

Purchase consists of a luff tackle with two single sheave blocks at the head of the hauling post (A) and a single sheave block at the opposite end of the hatch (B). At the centre of this purchase are three single sheave lead blocks which are secured at the first fold of the cover.

Folding type covers on the M.V. *Norse Coral*, a modern bulk grain and car carrier of 15,800 tons deadweight capacity. Photograph by kind permission of British Car Carriers Limited (U.K. agents R. Nerdrum Ltd.).

The Single Pull type is operated by means of a wire from a winch or by an endless chain powered by an independent electric or hydraulic winch unit housed behind the end coaming. When opening, the chain or wire pulls the end section towards the opposite end of the hatch which in turn pushes the other sections in the same direction. All the cover sections roll on their wheels in a channel on the coaming, pivoting at the end of the coaming into a vertical stowage position between the transverse coaming and the winch island or mast house bulkhead.

To close, the operation is reversed and in the closed position the covers rest on rubber jointing and are secured tightly by screw cleats or hydraulic locking cleats fitted at intervals round the coamings. When the covers are secured the rubber jointing is compressed and forms a water-tight seal.

Folding type covers are operated hydraulically or again by a wire from a cargo winch.

The diagram and photograph show the wire operation of this type of cover. In this case the cover sections are being lifted which requires a greater effort than that required to roll the Single Pull type.

For this reason a system of pulleys is introduced, reducing the strain on the hauling part to a figure applicable to the s.w.l. of the wire. The weight of the cover sections varies with the dimensions of the hatch, and the diagram shows the total effort required reduced to 4·4 tons on the hauling part. Securing the covers in the closed position is the same as in the case of Single Pull covers.

Like all other cargo-handling equipment normal maintenance is required. The cover wheels should be kept greased and free from dirt, and the coaming and drainage channels periodically inspected and cleared of any foreign deposits.

All securing cleats should be kept greased and at sea they should be inspected and tightened when necessary.

Chapter 8

TYPICAL CARGO SPACES

The entire hull of the ship is subdivided into compartments by watertight bulkheads, and each hold, except in 'single-deckers', is divided into lower hold and one or more 'tween decks. The lower hold extends from the tank top (the 'inner bottom') to the lower 'tween deck. A protective layer of planks is laid over the tank top, either in the square of the hatchway only, or from side to side and end to end of the hold.

Adjacent to the double bottom and running along both sides of the ship from forward to aft are the bilges, which drain off any water which collects in the holds. The bilges are connected with the bilge pump in the engine-room by pipe-lines. The bilges are sounded twice daily by the carpenter and are pumped dry as necessary. The sounding rod is lowered into the bilge by means of a sounding pipe from the weather deck. Bilges should be kept as dry and as clean as possible. Since the bilges are only accessible from the holds they can only be cleaned when the cargo has been discharged.

Bilge covers (limber boards) are unshipped when cleaning operations start, dirt and water are removed from every compartment and the strums (or rose boxes) fitted at the end of the bilge pipe-line and in the after end of each cargo hold (since the average ship is always 'down by the stern', and the water will therefore run aft) thoroughly cleaned. It is surprising the amount of filth which collects in bilges. 'Bilge-diving' is not, therefore, a pleasant job.

After cleaning the holds and bilges, liming the former and cement-washing the latter, dunnage is laid to protect the cargo from contact with steelwork in the holds. For this purpose dunnage wood, mats or separation cloth (burlap) are used, any or all of which can be employed according to the nature of the cargo. In the case of coal or iron ore it is not necessary to be very particular about the cleanliness of the holds, of course, but with grain and many other cargoes it is essential that they should be spotlessly clean. Before *any* cargo is loaded, however, the bilges should be cleaned. The dunnage is laid on the deck of the hold athwartships in order to allow moisture from the cargo to run to the bilges. If a second layer of dunnage has to be laid it should be laid across the bottom one, i.e. fore and aft.

General and bagged cargoes are kept clear of the ship's sides with what is known as spar ceiling, which are long lengths of timber about 102mm (4 in.) broad and 25mm (1 in.) thick,

MIDSHIP SECTION OF A CARGO SHIP

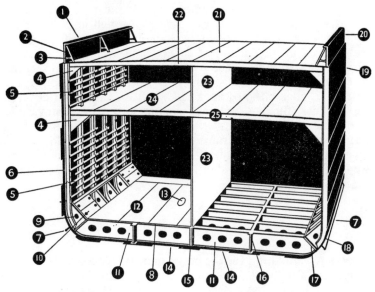

(1) Bulwark rail	(13) Manhole cover
(2) Bulwark stay	(14) Garboard strake
(3) Spur	(15) Keel plate
(4) Beam knees	(16) Intercostal
(5) Spar ceiling	(17) Margin plate
(6) Frame	(18) Bilge strake
(7) Bilge keel	(19) Sheer strake
(8) Reverse frame	(20) Bulwark
(9) Lightening hole in tank side bracket	(21) Upper deck plating
(10) Limber boards	(22) Upper deck beam
(11) Floor	(23) Centreline bulkhead
(12) Tank top plating	(24) Main deck plating
	(25) Main deck beam

which rest in cleats bolted to the frames. If these have to be taken out of the cleats for any reason at all they should be replaced before loading commences. Hold ventilators, stanchions, ladders and sounding pipes should be covered with mats when cargo liable to be damaged by 'sweat'—moisture caused by condensation on steel work—is to be loaded. Burlap is used for separation of the various cargoes.

Although a high percentage of bulk cargo is now carried in specially constructed bulk carriers, many of these vessels are too deep draughted to enter many ports and the cargo is off-loaded at places where these vessels can berth, and then transhipped in smaller cargo vessels to the final destination.

Special precautions are taken if bulk cargoes are to be loaded in general cargo vessels. Limber boards must be thoroughly sealed so that the cargo does not seep through into the bilges and block the strum. The limber boards are therefore caulked with oakum at the seams and corners and, in the case of grain cargoes, burlap is stretched over the entire bilge and is secured by means of wooden laths. Similarly, where the sounding pipe enters the bilge all gaps are caulked with oakum and covered with laths. Surplus dunnage should either be removed or stacked against the transverse bulkheads and covered with a tarpaulin. Better still, transfer it from the lower holds to the 'tween decks, where it is both readily accessible and out of the way. Mats and burlap should be collected and stowed away until required again.

HOLD VENTILATION

Adequate ventilation for the cargo must be ensured at sea at all times, and for this purpose ventilators are fitted in all holds—lower holds and 'tween decks. Some cargoes require a great deal of ventilation, rice, for example; others, iron ore and timber, require none at all. The ventilators are usually tubular airshafts which permit fresh air to enter the holds and stale air to be expelled. They extend above the upper deck and are arranged so that they can be turned in any direction. Lee ventilators are turned into the wind so that fresh air can enter, whilst the weather ventilators are turned away from the wind to facilitate the escape of stale air from the holds, whilst at the same time preventing spray from entering. In adverse weather, when there is the danger of rain or spray getting into the holds through the ventilators and damaging the cargo, all ventilators should be turned away from the wind (in other words backed) or the cowls should be covered.

Precautionary measures should be so familiar to experienced sailors that they will back the vents on their own without waiting to be ordered to do so by the officer of the watch, just as an eye is kept on halyards during heavy rain and they are slacked a little to prevent them parting when they shrink. In fine weather holds are partly opened up to improve the ventilation.

It is sufficient to knock out a few wedges, lift the tarpaulin and remove a corner hatch whilst the rest of the hold remains battened down. On ships fitted with steel hatchcovers, the covers can be quickly rolled back far enough to allow additional ventilation as and when required.

Fig. 1 shows the 'cowl' type of ventilator which is turned by hand either 'back to' or 'on to' the wind. This type of ventilator, if sited on the foc's'le or weather deck, is very vulnerable in heavy weather. If heavy weather is expected the cowls are removed, a wooden plug is inserted and a canvas cover is securely lashed over the top of the trunk (fig. 2). Most modern vessels now use the samson posts as ventilators (fig. 3). An electric fan is fitted in the trunk, sufficiently high up to be clear of any sea damage, and the motors are set so that air is drawn in on one side of the ship and expelled on the other, thus ensuring a continuous flow of air through the cargo spaces.

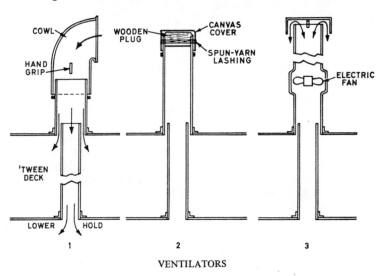

VENTILATORS

CARGO WATCHING

When general cargo is being taken aboard it is customary for a few seamen to be detailed to assist the officer in charge. Their duties are to act as cargo watchers and/or to tend all gear so that in the event of breakdowns occurring or replacements being needed they can be attended to with a minimum of delay to the ship. Spare runners should be available for the derricks, together with strops, nets, beam slings, can hooks, etc., both before a ship berths and at the start of each day's work. Laying dunnage and covering parcels of cargo is a continuing process, and whilst most of this work is normally undertaken by stevedores it is good practice for a representative of the ship to see that the work is carried out properly.

Seamen deputed to act as cargo watchers are primarily concerned with preventing pilferage, but they should also be interested in the proper stowage of the cargo. Damaged goods should never be stowed without the attention of the officer in charge being drawn to them. Cargo watchers must not leave the hold without being relieved. When work stops at meal intervals or at the end of the day's work the watchman should make sure that all workmen leave the hold.

The number of shore workers engaged in the hold should be noted and their activities carefully watched. Entering into conversation generally diverts the attention of the watchman and cargo can be broached in dark corners. The cargo watcher should select a good vantage point in the hold whence he can see all that is going on. If he has reason to suspect anything untoward he should report it at once—certainly before the workmen leave the hold of the ship.

OIL TANKERS

Oil tankers have no inner bottom and the entire space in each tank, down to the shell plating, is taken up by the oil cargo. Once this cargo has been discharged, the vessel is ballasted and proceeds to sea. During the passage to the loading port, the tanks have to be prepared for the next cargo.

Tank cleaning. Each tank usually has four tank-washing apertures and the covers of these are first removed and the washing machines, flexible hoses, hose saddles and safety lines got ready. The most common types of washing machines used in British ships are the Butterworth and the Victor Pyrate, both of which are activated by the flow of water through them driving impellers. The impellers cause the barrels to revolve so that the nozzles force water jets at high pressure all round the tank. The pressure and splash from these machines wash away the oil from the sides of the tank and loosen and remove rust and scale which absorb and hold gas pockets.

The 63mm ($2\frac{1}{2}$ in.) flexible rubber hoses are made in $15\frac{1}{2}$m (50 ft.) lengths and are marked at every 1·5m (5 ft.) by the makers. One end of the hose is coupled to the water main on the flying bridge and the other end is tightly screwed to

A BUTTERWORTH 'K' TYPE TANK
WASHING MACHINE
(By courtesy of Butterworth Corps.
Inc., New Jersey, and Messrs. J.
Edmiston Ltd., London.)

THE VICTOR PYRATE TANK
WASHING MACHINE
(By courtesy of Samuel Hodge & Sons
Ltd., London.)

the washing machine. 50mm (2 in.) or 63mm (2½ in.) manila
safety lines, of sufficient length to reach to the bottom of
the deepest tank, are then made fast to the machines. On the
Victor Pyrate, the safety rope is shackled to the lug on the
machine, but on the Butterworth it must be secured under the
top bolted flange where it will then support the whole machine.
If secured to the hose coupling it will only support the hose and
not the machine.

A word of warning about safety precautions when operating
these machines. They are made of non-ferrous metal but should
never be allowed to strike against any part of the tank. Static
charges of electricity can be built up by the lowering of these
machines into a tank and water should be slightly running
before putting through opening. Research has shown that they
are more easily generated when the tank contains steam. The
machines should therefore never be lowered into the tank until
the steam has been ejected. Charges can also be built up
when water passes through the hose and, to guard against
this, an earthing or bonding wire is incorporated in the inner
ply of the hose. Each hose should therefore be tested for electrical continuity before use.

When everything is checked, either two or four machines are carefully lowered down through the apertures to the required height, the hose securely clamped in the saddle and the safety rope turned several times round the saddle clamp. On most ships it is possible to wash two or more tanks at any one time. Whilst washing tanks, the slops are immediately stripped and pumped into a slop tank or over the side, if the vessel is in an area where it is permissible to do so. The machines are lowered carefully to different levels during tank washing to ensure that the entire tank is washed down.

Gas-freeing. Once the tank has been washed and stripped, it must be gas-freed. This is usually carried out by using either Axia or Meco compressed-air fans and by the use of windsails. The fans are designed to be mounted over the tank wash openings. Windsails are suspended from the ridge wires.

In order to establish that a tank is gas-free, an instrument in common use is the Mine Society Appliance Company's 'Explosimeter' which is designed to measure the degree of flammability of the atmosphere, but can also be used to find out if a compartment is sufficiently clear of gas to permit men to enter.

THE M.S.A. EXPLOSIMETER
(By courtesy of the Mine Safety Appliances Co. Ltd., Glasgow.)

The instrument is first adjusted to zero and the sampling tube lowered into the tank. The aspirator bulb is pressed several times and, if there is no response from the needle, the action is repeated. No response on the second test indicates that there is no gas. Before the men are allowed to enter the tank, the instrument should be used to test different levels within tank and tank corners, etc., where there may be pockets of gas. If any is detected, the area affected should be ventilated before the men enter the tank.

De-rusting. From time to time, tanks must be de-rusted and the diagram below shows the usual equipment set up for such an operation. Wooden or glass fibre shovels are used for scraping up the loose scale and residue left in the bottom of the tank. On the larger ships an air hoist is used instead of the 'armstrong's patent' for lifting the buckets.

Scaling may release gas and men working in the bottom of the tank must be under constant observation. Occasionally repeat

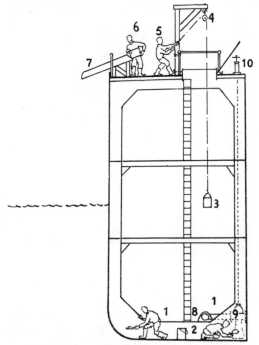

Equipment set up for the de-rusting operation.

 1. Men engaged in lifting scale and sediment
 2. Bucket into which scale is being shovelled
 3. Full bucket being hauled to deck
 4. Single tail block with gantline
 5. Man to heave out buckets (sometimes two required)
 6. Depositing contents of full buckets overside
 7. Wood chute (metal lined)
 8. Pipeline
 9. Suction valve
10. Suction valve control wheel

Explosimeter test (See posn. No. 1 on diagram). A man going to another's assistance in a gas-filled space must wear breathing apparatus and a lifeline. A crew member receiving a slight amount of gas may be revived by using capsules of amyl nitrite which should be crushed between the fingers and held under the victim's nose. 'Novita' oxygen equipment is used for more serious cases.

Loading. The Chief Officer is responsible for loading and during this operation will delegate the following duties:

Ullaging. Ullage is the depth of the oil (or liquid) below the level of the ullage pipe or sighting port. Many tankers are equipped with fixed tank-gauges, such as the 'Whessoe' (in which a metal float secured to the end of a tensioned steel measuring-tape runs up and down two guide wires extending

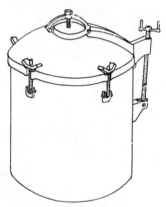

Domed tank lid about three feet high, fitted with worm-screw lifting gear and combined sighting and ullage port in the centre of the cover.

from the top to the bottom of the tank) and the Dobbie McInnes Teledip tank-gauging instrument, where the valves are automatically opened or closed at pre-set ullages. You will still be required, however, to operate hand measuring instruments, and

---

Opposite (*lower diagram*):

(a) A Fahrenheit thermometer (0°-160°) for oil measurement, encased in brass guard.
(b) An oil hydrometer for measuring specific gravities.
(c) An oil hydrometer—of slightly different design to previous illustration—immersed in oil contained in a measuring jar. Note 'meniscus' and true level at which reading is observed.
(d) A dip-can with brass-cased thermometer becketed securely to handle for lowering into oil in tank.

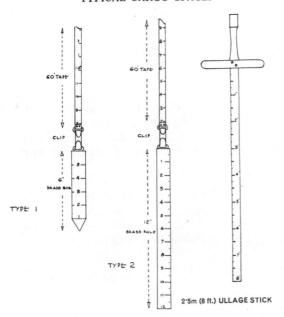

MEASURING TAPES 3.11

Measuring instruments—'Chesterman's' 18m (60 ft.) steel tapes of two different types, and a standard 2½m (8 ft.) wood ullage stick.

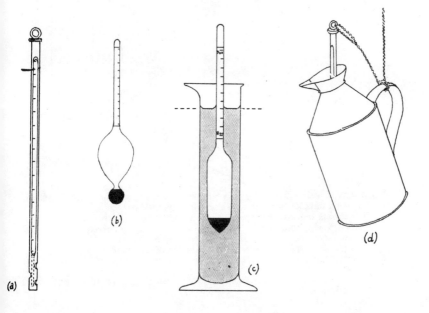

the most common are illustrated in the diagram at the top of page 103.

Samples. These are taken from each tank at different levels, when loaded and again before discharging, to ensure against contamination. It is particularly important when several grades of oil are carried.

Temperatures and specific gravities. These are taken at different levels to enable the Chief Officer to make his cargo calculations and to plan his distribution and the trim of the ship. The various instruments used are illustrated on page 103 (lower diagram).

Valves. These are used to control the flow of oil or ballast from tank to tank. All tank valves are controlled from on deck by means of extended spindles and universal joints. The diagram shows the arrangement of valves for one particular tanker and you should familiarise yourself with the layout of the valves

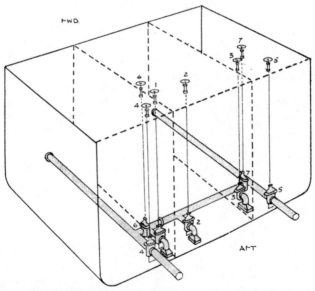

No. 4 tank in a ship fitted with twin bulkheads and a ring main pipeline system:
1. Port wing tank suction valve. Valve wheel painted red.
2. Centre wing tank suction valve. Valve wheel painted black.
3. Starboard wing tank suction valve. Valve wheel painted green.
4. Master valve—port line. Valve wheel painted white.
5. Master valve—starboard line. Valve wheel painted white.
6. Port to starboard crossover valve. Valve wheel painted black rim, white spokes.
7. Starboard to port crossover valve. Valve wheel painted black rim, white spokes.

and the pipeline system on the tanker on which you are serving as soon as you join it.

Tanker safety. Fire and explosion are the greatest potential dangers which the seaman has to face, due to the presence on board of large quantities of inflammable liquid and explosive gases.

The acuteness of these dangers is ever present and it is essential that high safety standards, together with rigid discipline and commonsense, should prevail. These dangers are greatest during loading, discharging, ballasting and gas-freeing.

The following safety points are listed for the benefit of those young seamen who sign on in these ships:

(1) Never smoke on tanker decks, passageways, alleyways, etc. Smoking may be permitted in smokerooms but, if the presence of gas is apparent, extinguish your cigarette. Do not dispose of cigarette ends through port holes or cabin windows.

(2) Only safety matches, issued on board the tanker, should be used.

(3) All seamen should familiarise themselves with the safety notices on board and with the alarm signals and bells; also with the positions and working of all portable fire-extinguishers and installations.

(4) All portable decklight and electrical fittings should have gas-tight fittings.

(5) Only approved gas-tight torches should be used.

(6) No deck repairs should be carried out that might produce a spark.

(7) Take a keen and thorough interest in all the Fire Drills held on board.

(8) A close watch should be kept on shipmates who have just returned from shore and who may unconsciously light a cigarette or strike a match near installations.

Chapter 9

ANCHORS AND CABLES

Ground tackle is a general term which includes anchors, cables, windlass, shackles, bow stoppers, etc. The weight of the anchors and the size and length of the cables depend upon the size and type of the ship. They are determined by the classification societies, Lloyd's Register, the American Bureau of Shipping, and Bureau Veritas being the main ones. The weight of the three bower anchors—one for each cable and one spare—of an average cargo ship is about 3 tonnes 48 kilos (3 tons), the length of each anchor cable is about 135 fathoms, size (diameter) of the cable being 63mm (2½ in.). Only the patent stockless anchor is used aboard merchant ships nowadays for anchoring purposes. (See the accompanying illustrations for the names of the various parts of the stockless and stock anchors.) Among the advantages of the former are (1) that it lies flat on the bottom of the sea when it is let go; (2) the shank is lifted up when strain comes on the cable, and the flukes automatically dig themselves into the ground; and (3) it is easily stowed. Bad holding ground, incidentally, usually means a hard rocky sea-bed in which the flukes cannot get a grip and the danger of dragging is ever-present.

When anchoring, therefore, the length of the chain should be in proportion to the depth of the water. Other factors have to be considered, however, among them being the quality of the holding ground, weather conditions and the strength of the tide if any. The anchor chain, serving as a connection between the anchor and ship, is most effective when it hangs in a bight. The weight of the chain operates so that the action of wind and sea can be effectively intercepted. In fact the weight of the chain hanging in a bight makes a very good shock absorber.

In matters of this kind generalization is probably best avoided, for so much depends on the experience of the individual concerned, and his viewpoint, as well as a variety of factors—ship's draught, force of wind, state of sea, quality of holding ground, strength of tide and the length of time the ship is expected to be anchored, for instance—which must be taken into account. But in order to provide the student with some guide as to the amount of cable employed when anchoring, 6 fathoms for each fathom of water is usually considered a safe proportion, with a minimum amount of three shackles (45 fathoms). Thus if the depth of water at an anchorage were 15 fathoms, six shackles of cable should normally be used, but if the depth were only 6 fathoms the ship should not be anchored with less than three shackles of cable in the water. In this case, of course, the proportion of cable to depth would be 8 : 1.

The cable consists of several 'shackles' (15-fathom lengths). All the links, except two in each shackle of cable, one at each end, are provided with studs for strengthening purposes and to prevent kinking, and lengths of cable are connected to each other by means of a joining shackle. The shackle joining the anchor to its cable is sometimes of a different shape to the shackle used for joining the 15-fathom lengths, but in most modern ships there is no difference between the shackle joining the lengths and that employed for attaching the cable to the anchor. The two non-studded links in each 'shackle' comprise one end link and one enlarged link, the purpose of the former being to allow the joining shackle to be unshipped and of the latter to compensate for strength lost through the elimination

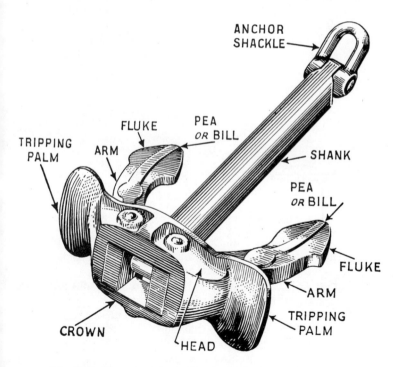

Merchant ships carry two working bower anchors and one spare.

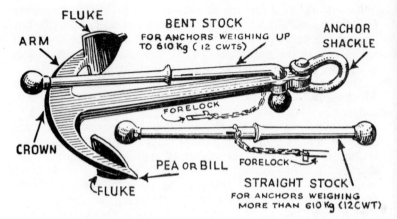

of studs. Many ships now use lugless joining shackles instead of the 'D' type shown below. The pins of joining shackles are secured by means of a piece of hardwood, known as a spiel, which is driven into holes in the lug of the shackle and the pin.

The joining shackles are placed in the studless end links of the separate chain lengths so that their bows (arches) are facing forward; thus there is no chance of them fouling when the anchor is let go. In order that the chief officer and carpenter

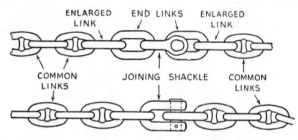

can recognize the number of shackles paid out, cables are usually marked as follows:

15 fathoms.   Turns of wire on the first stud from each side of the joining tackle.

30 fathoms.   Turns of wire on the second stud from each side of the joining shackle.

45 fathoms.   Turns of wire on the third stud from each side of the joining shackle.

60 fathoms.   Turns of wire on the fourth stud from each side of the joining shackle.

and so on.

Occasionally the appropriate link is painted white; this is very helpful in the dark when letting go or heaving in anchors.

The inboard end of the cable is either shackled to a heavy eyebolt on the collision bulkhead in the chain locker or secured to the eyebolt by a cable clench.

"KENTOR" EXPLODED SHACKLE

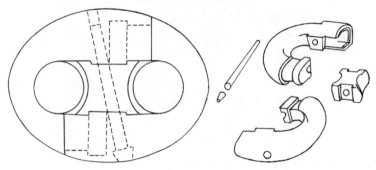

WINDLASS

The windlass is equipped and arranged so that the cable can be hove in or hove out, and so that the anchor can be readily let go from its stowed position in the hawse pipe. The drive of the windlass is similar in many respects to that of a cargo-cum-warping winch. The gypsies (or cable holders) on the windlass are provided with grips, which are adjusted to the form of the cable links and prevent turns from getting into the cable as it passes over the windlass. The gypsies lie loosely on the shaft and are readily put into gear, together or singly, for heaving by operating an engaging lever or clutch. The speed of the cable as it runs out is regulated by means of a friction brake.

Heaving anchor. First grease all working parts, paying particular attention to the sliding main wheels and cable lifters (gypsies). Open the drain cocks and turn on the steam gradually. Run the engine both ways and by means of the engine bring the main wheel clutch jaw around into position. Slide the wheel into gear with the cable lifter but DO NOT JAM.

Letting go anchor. Screw up the brake hard and by means of the engine work the main wheel clutch jaw clear of the cable lifter jaw. Slide the main wheel clear of the cable lifter and control the anchor with the brake.

Warping. Screw up both brakes tight and slide both main wheels clear of the cable lifters.

STEAM WINDLASS, AFTER SIDE

1, Port brake control; 2, port gypsy; 3, clutch; 4, clutch control; 5, stop valve; 6, clutch control; 7, gypsy; 8, starboard brake control; 9, warping barrel; 10, side frame; 11, bedplate; 12, drain cocks; 13, cylinder; 14, exhaust; 15, steam inlet; 16, valve chest; 17, cylinder; 18, drain cock; 19, warping barrel.

STEAM WINDLASS, FORE SIDE

1, Starboard brake band; 2, port brake band; 3, spurling pipe; 4, connecting rod; 5, big end; 6, driving disc; 7, bearing; 8, eccentric strap; 9, main drive pinion; 10, eccentric strap; 11, bearing; 12, driving disc; 13, port spurling pipe; 14, drum end shaft; 15, bedplate.

MAINTENANCE AND UPKEEP OF THE WINDLASS

All the bearings of the working parts should always be kept well lubricated. The bolts of the brake gear should be regularly removed and dipped in oil so as to ensure that the joints are free. Particular attention should be paid to the lubrication of the cable holders, the centres of which are hollow so that they may be flooded with lubricant. The teeth of all the gears should be well greased and the cable lifter disconnecting gear kept free and easy for sliding the main wheel on the main shaft. The cylinder drain cocks should always be kept open when the windlass is out of use so as to prevent corrosion in the cylinders and steam chest—which should be opened out periodically to see that the bores, valves and chest are in good condition. All the bearings should be kept properly adjusted and periodical attention should be given to the painting of the underside of the cylinders, the bedplate being cut away for this purpose.

Both ends of the main shaft are fitted with warping ends so that when the windlass is in gear mooring lines can be hauled in at the same time as the anchor, or when out of gear and the anchors are secured by the friction brakes and/or bow stoppers (whatever form they may take) the warping ends can be operated independently, as when docking or undocking.

BOW STOPPER

This self-holding and automatically releasing patent roller bow stopper was introduced by Clarke, Chapman & Co. Ltd., Gateshead. The roller on which the cable runs eliminates the cable nip normally experienced at the hawse pipe deck casting, a more constant load is transferred to the windlass, and cable and hawse pipe wear and tear are considerably reduced.

A few words about stowing the chain in the chain locker. Before heaving commences two hands should be stationed in the locker. They should each be equipped with a chain hook, and should make sure that the locker is well lit. When they are in position they should inform the carpenter accordingly (they are at the bottom of the spurling pipe, of course, and the carpenter is standing by the windlass at the top) and they should not hesitate to ask 'chippy' to heave more slowly if the chain is coming into the locker so fast that they cannot properly stow it. It is essential that the chain be stowed in such a manner that it can run free when the anchor is let go.

Before the carpenter takes the windlass out of gear he should order the hands out of the locker in case the anchor 'goes with a run' as he is making the change. The chain is washed down with the deck hose as it comes up the hawse pipe and passes over that part of the fo'c'sle head between the inboard end of the hawse pipe and the windlass. As the cable is running out or coming in the bridge is notified of the amount in the water by striking the fo'c'sle bell once for each shackle that is out. The anchor ball or light(s) must be hauled down as soon as the anchor is off the bottom—indicated when the chain hangs vertically from the hawse pipe. On the other hand, when anchoring, as soon as the 'pick' is let go the black ball or anchor light(s) should be immediately hoisted so that passing vessels can take steps to keep out of the way.

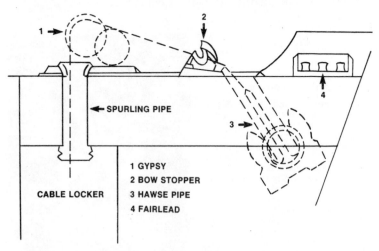

← SPURLING PIPE

CABLE LOCKER

1 GYPSY
2 BOW STOPPER
3 HAWSE PIPE
4 FAIRLEAD

This sketch shows the starboard anchor stowed in hawse pipe, bow stopper, cable passing over gypsy on windlass and through the spurling pipe into the cable (or chain) locker.

Hanging off an anchor. At many ports your vessel will have to moor to a buoy or buoys. If mooring to a single buoy one of the anchors will have to be 'hung off' and the free end of the cable used to make fast to the buoy. The windlass is put in gear and the anchor 'walked' out until the anchor shackle is just clear of the hawse pipe. A mooring wire is then passed outboard through the fairlead and secured to the anchor shackle. When secure, the wire is hauled hand-tight and made fast on the bitts. The cable is then 'walked' out until the anchor's weight is taken on the wire. On some ships the position of the fairlead may be such that the anchor is too close to the hawse pipe. If this is the case, a second wire is passed out through the after fairlead, secured to the anchor shackle and the anchor hove aft clear of the hawse. When in the required position, the second wire is stopped off and secured to convenient bitts.

So that the cable does not run down the hawse pipe as more cable is being flaked out on deck, a wire lashing is passed through a link near the hawse pipe and secured to a convenient point on deck. Although chain cable is made up of lengths of 15 fathoms, the first length is often made up in two lengths of 5 fathoms and 10 fathoms so that only a short length has to be brought up out of the chain locker to enable the joining shackle to be disconnected. When the first joining shackle is on deck, forward of the windlass, the shackle is disconnected, and the cable end passed out through the hawse pipe ready for shackling to the buoy.

Approaching the buoy, a rope hawser is first passed down to the boatmen at the buoy, and this is made fast and secured on board to hold the vessel while the anchor cable is being secured. A slip wire is then sent down from the opposite side to that of the 'free' cable, passed through the buoy ring and brought back to be secured to the cable end. The cable is then 'walked out' and hauled to the buoy by the wire which is being hove in on the windlass drum end. When secured to the buoy the slip wire and hawser are released and the cable secured.

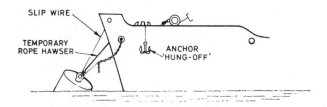

Mooring. If anchored in a river with a very strong tide, one anchor may not be sufficient. In this case, the ship is sheered away from the first anchor by means of the rudder (which acts, in a tideway, as if the ship were under way) and the second anchor is let go. Again, if in a crowded anchorage where space is restricted, the ship may be moored either by a running moor or an ordinary moor. In an ordinary moor, one anchor is dropped and the vessel given sternway until sufficiently far from the first anchor when the second one is dropped. By heaving on the first cable and paying out on the second the ship is finally brought up about midway between the cables. With a running moor, the first anchor is dropped and cable payed out as the ship moves ahead. When sufficiently far ahead, the second anchor is dropped and, by paying out on the second cable and heaving in on the first, the vessel is brought up in the required position. In both these cases the ship will then swing in a restricted circle, the radius of which is the length of the riding cable.

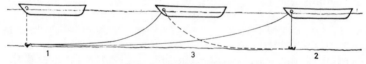

STANDING OR ORDINARY MOOR

The starboard anchor is let go when vessel has slight sternway (1). The cable is payed out as ship moves astern either by tide or under power until, at position (2), the brake is applied and port cable let go. The starboard cable is now hove in and port cable payed out until ship is in required position (3) when cables are secured.

RUNNING MOOR

While slowly moving ahead, the port anchor is let go and payed out (1). When the required number of shackles are out and headway is off the ship, the second anchor is let go (2). The first cable is hove in and the second cable payed out until ship is in required position (3). *Note.* There is no hard and fast rule for which anchor to use first.

Foul hawse. In a tideway, the ship will swing to each new tide and, at each second tide, the ship should be given a sheer towards the side of the last swing so that the cables remain clear. This may not always be possible, however, perhaps owing to a strong cross-wind, and on lying to the new tide it will then be found that the cables have fouled one another, as shown in the diagram below.

To clear a foul hawse, the cables should be lashed together below the turns and a mooring wire shackled to the lazy cable, two links forward of the joining shackle. The wire is hove taut, turned up on the bitts and the joining shackle disconnected. A second wire is passed out through the fairlead and secured to the same cable below the lashing. When secure it is hove taut and turned up on the bitts. This wire acts as a preventer wire in case the lashing should part. The first wire is then slacked away on the bitts so that the cable end falls outboard clear of the hawse pipe. The turns in the cable are then taken out by using two more wires, as shown in the diagram, and when clear, the first wire is re-connected and the cable hove on board and re-shackled. All other wires are disconnected and the man in the chair must take great care when cutting the lashing to see that he is clear of the cable as it falls away.

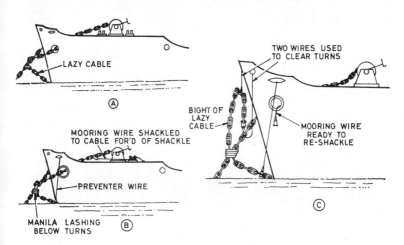

Anchor buoys are wooden floats used to mark the position of the anchor so that, in the event of the cable parting, the posi-

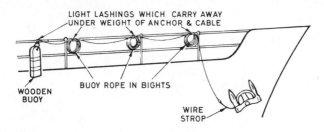

tion of the anchor is clearly marked for eventual recovery. The buoy rope must be long enough for the greatest depth of water in which the ship will anchor.

Securing the anchors for sea. On leaving the final loading port the anchors must be properly secured and the spurling pipes efficiently sealed so that any water which comes on board does not flood the chain locker. The windlass is put in gear and both anchors hove hard up in the hawse pipe. Compressors are secured, and devil's claws attached and hove tight by means of their bottle screws. Both hawse-pipe covers are slid into place and securely lashed. Both brakes are tightened up and the windlass put out of gear. The spurling pipes are packed with burlap and a 76mm (3 in.) layer of sand and cement, mixed in the ratio of 5 : 1, placed on top of the burlap and levelled off evenly with the top of each spurling pipe. The steel covers are slid into place and the canvas covers are then placed in position and securely lashed.

Chapter 10

THE MAGNETIC AND GYRO COMPASSES

The principle governing construction of the compass is simple. A magnetized bar of steel or iron called the needle is balanced on a pivot so that it will rotate freely, coming to rest in the line of the magnetic meridian at any place where it is free from other disturbances. Aboard ship the needle is deflected from the magnetic meridian by the unequal attraction of the surrounding iron and steel in the ship herself. This deflection is known as deviation. Compasses are adjusted by placing correctors— Flinders Bar, soft iron spheres (quadrantal correctors), fore and aft, thwartship and vertical magnets—in such positions in or on the binnacle about the needle that they act in a direction opposite, and of equal force to, the deflecting materials in the ship.

In addition to deviation the compass is deflected to one side or the other of true north by an angle known as magnetic variation. At different places on the earth's surface the needle —pointing approximately to the magnetic pole which does not coincide with the true pole at the axis of the earth's meridian— forms an angle with the true meridian. This angle is shown on charts by means of a compass rose and by lines of equal variation for a particular year together with an indication of the annual increase or decrease for this particular place. The foregoing are the fundamental errors of the compass, and when these are understood present designs can be elaborated.

The simple bar or needle has been superseded by mounting two, three or four needles in parallel on each side of the pivot. To these needles a light graduated compass card is attached. A dry compass card consists of a segmental circle of rice paper mounted on an aluminium ring and suspended from an aluminium centre piece by thirty-two silk cords—one for each point of the compass. The needles are suspended below the card and depend from the card ring by a second series of silk cords. (See accompanying illustrations.) This brings the weight of the needles down low and conduces towards a steady card.

COMPASS AND COMPASS BINNACLE

The iridium-pointed pivot supporting the jewelled (sapphire or agate) cap fixed in the boss of the card rises from the bottom of the brass compass bowl, on which the lubber line is marked.

The bowl in turn is carried on gimbals, both gimbals and bowl being supported by knife edge or roller bearings. The bearings on the bowl resting on the ring are fore and aft. Those on the ring resting on the binnacle are athwartships, thus ensuring that no matter how the ship may pitch or roll the compass pivot

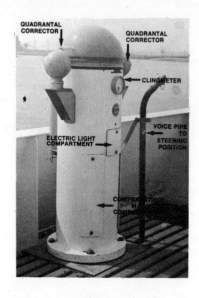

remains vertical—and the card horizontal. In the dry compass the card is made as light as possible to minimize friction on the pivot. To steady the bowl in a seaway the bottom is partly filled with fluid.

Liquid compasses differ in construction from dry card compasses in that the needles are formed by bunching magnetized wires in the form of small cylinders and the metallic card—much heavier than a dry compass card—is carried by these

KELVITE 254mm (10 in.) DRY COMPASS CARD Note the thirty-two silk cords subtended from aluminium centre-piece.

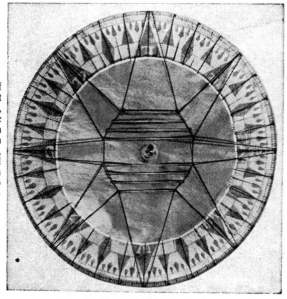

Reverse side of card showing eight parallel needles, the way they are suspended from the aluminium ring by silk cords, and the jewelled cap in aluminium centre-piece to take the iridium-pointed pivot.

magnets. The boss is carried by a cylindrical metallic float, being also attached to the magnets. Whereas a dry-card compass has from two to eight needles there are usually only two magnets in a liquid compass, one on each side of the pivot.

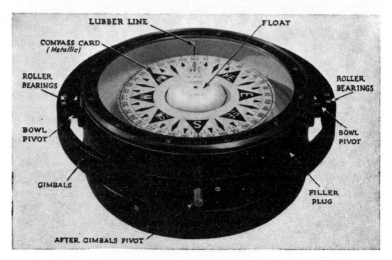

LIQUID COMPASS BOWL, FITTINGS AND ACCESSORIES

The bowl is covered with glass, all air being excluded, and the card swings freely in liquid—a mixture of glycerine and water, of alcohol and water, or of alcohol alone—which, in the course of manufacture, is forced into the bowl under pressure. The liquid compass has been developed to a high degree of efficiency, and it has many advantages, particularly in so far as steadiness and economy are concerned. In the Royal Navy, in fact in all the world's navies, magnetic compasses are of the liquid type; indeed, it seems to be regaining its former popularity in the Merchant Navy, particularly in motorships where there is frequently a great deal of vibration on the bridge. Its main disadvantage is that it is impracticable to fit a card with a diameter in excess of 203mm—51mm (8 in.—2 in.) less than a dry-compass card. *In many ships the magnetic compass has gradually taken a 'back seat', as it were, since the advent and increasing use of the gyro compass, but it should always be borne in mind that it is the only navigational instrument aboard the ship which is self-sufficient; in other words, it is entirely independent of the ship's main or other sources of power. It should always be treated with the care it deserves; it should never be roughly handled and loose iron and steel should as far as possible be kept away from it.*

THE REFLECTOR BINNACLE AND COMPASS

The standard compass, is sited on the monkey island, and is used for taking bearings and setting and checking courses.

The reflector binnacle is in fact an inverted periscope fitted in the wheel house in front of the wheel. Thus the compass card and lubber line of the top compass are reflected down the tube as shown in the diagram and the helmsman in the event of a gyro break-down is able to steer the vessel by the magnetic compass on the monkey island through the periscope.

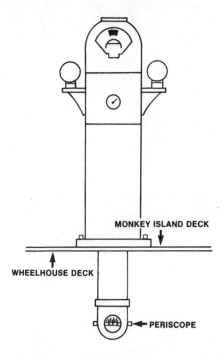

The azimuth mirror fits on to either the standard magnetic compass or the gyro repeaters, and is used for taking bearings of both terrestrial and celestial objects. When taking bearings of terrestrial objects, turn the prism to 'arrow down', look at the object over the top of the prism and read off the bearing as

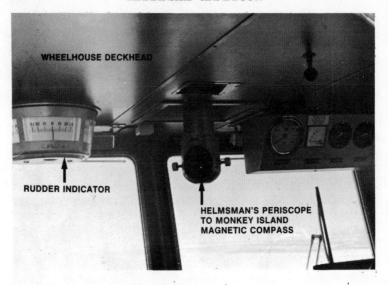

WHEELHOUSE DECKHEAD

RUDDER INDICATOR

HELMSMAN'S PERISCOPE
TO MONKEY ISLAND
MAGNETIC COMPASS

seen from the reflected compass-card image. When taking celestial bearings, turn the prism round so that the arrow points up. Look down the barrel towards the compass card and read off the reflected image against the card reading.

Note. The azimuth stand may be either triangular (as shown in the diagram) or circular. Most gyro-repeater azimuths have a circular stand.

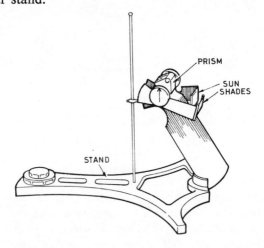

PRISM

SUN
SHADES

STAND

Boxing the compass. In order to be able to read off any course and to know at once which way the wheel should be turned on an alteration of course order being given, a knowledge of the compass card's subdivision is indispensable to the helmsman.

Starting from the North point of the compass as determined by the magnetic needle, then South is in exactly the opposite direction, East being to the right of North and West to the left of it. If a line is drawn from North to South and another from East to West the circle will be divided into four equal parts, and these are called quadrants. By halving the North-East quadrant again the N.E. point is derived. By further halving of the parts from North to N.E. and N.E. to East the N.N.E. and E.N.E. points are obtained. Halve these again and the points to the nearest principal points of North, North-East, East, are designated as follows: North by East, North-East by North, North-East by East, and East by North. The eight points in the other three quadrants, East—South, South—West, and West—North, are determined in a similar manner, and the thirty-two points become:

North	East	South	West
N×E	E×S	S×W	W×N
NNE	ESE	SSW	WNW
NE×N	SE×E	SW×S	NW×W
NE	SE	SW	NW
NE×E	SE×S	SW×W	NW×N
ENE	SSE	WSW	NNW
E×N	S×E	W×S	N×W
East	South	West	North

North, East, South and West are known as cardinal points; NE, SE, SW and NW are inter-cardinals; NNE, ENE, ESE, SSE, SSW, WSW, WNW and NNW are 'three-letter' points; and N×E, NE×N, NE×E, E×N, E×S, SE×E, SE×S, S×E, S×W, SW×S, SW×W, W×S, W×N, NW×W, NW×N and N×W are 'by' points.

DIVISION INTO DEGREES

As well as being divided into points the compass card is divided into degrees, counting from the North, zero, clockwise through the whole 360 deg.; or assuming a division into four quadrants, then counting each 90 deg. to East and West from North and South respectively. In the former case it is sufficient to indicate the number of degrees in order clearly to determine the course at a given time, whilst in the latter case, quadrantal division, the quadrant in question must be stated. For instance, if a S.W. course is steered, according to the division into degrees, this would be 225 deg., whereas it would be S.45 deg. W. by the quadrantal division. In ships where a gyro compass is fitted courses are given to the helmsman in degrees only.

THE GYRO COMPASS

The magnetic compass has been the navigator's aid for more than four thousand years, and as far as can be seen ahead it will remain an essential part of a ship's navigational equipment

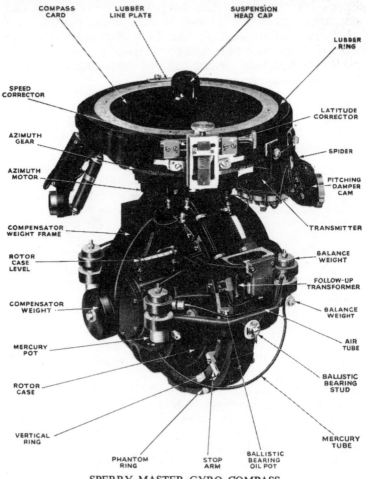

SPERRY MASTER GYRO COMPASS

because, as has already been stated, it is the only one absolutely independent of power supplies. Even so it has not the same absolute importance it possessed only a few years ago—before the advent of the gyro compass, a comparatively new and powerful indicator of direction which has been fitted to most new ships for the past two decades or so. The gyro compass depends only on a spinning wheel, the force of gravity and the rotation of the earth. But power is required to start the wheel spinning and to maintain it spinning at a uniform rate. This is the gyro's main drawback, since if for any reason the power supply is cut off the compass becomes useless. Another point is that it requires more attention than a magnetic compass. Although a ship may be equipped with a gyro compass the magnetic compass should never be ignored or neglected. It should be adjusted regularly and its error ascertained frequently —every watch, when practicable—so that if at any time the gyro fails the magnetic compass can be immediately used with confidence and safety.

Gyro compass equipment. Each compass equipment consists of a master gyro, its auxiliaries and accessories. The master compass contains the gyroscopic or true north-seeking element and the mechanism by which its indications are transmitted to' the accessories located in various parts of the ship.

Auxiliaries. These usually comprise a motor generator, a control panel, an amplifier panel and a current-failure alarm. These units supply the master compass with current of the proper characteristics and provide a warning on the bridge in the event of current failure.

Accessories. A complete equipment usually includes: (1) a steering repeater for each steering position; (2) one or more bearing repeaters; (3) a repeater with the Radio Direction Finder; (4) a course recorder; and (5) a gyro-pilot automatic steering equipment.

Steering repeater. This is mounted in a yoke attached to the top of the gyro-pilot steering hand or bridge unit where it may be used either for manual steering with the ship's wheel, for electric follow-up steering with the wheel on the gyro-pilot, or as a reference when steering 'automatic'. In ships which are not equipped with the gyro-pilot the steering repeater may be mounted on a suitable stand or in a bracket built out from the telemotor steering stand. The yoke on which the steering repeater is mounted is readily adjustable to the most convenient position for the helmsman, a cover being supplied to mask all the repeater dial except a sector adjacent to the lubber line, the card having large-scale markings to assist the helmsman.

Bearing repeater. Is gimbal-mounted in a stand which is convenient for obtaining bearings of celestial and terrestrial objects or of other ships. One is usually mounted on the monkey island and sometimes on each bridge wing, with the repeater's lubber line parallel to the fore and aft line of the vessel.

OPEN-SCALE STEERING
REPEATER

STANDARD BEARING
REPEATER

Direction finder repeater. This provides a means whereby direction-finder bearings can be read directly on a 'live' compass card which is energized by the master compass. The repeater compass may be mounted as a complete unit under the rotatable

RUDDER ANGLE INDICATOR
A self-synchronous instrument indicating rudder angle with no time lag.

COURSE RECORDER
Providing a permanent transcription of a ship's headings throughout a voyage.

index of the radio set, or the repeater motor only may be supplied to the D.F. makers who built it into their set. Where it is not practicable to incorporate a repeater in the D.F., a repeater compass from which the ship's heading can be read is mounted alongside the D.F. apparatus.

Course recorder. This automatically provides on a moving chart a chronological, graphic record of all movements of the ship's head. From this record the quality of the steering, the mean course steered, and the times and amounts of alterations of course may be ascertained either at the time of recording or at any subsequent time.

Gyro-pilot. Although the use of the gyro compass has greatly improved the quality of manual steering owing to the 'dead-beat' nature of the compass, certain human shortcomings such as the tendency of the helmsman to favour one side or the other of the course remain. The gyro-pilot favours neither side but maintains a given heading with such precision that even a change of only one-quarter of a degree is immediately noticeable on the record. The gyro-pilot detects the 'off-course' movement in its early stages and applies the small amount of corrective rudder necessary to return the vessel to her course before the yaw achieves appreciable proportions. The ship can be kept

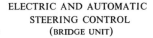

ELECTRIC AND AUTOMATIC
STEERING CONTROL
(BRIDGE UNIT)

closer to her prescribed course by the gyro-pilot than by the human helmsman, and course alterations can be effected with greater facility. When used in a ship which is equipped with shaft or hydraulic telemotor steering control the gyro-pilot parallels that control without interfering with it in any way. The lever on the side of the bridge unit has three positions, 'gyro', 'hand', and 'off'. When in the 'gyro' position the ship is steered automatically in response to the indications of the gyro compass; when in the 'hand' position the steering is in response to the movement of the steering wheel in the hands of a helmsman; and when in the 'off' position the gyro-pilot is disconnected, the magnetic clutch in the power unit opens automatically, and steering control reverts to the ship's wheel, permitting full use of the telemotor. A feature of the Sperry gyro-pilot electrical telemotor is that synchronization of rudder and wheel positions is automatically effected when the steering control is taken over by the gyro-pilot. To change from gyro-pilot to ship's telemotor it is necessary only to throw the lever on the gyro-pilot steering stand to its 'off' position and close the telemotor stand. Both operations can be executed instantly.

Chapter 11

STEERING GEAR

In all but the smallest ships the wheel is on the bridge—in deep-sea craft, in a wheel house provided for this purpose. Turning the wheel turns the rudder in the same direction and, therefore, the ship's head. Since manual operation alone is inadequate in fast, heavy ships a steering engine is provided at some point between the wheel and rudder. It is usual for the engine to be in a 'steering flat' on or below the poop. In all modern ships either the telemotor or electrical systems are employed. The former is hydraulic and depends for its operation on the pressure generated on a mixture of water and glycerine in various proportions, or on special telemotor oil, contained in thin copper pipes from the wheel house to the steering engine rams. As this system is widely used throughout the Merchant Navy a few words regarding it will not be out of place.

TELEMOTOR—HOW IT WORKS

DONKIN'S STANDARD
TELEMOTOR TRANSMITTER

1. Helm indicator
2. Wheel
3. Casing
4. Hand-operated equalising valve
5. Copper pipes to steering engine
6. Holding-down bolts
7. Inspection door
8. Copper pipe
9. Automatic equalizing valve
10. Air cock
11. Gauge glass
12. Charging tank
13. Pressure gauge
14. Electric light

NOTE.—Casing contains hydraulic cylinder and ram operating gear from wheel

The object of a telemotor is to provide an alternative means of controlling the steering gear, which is usually placed at the further end of the ship, from the bridge or any other distant part of the ship at which a steering position is required. The telemotor installation consists of a transmitter, connecting pipes and receiver. The transmitter, in which the steering wheel is incorporated is sited on the bridge, or in any other steering position. In modern times the transmitter and thus the system, is more often activated by an electric motor in the steering wheel housing. It drives a small pump providing the necessary pressure to be generated on the water or glycerine or telemotor oil mentioned above. The change is usually effected by means of a lever which automatically throws out the gyro steering, movement of the wheel then starts the electric motor and the telemotor system goes into operation. The receiver—placed on or near the steering gear, connected to the transmitter by a double line of copper piping—is mechanically coupled to the control valve pump/mechanism or switch of the steering gear, according to the type of gear which is being controlled. The hydraulic fluid flows through the copper pipes on one side or the other, and causes a corresponding movement of the receiver rams which operate the control of the steering engine. It is essential for accurate steering that the pressure on the rams of the receiver is equal. In order to ensure this, the receiver rams are spring-loaded in the midships position. By-passing on the transmitter to equalise the pressure occurs automatically every time the wheel is brought to the midships position. In addition to intercommunicating the two sides of the system in the midships position to allow equalisation, the by-pass may open the system to a make-up tank which allows liquid to flow off through a relief valve if it is at too high a pressure or to suck in 'make-up' liquid from the tank if the system is not fully charged.

Such variations of the amount of liquid required are due to expansion and contraction through variation in atmospheric temperature or to actual loss of liquid caused by leaking glands.

THE PRINCIPLE OF THE COMBINED STEERING CONSOLE (a typical combined modern steering unit)

The combined unit provides in one Bridge Mounted Console two entirely independent steering systems.
1. Any required make of Hydraulic Telemotor Transmitter.
2. The 'Brown' Automatic Helmsman operated from a datum provided by the Gyroscopic Compass—familiarly known as 'IRON MIKE'.

In turn, the latter system can also be operated by a small handwheel independently of the gyro compass thus providing a third alternative in the form of manually operated electric steering.

S. G. Brown Ltd, and the telemotor steering manufacturer concerned each provide a handbook respectively dealing with the maintenance and servicing of their units.

General description

Bridge Unit. A vertical partition divides the console into two parts; that forward of the operating position housing the Bridge Telemotor Transmitter Unit, accessible on opening the forward door, and to aft (nearest the large and small handwheels) the apparatus associated with the Brown Automatic and Hand Electric Steering systems, cable connections, etc. These are fully accessible on opening the Port and Starboard doors.

Surmounting the unit is the Brown Multiple Steering Repeater with expanded scale giving degree readings a quarter of an inch wide.

Photograph by
courtesy of Decca

Controls. On the port side of the console a lever having three definite locating positions provides for steering by:

1. *'Hydraulic'*—in this position steering is effected by appropriate movement of the large handwheel to port or starboard, when the rudder position obtained is indicated by the large mechanically operated pointer as normally supplied with telemotor equipment. There is no connection electrically or mechanically with the gyro compass, but the ship's head may be read from the indication of the Steering Repeater when the gyro compass is running.

   In this position of the main control lever the by-pass valve is fully closed.

2. *'Hand Electric'*—In this position of the control lever, the by-pass valve is *open*, and at the same time electrical connection is made to the appropriate units in the Brown System. Steering is thus effected by turning the *small* hand-wheel (concentric with the large) when the appropriate connections are made via the hand-driven impulse transmitter, the breaker switches, and aft power units (see later) which allows of the latter moving the operating valve of the steering engine.

3. *'Automatic'*—in this position of the control lever, the by-pass valve is *open*, and at the same time the necessary electrical connections are made to the Brown Gyro Compass repeater system. Steering is entirely automatic from the datum provided by the gyro compass. If the rudder angle control has been set to *zero* then it will be necessary to revert to the appropriate setting, and also adjust the *Yaw Control* to suit the weather conditions prevailing. Both settings are immediately accessible on opening the starboard door.

   Rudder movement and position is shown by an electric helm indicator.

   Indicating Lamps. When in Automatic or Hand Electric Steering, operation of the breaker switches also lights the appropriate Indicating Lamp, port or starboard, thus showing that the correct circuit is energised to apply the required rudder.

   Alarm Unit. This is an improved pattern giving visual and audio indication of failure of the repeater system. In the rare event of this happening, the small red indicator mounted on the front panel of the bridge unit will glow, and the internally mounted bell ring. The bell may be silenced by turning *off* the switch, but the red indicator light will only extinguish when the fault has been cleared and relay re-set by pressing the re-set button.

   If the alarm operates, the main control lever should be placed in position 1 above, 'Hydraulic' and manual steering resumed.

The relay associated with the above is provided with a cover, and is unlikely to require any adjustment. It is situated inside the aft compartment and mounted at the base of the panel. Access can be obtained by opening the port door.

Associated Apparatus in Steering Flat Aft (not shown on stand)

The Telemotor Receiver is the standard pattern and mechanically coupled to the control-valve of the steering-engine.

The Charging Tank and Pump will be found adjacent to the Telemotor receiver, to which system it is coupled, and is used to bleed the system of air as may be necessary from time to time.

The Brown Aft Power Unit—this is coupled to the steering engine control valve, in such manner that when the bridge unit control lever is in position 2 or 3, above, the rack drives the valve of the steering engine, and, due to the by-pass valve being 'open' the telemotor receiver idles. Similarly, when 'hydraulic' steering is used (position 1 of the Bridge Unit control lever) an internal magnetic clutch disconnects the mechanism, and the unit idles.

The rudder is attached to the sternpost by means of pintles and gudgeons, the former on the rudder, the latter on the sternpost. The rudder stock leads through an opening (rudder trunk) in the hull and its upper end is keyed on to the quadrant. The angle of the rudder blade at any given time is made known to the helmsman on the bridge by an indicator set on the after part of the steering standard, or by other means, one being by green (for starboard helm) and red (for port helm) lights.

Auxiliary steering gear. Apart from the main steering arrangements there is in every ship auxiliary gear for use in an emergency, and in all well-run ships this is brought into use at regular and frequent intervals. Sometimes it is a Saturday morning duty to steer with the emergency gear for half an hour or so.

Electrical systems. There are so many different systems of electrical steering in use at the present time that it is impossible to describe them individually in a book of this size. The helmsman may have to steer by using press-buttons, by lever, or even by small tiller, each of which, from the bridge console, operates the controls on the steering motor and turns the rudder as required. On several ships which are employed on steady runs to river ports, particularly the West African trade, an additional feature for sharp turns, or when mooring, is the fitting of an auxiliary propeller in a boss in the rudder. Controlled from the bridge, this extra propeller pushes along the fore-and-aft line of the rudder giving extra turning power on sharp bends, and, if the rudder is turned hard to port or starboard, additional power in pushing the bow or stern on to or off the quay as required.

The young seaman should familiarise himself with each different type of steering which he encounters, particularly the method used in the steering flat for operating the rudder.

Chapter 12

HELMSMANSHIP

Steering is one of the seaman's most responsible tasks. A helmsman is not only required to be familiar with the steering qualities of his ship and a complete knowledge of the compass, but also to be absolutely reliable, trustworthy and capable of concentration. A good, intelligent quartermaster is highly regarded in every ship by the master and officers, and every young sailor should aspire to become a helmsman upon whom officers and pilots can rely implicitly. A mistake on the helmsman's part which is not at once detected, and corrected, can lead, and often has done, to disaster.

Every alteration of course is naturally important, but some are more important than others, and for this reason it is a basic principle that helm orders given by an officer should be repeated by the helmsman. When the wheel is being relieved the quartermaster whose 'trick'—a two-hour spell—is over gives the course to his relief, who repeats it back. The new helmsman compares the course he has been given with the direction of the ship's head and the course on the steering board. If there is any doubt in his mind he should immediately summon the officer of the watch. The quartermaster going off watch must give the officer of the watch the course before he leaves the bridge. The officer. in turn, repeats it. These verbal checks and cross-checks are carried out in every ship irrespective of size.

HOW TO STEER

The art of steering a ship is simply moving the wheel, the rudder and the ship's head so that the lubber line corresponds with a selected point on the compass rose. To beginners this gives rise to the idea that the compass rose is turning, whereas, of course, the card is stationary, or almost so, and it is the ship which is turning. If the North point of the compass appears to move to the right, what has actually happened is that the ship has veered to the left and the wheel must be turned to starboard in order to get the ship's head in line with the North point.

Suppose the course North has been set by steering compass, the helmsman's job is to see that the lubber line lies exactly in line with the North point of the card. Owing to the direction and force of the wind, state of the sea and movement of the ship, the vessel is constantly being forced off this course. Deviation from the course is indicated by the real movement of the lubber line, and it is the helmsman's task to correct it immediately by turning the wheel and hence the rudder in the required direction.

The successful helmsman is one who maintains a steady course with the least possible movement of the wheel. To this end his undivided attention is essential. If, through inattentiveness or inexperience on the helmsman's part, a ship yaws from side to side of her course, the steering engine is continually on the move. This is not very pleasant for the watch below if the 'fo'c'sle' happens to be directly below the steering engine, nor does it contribute towards either maximum efficiency as far as the engines and fuel consumption are concerned, or to the helmsman's own task. Naturally it is better for him if he turns the wheel a little than if he turns it a lot.

Assume that when a helmsman takes the wheel a course of N.E. is given to him and the helm is amidships. Soon the lubber line strays to starboard and the ship's head is now at N.E.¼E., i.e. quarter of point to starboard of the proper course. At the moment this deviation is noticed on the compass the wheel should be turned one or two spokes to port, but if the ship's head continues to swing to starboard a few more spokes of port helm should be given. As soon as it is noticed that the swing has stopped the helm should be taken off and the rudder put amidships.

This action, if taken at the right time, may result in the ship coming back slowly on to her course. (A point to remember is that the compass card 'drags' a little and the ship will be coming back on to her course before it is indicated on the card.) However, if a ship is 'met' at the right time she returns slowly on to her course, but if it is considered that she may go past it, a little starboard helm may be given, following which the wheel should again be set amidships.

Steering by a point of land or a star is easier because any movement of the ship's head can be detected immediately. When piloting, a good leading mark (light, tower, beacon, buoy, mountain peak, tree or the like) is selected ahead, preferably just a little, say two degrees, on one side or the other of the foremast when the ship is steady on her set course. If the mark appears to swing to the right the wheel must be set to starboard, but if it strays to the left, then the helm must be set to port. This movement of the steering or leading mark is of course only apparent, and the wheel and rudder should immediately be put towards the side to which the steering mark appears to have strayed. The course steered by magnetic compass by the quartermaster is termed the compass course; this is not necessarily the true course, in fact it very rarely is. In the case of the gyro compass, however, the compass course is also the true course.

HELM ORDERS

Midships — Place the wheel in the 'midships position.

Starboard — Set the wheel half-way between 'midships and hard-a-starboard.

Hard-a-port — Set the wheel hard over to port, that is as hard over as it will go to the left.

Hard-a-starboard — Opposite to hard-a-port.

Steady — Note her heading at the time the order is given. Turn the wheel in the opposite direction to that in which the ship's head is swinging, until the swing is arrested, then put the helm amidships and apply helm as required so that the ship steadies on the course ordered.

As She Goes — Steer the course on which the ship has steadied.

Starboard 5 — Turn the wheel to starboard until the helm indicator rests at 5 deg. to starboard.

Port 10 — Turn the wheel to port until the helm indicator shows that the rudder is 10 deg. to port.

Starboard a little, port a point, steer N.E., are other typical helm orders which are self-explanatory. Each order is immediately repeated aloud by the helmsman, and as soon as it is carried out. For example, the master, officer of the watch or the pilot orders hard-a-starboard, the helmsman repeats the order immediately, and then, when the order has been carried out, calls: 'Helm's hard-a-starboard, sir.' If the effect of a wheel movement is not apparent the helmsman should report it at once.

If, for example, the order 'hard-a-port' has been given and the quartermaster notices that the ship is not turning to port he should let the master, officer of the watch or pilot—whoever is giving the helm orders—know at once. A conscientious helmsman will only hand over to a relief when a manœuvre has been completed and the ship has been steadied on her course. An indication of how the vessel is steering, that is, carrying port or starboard helm, steering good or steering badly, should always be given by the man-at-the-wheel to his relief. If the wheel is handed over in a proper manner it will make things easier for the new helmsman.

Chapter 13

LOG AND LEAD

The patent log has long superseded other methods of finding the distance covered through the water; no instrument yet available gives the distance travelled 'over the ground'. The towing log, developed by Walkers, of Birmingham, comprises three primary parts. First the rotator, which is a metal tube to which are affixed four vanes set at such an angle that a certain number of revolutions are made per nautical mile; secondly the log line by which the rotator is towed and which transmits the turns made by the rotator to the third component of the log, the register. This comprises a suitable reduction mechanism and indicates on a clearly marked dial the distance travelled in nautical miles through the water.

The installation is simple; hull fittings are not required, and when not in use the rotator is hauled in and the register stowed away. For merchant ships the Walker 'Trident' electric log has been developed. This comprises a register mounted aft, embodying electrical contact mechanism which gives repeated readings in the chart room or anywhere else as may be desired. In cases where it is not desired to repeat the log reading the standard log is the 'Cherub', which will run the longest passage with little or no attention. The register is mounted on the taffrail; in open deck ships of 122m (400 ft.) or upwards in length it can be streamed amidships by means of a 'Viking' connector fitted on a boom 7½m to 9m (25 to 30 ft.) in length, usually directly under the bridge. The revolutions of the log register are conveyed from the connector by a light aerial wire to the log register which is mounted in the wing of the bridge. The advantage of this method is that the rotator is always in sight of the officer of the watch and the register is read from the bridge.

The efficiency of the log depends partly on the use of an accurate rotator and partly on the correct length of the line being streamed. The length of line varies with different ships and will sometimes vary with different loadings of the same ship. Lengthening the line increases the log registration and vice versa. The actual length of line does not affect the readings as much as the length of line actually *immersed in the water*. For good results it is essential that the rotator is towed clear of the vessel's wake, so that it is in an area of comparatively undisturbed water, and also that the rotator should be towed at a

Log streamed from amidships, a method which is decreasing in popularity, since one of its main advantages, reading the log on the bridge, is now achieved by means of the 'trident' electric log.

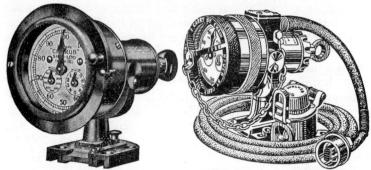

WALKER'S 'CHERUB'　　　　　'TRIDENT' ELECTRIC REGISTER
LOG REGISTER　　　　　　　　　AND FITTINGS

sufficient depth to prevent it from breaking the surface. When the log is streamed amidships from a boom the length of line is even more important as too much line may allow the rotator to be drawn into the propeller.

An important factor as regards the accuracy or otherwise of the log is the position of log shoe in reference to turbulence caused by propeller slip; water disturbance caused by vessel's skin friction can be disregarded as negligible, $91\frac{1}{2}$m (300 ft.) or more astern. Shoes should be as far outboard at the stern as is practicable. In practice it has been found that the shoe position should be at least 9m (30 ft.) from the stern, thus allowing the rotator to be streamed well clear of propeller wash. Moving the shoe position a few feet forward, and so increasing outreach a little, has been found to give considerable improvements in log readings.

The log should always be streamed from the lee quarter as the wind and sea assist in keeping the rotator clear of the wake, whereas when streamed from the weather quarter it is forced

CHARTROOM
RECEIVER

ROTATOR

into the propeller wash. The length of line is second in importance only to shoe position. Correct length is dependent on the ship's speed and the height of the register above the waterline. The basis of calculation for length to be streamed is 40 fathoms of line at a speed of 10 knots for a height of 7m (20 ft.). An increase in either speed of ship or height above water necessitates an increase in log-line length. For every knot increase of speed the line should be lengthened by 4 fathoms, and for every foot increase in height above water by 914mm (3 ft.).

These figures are only a very rough approximation as in practice other factors come into operation, i.e. the number of propellers, type of stern, propeller slip, etc. Also there is a limiting factor to the length of line. By lengthening the line log readings are increased, but if the line is lengthened too much it will be too heavy for the rotator to turn and rotator slip will ensue, giving a log under-reading. Once the correct length of line for a particular vessel has been found it should not be altered except for extreme variation in draught. A new line should be streamed for a while before being measured; for new lines stretch a good deal when used for the first time.

In order to transmit the revolutions as uniformly as possible to the register a wheel known as the governor is fitted between the register and the line. When streaming the log or hauling it aboard, care must be taken to see that the blades of the rotator are not damaged; especial care is necessary when the log is streamed amidships from a boom. When hauling the line aboard at the end of a passage all turns are taken out before an attempt is made to coil it down. This is accomplished by passing overboard from the weather quarter the end which has been unhooked from the clock, and this should be paid out until the rotator is inboard. Then the line is coiled down, rotator first, employing large turns, by hauling in the line. The line should then be taken to the bridge and hung up to dry, and the register, rotator and governor stowed in the wheelhouse; the register

GOVERNOR

should be cleaned and greased, and the rotator washed in fresh water and wiped with an oily rag. In large, fast liners, say up to 20 knots—the towing log is unreliable above this speed—the log is usually read every hour, or every half-hour. In tramps and similar craft readings are taken at the end of every watch, except when coasting, when officers may require more frequent readings. The log should always be streamed and kept on the lee side, so that after a large alteration of course, or a shift of wind, it should be transferred as soon as possible, if only to prevent the governor chafing on the taffrail. Rotators have a habit of becoming attached to any floating rubbish which is thrown overboard. Regular reading and inspection of the log will soon indicate when the rotator is foul. In the Sargasso Sea, where there is a great deal of Gulf Weed, the rotator fouls so frequently that in most ships which stream a towing log, no attempt is made to keep it running, and it is taken in on entering the area, and streamed again when leaving it.

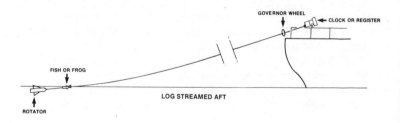

GOVERNOR WHEEL

← CLOCK OR REGISTER

FISH OR FROG

LOG STREAMED AFT

ROTATOR

LOG READY TO BE STREAMED AFT

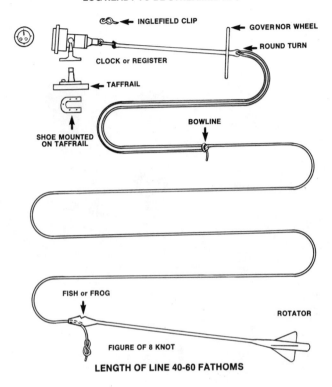

THE CHERNIKEEFF LOG

The Chernikeeff submerged log has gradually become a standard fitting in the majority of ships in the British Navy and in a large number of commercial vessels, especially those which operate at high speeds, or at very low speeds, such as tugs, fishing vessels and cable ships. It has many advantages, the main being (1) it is guaranteed to record distance to 805m ($\frac{1}{2}$ mile) per cent and speed to $\frac{1}{2}$ knot in any state of weather and at any draught; (2) it will record distance run at both very low speeds—down to $\frac{1}{2}$ knot— and very high ones; (3) being well beneath the surface of the water it is clear of all floating objects such as rubbish thrown overboard and Gulf weed; (4) no special knowledge is required as regards maintenance; (5) the submerged part can be quickly withdrawn for inspection in a few seconds; and (6) it will last indefinitely with normal care.

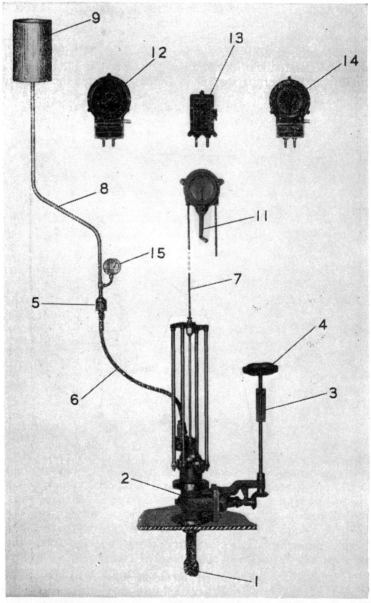

1, Impeller; 2, sluice valve (3-in. bore); 3, valve 'shut' and 'open' indicator; 4, valve operating handwheel; 5, oil filter; 6, flexible oil hose connector; 7, raising and lowering cable; 8, oil pipe; 9, oil supply tank; 11, shipping gear and log position indicator; 12, distance recorder; 13, log switch; 14, speed indicator; 15, oil pressure gauge.

The standard log equipment consists of the following:

Gunmetal hull fitting which includes sluice valve, i.e. sea cock, and watertight chamber through which the log tube is passed by means of a glanded shaft so that the retractable log may be shipped or withdrawn inboard. To remove the log for servicing, etc., it is only necessary to draw the log tube inside the hull fitting to close the sea valve, and the log can then be simply removed without any risk (the fitting is approved by both Lloyd's and the D.T.I.). The hull fitting is usually installed in the bottom of the ship as near to the centre-line as convenient (except in the case of ships having a bar keel), the best position for high-speed ships being just forward of amidships about the turning point, but the log will operate quite satisfactorily in any part of the ship's bottom, though not too close to the propellers.

Recording instruments are arranged for wheelhouse connection and consist of a distance recorder reading 0—16,000 Km (0–10,000 miles) which can be reset, and speed indicator reading 0-25 or 0-40 knots for commercial ships, and in the case of very fast M.T.B.s 6-55 knots. Repeater instruments of both kinds can be provided for installation in any other part of the ship such as at the engine-room control panel, etc. The different parts of the log, i.e. the log tube in the hull and the instruments in the wheelhouse, are connected by ordinary electric cable of small section. The log normally operates at 6 or 20 volts from its own supply, either off a dry battery or charging board and accumulators.

Construction is based upon the principle of a loadless impeller —i.e. a screw which has practically no work to do or appreciable internal friction to overcome—which, having no slip, has no variable error. The only work this impeller has to perform is to 'make' and 'break' contact between an extremely light pair of springs. These contacts are made by the submerged mechanism at at predetermined interval, the standard being 11¼ revolutions of the impeller; this corresponds to 4·6m (15·2 ft.) of distance run, or one four-hundredth part of a nautical mile. As each contact occurs an electrical impulse is transmitted to the distance recorder and the decimal hand is moved up one division (one four-hundredth part of a mile). This action, in turn, moves forward all the indicating hands of the distance recorder as the mileage increases. The impulses are then passed through a distributor in the distance recorder to the speed indicator and, by a combination of distance and time, the actual speed of the ship is then indicated.

Upkeep costs of the Chernikeeff log are extremely small,

maintenance is simple and can be attended to on board. It consists mainly of giving attention to the lubrication system which supplies the submerged mechanism situated at the outboard end of the log tube. As this little mechanism is really the heart of the log and is working beneath the ship's bottom at a pressure even in excess of the ship's maximum draught, it should be realized how important it is that oil pressure is maintained according to the manufacturers' recommendations. Apart from the standard injector system of lubrication by manual screw-down applied pressure, there is also an automatic system working on a simple arrangement employing gravity pressure. This, shown in the accompanying diagram on page 143, is used invariably in merchant ships.

With regard to the retractability of the log a remote-controlled means of raising and lowering the log tube was introduced. It can be operated either manually from main-deck level or by electrical power from the bridge, so that at all times the log is under the direct control of the navigating officer. Installation of the log is simple, requiring only the cutting of a 89mm ($3\frac{1}{2}$ in.) (diameter) hole in the ship's bottom and the attachment of the sluice valve. This, of course, has to be done in dry-dock, but the remainder of the equipment can easily be installed whenever a ship visits port in the course of her normal trading employment.

THE LEAD

The lead is employed to ascertain the depth of water and the nature of the sea bottom. The greater the depth the heavier the lead must be. Of the two leads, hand lead and deep-sea lead, only the former is used nowadays because deep-water soundings are obtained by means of the patent sounding machine or an echo-sounding device. To all intents and purposes there is now no such thing as a deep-sea lead, although passenger ships are still required to carry one.

The hand leadline is made of 25 fathoms of untarred, left-hand-laid hemp, the lead itself weighing about 3kg (7 lb.) Ships carry two lines and leads. A length of 20 fathoms of line is subdivided, the remaining five (or more) being necessary to reach from the deck, whence the soundings are taken, to the waterline. The line is marked as follows:

At	2 fathoms	..	Two strips of leather
,,	3 ,,	..	Three strips of leather
,,	5 ,,	..	Strip of white rag (linen)

,,	7	,,	..	Strip of red rag (bunting)
,,	10	,,	..	Piece of leather with hole in it
,,	13	,,	..	Strip of blue serge (or flannel)
,,	15	,,	..	Strip of white rag (linen)
,,	17	,,	..	Strip of red rag (bunting)
,,	20	,,	..	Cord with two knots

(it has been advocated that the line should be marked in metric measure. This at present is only a recommendation, but will probably eventually go into operation. See following table).

1, 11 and 21 metres—one strip of leather.
2, 12 and 22 metres—two strips of leather.
3, 13 and 23 metres—blue bunting.
4, 14 and 24 metres—green and white bunting.
5, 15 and 25 metres—white bunting.
6, 16 and 26 metres—green bunting.
7, 17 and 27 metres—red bunting.
8, 18 and 28 metres—blue and white bunting.
9, 19 and 29 metres—red and white bunting.

10, metres	—leather with a hole in it.
20, metres	—leather with a hole in it and 2 strips of leather.
30, metres	—leather with a hole in it and 3 strips of leather.
40, metres	—leather with a hole in it and 4 strips of leather.
50, metres	—leather with a hole in it and 5 strips of leather.
All 0·2 metre markings	—a piece of mackerel line.

The idea behind the use of pieces of different material is supposed to be that soundings may be taken at night and the leadsman can 'feel' the sounding due to the different textures of linen, bunting and serge. One, 4, 6, 8, 9, 11, 12, 14, 16, 18 and 19 fathoms are known as deeps, and sometimes they are indicated by small lengths of marline, but this is by no means standard practice.

CALLING SOUNDINGS

The number of fathoms should always form the *last* part of the call, thus 'deep six', 'and a quarter six', 'by the mark thirteen', 'a quarter less thirteen', etc. If the bottom is not reached the

SECURING LINE TO LEAD

call should be 'no bottom at twenty fathoms'. Incidentally the leadline should be measured, and accordingly subdivided, from the end of the line—not from the bottom of the lead. The length of the lead thus provides a small safety margin, called the 'benefit of the lead'. This is rather like the arguments for keeping a clock five minutes fast, but it is the method used in all merchant ships.

Before new leadlines are marked they should be stretched and thoroughly wet. They should be marked when wet—since they are bound to get wet when in use! Into one end of the line an eye is spliced. This is rove through the grommet on the lead and over the lead itself, as shown in the accompanying illustrations. At the bottom of all leads there is a cavity which is stuffed with a mixture of tallow and white lead before a cast is taken. By this means the nature of the sea bottom can be ascertained when a cast is being taken, and both the depth of water and the nature of the bottom used to assist in determining the ship's position by reference to the chart. But more often than not arming the hand lead is omitted since the principal use of this lead in these days of well-charted channels and entrances to ports is not so much to determine position as a quick way of getting the depth of water.

When sounding with the hand lead the leadsman is stationed in the 'chains', which is a platform on the ship's side at deck level; the line is grasped with the right hand and paid out until the lead is just clear of the water's surface, and then held firmly at this length with one turn around the right thumb. At the same time a few bights are taken in the left hand and the lead is now hove a few times until it has acquired enough momentum to be cast far enough ahead. At this stage the line is allowed to slip through the right hand until, by picking up the slack as the ship moves ahead, the lead can be 'bumped' on the bottom and it is known that a good sounding has been obtained. If no. bottom is reached when the line has been paid out to the limit then the appropriate call is made to the bridge.

Chapter 14

MOORING

Head, stern and breast ropes as well as the fore and after back springs, serving to keep the ship in position when alongside, pass around fairleads or through Panama leads. The fore back spring leads in the opposite direction to head ropes, i.e. from forward to aft, whilst the after back spring leads in the opposite direction to the stern ropes, in other words from aft to forward. Wire springs are employed to eliminate or minimize ranging to and fro. They are led through fairleads in the ship's side, usually situated in the forward or after corners of the fore and after decks, and care must be taken, (*a*) so that they do not jam under the rollers, and (*b*) lead towards the bollards or winch in as straight a direction as possible, a snatch block being employed if necessary.

Large hawsers 152mm–228mm (6–9 in. in circumference) are used for head, stern and breast ropes and large eyes are spliced in each end. The mooring lines are brought on deck before the ship comes alongside and are placed with the eye through the fairleads and then either put ashore by means of heaving lines or lowered into a boat. The heaving line is made fast to the eye of the rope with a bowline. If the rope is to be taken ashore in a boat the eye is taken in the bottom of the boat, a few loops being coiled over the thwarts.

The rope is paid out from the ship according to the amount of slack floating in the water. As the boat nears the shore the boatman throws overboard the coils of rope from the thwarts and passes the eye ashore. If mooring rings are employed ashore for securing the ropes the eye is rove through the ring and made fast on its own part. In the case of wires the eye is always shackled to the standing part; as the eye is not shackled to the ring a direct pull on the pin is avoided and there is no possibility of it being bent and making casting off difficult, if not impossible, without cutting the wire. In the case of shore bollards the eye is hooked over, and for this the bowline is found handy. When the hawser has been hauled far enough ashore with the heaving line for the eye to be grasped the bowline is slipped back to the point of the eye and the rope is hooked over the bollard; the heaving line is then let go and hauled back aboard.

If there are already on the bollard another ship's lines which

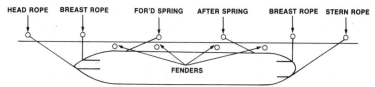

HEAD ROPE   BREAST ROPE   FOR'D SPRING   AFTER SPRING   BREAST ROPE   STERN ROPE

FENDERS

may have to be cast off first, the eye should be passed up through the eyes of the other ship's ropes and then hooked over the bollard. If this is done the ropes of the other ship can be let go from the bollard without having to cast off the ropes that were attached last, as the sketch below shows.

Slip moorings are effected by passing the eye through the ring of a buoy or round a bollard ashore, bringing it back on board and turning up on the bitts. Heave taut and make fast in the usual manner. As far as possible ropes should be distributed on different rings or bollards, so that if one carries away the others are not affected. Likewise aboard ships, ropes should be made fast on all available bitts, so that the strain is evenly distributed and, moreover, so that hawsers can be used independently of each other. Finally, a strong lashing should be placed around the turns at their crossing point, so that the upper turns cannot jump off, or all the turns render round the bitts when strain comes on the rope. This is only necessary in the case of wire ropes.

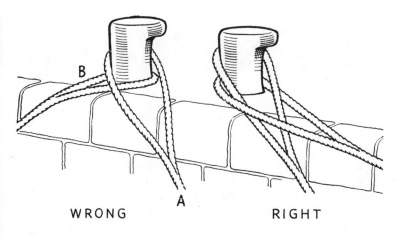

B

A

WRONG   RIGHT

ROPE 'A' MUST BE TAKEN OFF BEFORE ROPE 'B' CAN BE SLIPPED.

EITHER ROPE CAN BE SLIPPED BY USING THIS METHOD.

If a rope, after having been hove taut, has to be transferred from a capstan or winch barrel to the bitts the rope must be 'stopped' to prevent it easing up. A short chain with rope pennant is always used as a stopper for wire ropes, and this is made fast around one of the bitts to which the hawser has to be secured or through a convenient ringbolt on deck. For fibre and nylon ropes a chain stopper should never be used as it may cut or nip the strands. Use a stopper of 89mm (3½ in.) or 102mm (4 in.) manila. A rope stopper should be about 2 fathoms in length.

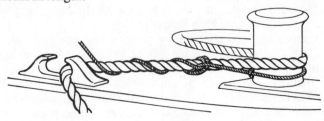

The top diagram shows the best type of stopper to use on a mooring rope. It is, in effect, the first two turns of a rolling hitch with the stopper then turned two or three times round the rope with the lay of the rope and the end held in the hand. Occasionally one will see a second half-hitch put on after the locking turns of the rolling hitch but, when the rope has been secured to the bitts and the ship is falling off the quay, speed may be an essential factor in slipping the stopper and the method illustrated is easier to slip.

The lower diagram shows how to put a chain stopper on a wire—'against the lay of the wire'. Note that the two half hitches make up a Cow Hitch and that the stopper is then turned round the wire and held in the hand. To release this type of stopper take off the turns and flick the chain towards the bitts. By so doing the tension is eased and the two hitches are easily removed. At this stage it should be said that the most common error in putting on a chain stopper is to make the two half hitches up as a clove hitch. This is a jamming knot and is most difficult to release. In fact, a clove hitch should never be used on board ship unless you require it for a hitch which is to be reasonably permanent.

Chapter 15

FIRE APPLIANCES

Fire is as dangerous as it is useful. To extinguish fires effectively and speedily the following simple facts should be understood. There are three main types of fire. These are classified ʿ.. A, B and C. Class A fires are those involving carbonaceous substances such as wood, paper, textiles, rubbish, etc. Class A fire risks are present almost everywhere, indoors and outdoors, in large premises and small, offices, houses, shops, factories, mines—and in ships. Class B fires are those involving inflammable liquids, fuel, lubricating and quenching oils, paints, varnishes, grease, fats and tar. Class C fires are those in electrical equipment. It will be seen that these three classes of fire are applicable to all classes of ships, and fire is indeed an ever-present shipboard danger. Fire is the process whereby one chemical element combines with another to produce heat and flame. It depends on three factors (1) material (fuel); (2) heat; and (3) air (oxygen). The removal of one or more will therefore put a fire out. Sometimes it is possible to remove the material, i.e. the burning substance, but most fires have to be put out by reducing the heat, or the air, or both. To reduce heat, water is commonly used because of its good cooling properties. Class A fires are fought with water. Class B are blanketed by foam, which cuts off the inflammable vapours from the surrounding air. Class C fires are smothered by a gas blanket which reduces the air supply to a level insufficient to sustain the fire.

Fire drill should be carried out at regular and frequent intervals aboard ship and every member of the crew should be familiar with his duties in the event of an outbreak.

Provision of fire appliances. The D.T.I. regulations governing the type and number of fire appliances cover all classes of merchant shipping. Fire-extinguishing gear required to be carried by, and fire precautions to be taken in, ocean-going passenger ships of Class I are necessarily more numerous, varied and elaborate than for, say, fishing craft of Class X. For example, fire patrols have to be kept in deep-sea passenger ships, but it would be unreasonable to expect them to be kept in other classes of tonnage. Clearly it is neither desirable nor necessary in a book of this kind to detail *all* the equipment to be carried by *all* classes of ships, so a happy medium has been struck, and the various appliances to be carried by a ship of Class VII, which is a cargo-carrying, foreign-going steamship or motorship not certified to carry passengers, are dealt with, and detailed, below.

Every ship of Class VII of 2,000 gross tons and upwards, unless otherwise stated, must be provided with:

(1) Apparatus whereby fire-smothering gas sufficient to give a minimum volume of free gas equal to 30 per cent of the gross volume of the largest hold in the ship can be promptly conveyed by a permanent piping system into any compartment in which cargo may be carried, provided that in steamships and motorships which have available a boiler or boilers possessing an evaporation of not less than 454gms (1 lb.) of steam per hour for each 340 cu. decimetres (12 cu. ft.) of the gross volume of the largest hold in the ship, steam may be provided as an alternative to gas. In oil tankers, froth may be substituted for gas.

(2) **Two power pumps** each capable of providing a full supply of water to the fire hoses, together with apparatus whereby at least two powerful jets of water can be rapidly and simultaneously directed into any part of the ship. Such apparatus shall include *two fire hoses*, each complete with couplings and conductor and a spare 9·1m (30 ft.) length of fire hose. Provided that in ships of less than 1,000 gross tons, apparatus for only one powerful jet of water need be provided, together with *one fire hose* complete with coupling and conductor; also a spare 9·1m (30 ft.) length of fire hose complete with coupling and conductor which shall be kept in a different part of the ship.

(3) Sufficient portable fluid fire extinguishers to ensure that at least one is available for immediate use in each space occupied by the crew, and passengers if any. In any case *a minimum of five extinguishers must be carried in ships over* 1,000 *g.r.t.*

(4) **At least two approved outfits,** each consisting of a breathing apparatus, smoke mask or smoke helmet, safety lamp and fireman's hatchet, which shall be kept ready for use in widely separated places, provided that in ships of less than 4,000 gross tons only one such outfit need be carried.

(5) In every ship of Class VII (except in tankers) where electric power is available, appliances shall include a *portable electric drilling* machine for providing emergency means of access to fires through decks, casings or bulkheads.

(6) In every ship of Class VII fitted with oil-fired boilers or internal-combustion machinery the arrangement of the pumps, and the sources of power for operating them, must be such as to ensure that a fire in any one compartment will not put all the fire pumps out of action.

(7) Every ship of Class VII fitted with oil-fired boilers or internal combustion machinery shall be provided in the machinery and boiler spaces with at least two fire hydrants, one port and one starboard, and for each hydrant a hose complete with coupling and conductor, together with a nozzle suitable for spraying water on oil without undue disturbance of the surface.

(8) Every ship of Class VII in which oil only is used as fuel for the main or auxiliary boilers shall be provided in the boiler and machinery spaces with:

(a) A receptacle containing at least 283 cu. decimetres (10 cu. ft.) of sand, sawdust impregnated with soda, or other approved dry material in each firing space, and scoops for distributing such material.

(b) For each firing space in each boiler-room, and in each machinery space in which a part of the boiler oil-fuel installation is situated, at least two approved portable extinguishers constructed to discharge froth or other approved medium for quenching oil fires. In addition to these, one or more extinguishers of the same description with a total capacity of 9 litres (2 gallons) (or the equivalent) for each burner, provided that the total capacity of the additional extinguishers need not exceed $45\frac{1}{2}$ litres (10 gallons) for any one firing space.

(c) Means for admission and distribution of froth rapidly over the whole area of the boiler-room to a depth of $152\frac{1}{2}$mm (6 in.) or fire-smothering gas or steam in sufficient quantity in the boiler space with control from an easily accessible position or positions which will not be readily cut off from use by an outbreak of fire.

(9) Every steamship of Class VII in which oil and coal are used simultaneously as fuel for the main or auxiliary boilers shall also be provided in the boiler and machinery spaces with:

(a) Appliances in accordance with paragraphs (a) and (b) above.

(b) If the tank top is effectually subdivided by vertical, longitudinal and transverse plates at each boiler to prevent spread of oil, and does not exceed 92 sq. m. (1,000 sq. ft.) in total area, one approved extinguisher of at least 36 litres' (30 gallons') capacity constructed to discharge froth, complete with hose. If the area of the tank top exceeds 92 sq. m. (1,000 sq. ft.)

the capacity of the extinguisher or extinguishers shall not be less than 273 litres (60 gallons). In each case means shall be provided for the admission of steam to the boiler-room. If the tank top is not subdivided there shall be provided in substitution for steam to the boiler-room means for admission and distribution of froth rapidly over the whole area of the boiler-room to a depth of 152½mm (6 in.) or fire-smothering gas in sufficient quantity in the boiler space or spaces with control from an easily accessible position or positions which will not be readily cut off from use by an outbreak of fire.

(10) Every motorship of Class VII shall be provided in the machinery spaces with:

(a) One approved extinguisher of at least 45½ litres (10 gallons) capacity constructed to discharge froth.

(b) Approved portable extinguishers constructed to discharge froth or other approved medium suitable for quenching oil fires, in accordance with the following scale:

B.H.P. of main engines	Number of portable extinguishers
Not exceeding 1,000..	2
Exceeding 1,000 but not exceeding 2,000	3
Exceeding 2,000 but not exceeding 3,000	4
Exceeding 3,000 but not exceeding 4,000	5
Exceeding 4,000	6

GENERAL RULES APPLYING TO ALL SHIPS

Ready availability of fire appliances. All fire-extinguishing apparatus and appliances shall be kept in working order and available for immediate use before the ship leaves port and at all times during the voyage.

Pumps. (1) Power fire pumps shall be independent of the main engines and each shall be capable of delivering the requisite jet of water in any part of the ship as the rules may require and in such quantity as the D.T.I. may deem sufficient. Sanitary, ballast, bilge or general service pumps may be accepted as fire pumps if they comply with the provisions of the rules.

(2) Effective escape valves shall be provided in connection with all power fire pumps. These valves shall be so placed and adjusted as to prevent excessive pressure in any part of the fire main system.

(3) Fire pumps not specifically required by the rules to be power pumps may be of the manual type, capable of delivering a sufficient jet of water in any part of the ship.

Water service pipes. (1) Water service pipes shall be made of wrought material, and if of iron or steel shall be galvanized.

(2) The diameter of the pipes shall be sufficient to enable adequate water to be supplied to the fire hose, or to both fire hoses when two are required to be provided for simultaneous operation.

(3) The pipes and hydrants shall be so placed that the fire hoses may be easily coupled to them. In vessels where deck cargo may be carried the positions of the hydrants shall be such that they are always readily accessible, and the pipes shall be arranged as far as practicable to avoid risk of damage by such cargo.

(4) Cocks or valves shall be fitted in such positions on the pipes that any of the fire hoses may be removed while the fire pumps are at work.

Fire hoses. (1) Fire hoses shall be of leather, seamless hemp, flax canvas of first-class quality, or other approved material, and sufficient in length to project a jet of water to any of the spaces in which they may be required to be used, and shall be provided with the necessary fittings.

(2) Hoses specified 'complete with couplings and conductor' shall, together with the necessary coupling wrenches and gooseneck connections, be kept ready for use in conspicuous positions near the water-service hydrants or connections. Such fire hoses shall be used only for the purpose of extinguishing fires or testing the fire-extinguishing apparatus at fire drills and surveys. Where hoses are not specified as 'fire hoses' they shall always be available, but may be used also for other purposes.

Fire buckets. Where fire buckets are specified they shall be of about 9 litres (2 gallons') capacity and shall be reserved for the purpose of fire extinguishing. Such buckets shall be painted red and marked 'FIRE' and be kept ready for use in readily accessible positions. At least half the number of fire buckets required to be provided shall be fitted with lanyards.

Portable fire extinguishers. (1) Portable fire extinguishers shall be of an approved fluid type, except when supplied as an alternative to extinguishers discharging froth for use on oil fires as required for motor engine-rooms and oil-fired boiler-rooms. The capacity of the extinguishers shall be not more than $13\frac{1}{2}$ litres (3 gallons) and shall be not less than 9 litres (2 gallons).

(2) The portable fire extinguishers provided (other than those supplied in boiler-rooms, etc., specially for use in connection with oil fuel fires) shall not be of more than two types.

(3) A spare charge shall be provided for each portable fire extinguisher.

(4) Extinguishers in which the medium is stored under pressure shall not be provided for use in passenger or crew accommodation.

(5) Fire extinguishers shall be tested at intervals not exceeding four years. Fluid extinguishers under inspection shall be emptied of their contents and examined, and a trial of one shall be made. Fluid extinguishers discharging froth shall be kept in as cool a place as possible.

(6) Fire extinguishers shall, where possible, be stowed near the entrance to the space in which they are intended to be used. In small motorships one of the extinguishers shall, where possible, be stowed near the entrance to the motor space.

Fire-smothering gas or steam for cargo spaces and boiler-rooms. (1) Where provision is made for the injection of gas or steam into cargo spaces or boiler-rooms for fire-extinguishing purposes the pipes for conveying the gas or steam shall be provided with controlling valves or cocks which shall be readily accessible from the deck in any circumstances, and so marked as to indicate clearly the respective compartments to which the pipes lead. Suitable provision shall be made for locking these valves or cocks so as to prevent inadvertent admission of the gas or steam to any compartment. If any pipe is led to a space to which passengers may have access, it shall be furnished with an additional stop valve or cock also capable of being locked.

(2) Piping shall be arranged so as to provide effective distribution of the fire-smothering gas or steam, and in large holds where steam is used there shall be two pipes, one at the forward part and one at the after part led well down in the space. In tankers the arrangements for steaming out cargo tanks shall provide for steam being distributed over the surface of the contents of the tanks.

(3) When carbon dioxide is supplied as the extinguishing medium in holds the quantity of gas available shall be sufficient to give a minimum volume of free gas equal to 30 per cent of the gross volume of the largest hold in the ship. When carbon dioxide is supplied as an extinguishing medium for boiler-rooms the weight of gas carried shall be sufficient to give a gas saturation of 30 per cent of the gross volume of the largest boiler-room measured to the top of the boilers.

(4) When steam is the extinguishing medium in holds the boiler or boilers available for supplying steam shall have an evaporation of at least 454g (1 lb.) of steam per hour for each

340 cu. decimetres (12 cu. ft.) of the cubic capacity of the largest cargo compartment in the ship.

(5) Means shall be provided for closing all doorways, ventilators and other openings to spaces in which fire-smothering gas or steam can be used as a fire-extinguishing medium.

Breathing apparatus and smoke helmets. (1) Breathing apparatus or smoke helmets shall be of a type approved by the D.T.I. and shall be equipped with a life and signalling line at least 3·5m (10 ft.) longer than the total length of air hose required under paragraph (2) of this rule. The life-line shall be efficiently attached to a strong leather or canvas harness to be worn by the wearer of the helmet when the latter is in use and shall be made of hemp-covered wire rope of about 32mm ($1\frac{1}{4}$ in.) circumference. The wire incorporated in the rope shall have a breaking strain of approximately one ton and shall be either copper or galvanized steel.

(2) Where smoke helmets or masks fitted for air hoses are provided, the length of air hose supplied shall be sufficient to enable the wearer to go into any part of the holds or machinery spaces from a position on the open deck well clear of hatch or doorway, so as to avoid smoke being carried to the wearer.

Safety lamps. The safety lamp provided shall be of a type approved by the Department of Trade and Industry and Power for use in mines and shall have a minimum burning period of three hours. Where a tanker is required to carry a safety lamp it shall be of the electric-battery type.

Alternative appliances. Where any special appliance, apparatus, extinguishing medium or arrangement is referred to in the Merchant Shipping (Fire Appliances) Rules, 1952, the D.T.I. may approve any alternative appliance, apparatus, medium or arrangement if he is satisfied that it is not less effective than that prescribed in the rules.

USE OF EXTINGUISHERS

A few words about the use of extinguishers and smoke helmets with which every foreign-going, cargo-carrying steamship or motorship must be equipped, are thought to be advisable. It is not feasible to deal with every type and make of fire extinguisher and smoke helmet, but the Nu-Swift 'Universal Royal Navy Model' extinguisher and the 'Spirelmo' helmet are particularly suitable for shipboard purposes, and are supplied to many hundreds of naval and merchant ships, so they have been selected for instructional purposes.

The extinguisher shown on page 163 is made ready for use by filling the outer container with 9 litres (2 gallons) of plain water, inserting a pressure charge (E) and screwing the wheelhead (C) firmly into position. The extinguisher is used in an upright position and operated by pushing over the safety guard (A) and striking the knob (B). The piercer (D) perforates a metal diaphragm in the charge (E). Carbon dioxide is instantly released and exerts a downward pressure on the water, which is propelled at a terrific pressure up the dip-tube (F) and through the hose. A $10\frac{1}{2}$m (35 ft.) jet is forced from the nozzle at an initial speed of 95 miles per hour.

The following are some of the ways in which the extinguishers may be used to the best advantage aboard ship:

(1) Extinguishers should be secured on bulkheads so that the bottom of the extinguisher is about 609mm (2 ft.) from deck level with a bracket of four spare charges sited adjacent. In this position the extinguisher may be operated without removal from the bulkhead to cover fires in the immediate vicinity, the spare charges being immediately available to refill rapidly the extinguisher.

(2) It will be noted that it is provided with a double-acting nozzle button (indicated at (G) in the accompanying illustration), as a spray is used aboard ship for extinguishing oil fires by either the 'sweep away' or emulsification method. In addition to this the spray may be used to enable members of the ship's company to progress down smoke-filled passages by holding the extinguisher under one arm and the spray being directed just ahead of the nose of the operator to drive away smoke and allow sufficient air to support life.

(3) The extinguisher is designed so that several extinguishers may be operated by one person simultaneously. Unlike many other extinguishers Nu-Swift Royal Navy models do not have to be held during operation. All that is required is to strike the knobs and hold the discharge hoses in either hand.

(4) The Nu-Swift Water/CO_2 extinguishers especially fulfil requirements for fighting ship fires, which differ radically from those which obtain on shore where unlimited quantities of water may be applied to a fire since stability considerations do not have to be taken into account. The problem aboard a ship is totally different and the amount of water which may be used to fight a fire with consequent effect upon heat or trim, together with the

danger resulting from the movement of free surface water, must be closely considered. In these circumstances the maximum fire-fighting effect must be obtained from minimum water.

(5) In emergency this make of extinguisher may be refilled with sea water, but should be washed out and refilled with fresh water as soon as possible to prevent corrosion.

(6) Nu-Swift extinguishers are simply and easily maintained by removing the head, ensuring that the extinguisher is filled with water to the correct level and that an unexpended charge is in position. The rubber hose and fittings should be examined to ensure that they have not been damaged.

(7) The extinguisher will not self-operate due to stress of weather and no amount of rolling or pitching will cause it to operate when not intended.

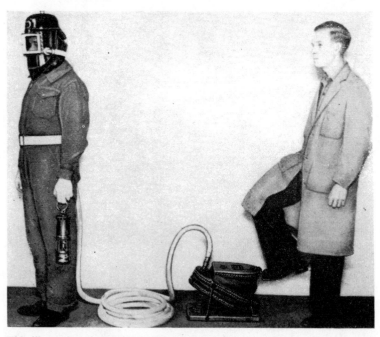

This illustration shows the 'Spirelmo' smoke helmet and accessories, air hose and bellows, also the safety lamp. Not shown is the combined signalling and lifeline which forms part of the equipment. It is required to be attached to the wearer by means of a strong leather or canvas harness, and must be at least 3m (10 ft.) longer than the total length of air hose. One sharp pull on the lifeline by the wearer means that he requires more air, two sharp pulls that he requires less air, and three that he requires pulling back.

Smoke helmets. The object of wearing the helmet is, of course, to enable the wearer to penetrate dense smoke and to get at the seat of the fire with fire-fighting appliances. The 'Spirelmo' smoke helmets are blocked out of hide, are fitted with strong, clear mica windows in aluminium hinged frames, and with air inlet connections and valve for escape of excess and vitiated air. A simple arrangement inside the crown of the helmet enables it to be adjusted for all head sizes, and a flexible leather extension, which is tucked under the wearer's overall, jacket or vest, effectively seals the lower part of the helmet. An ample supply of air is delivered by means of double-acting bellows through the non-collapsible air tube having embedded wire, or armouring, and metal couplings. Strong waist belts are provided for the wearer and for the man working the bellows (when the hand type is employed), that for the former being fitted with a device for keeping the air tube in position and preventing it from pulling down on the helmet.

Compressed-air breathing apparatus. Many vessels now carry self-contained breathing apparatus as part of their fire-fighting and gas freeing equipment. The AirMaster, see page 166, is supplied as a complete unit for shipboard installation and consists of one complete set, two spare cylinders, a test gauge and $36\frac{1}{2}$m (120 ft.) of hemp-covered wire lifeline. The compressed-air cylinder is secured by an adjustable quick-release metal strap to an anodized alloy metal back-plate, and this apparatus is supported on the wearer's back by an adjustable terylene harness. The lifeline is secured to a ring on the back-plate. Air passes from the cylinder to a reducing valve and the reduced air is then fed along a low pressure hose to a wide vision face mask. A warning whistle to indicate the approaching exhaustion of air in the cylinder can be inserted in the pressure gauge air pipe as an optional extra. A demand valve on the mask operates the flow of air. This apparatus provides complete respiratory protection, independent of the surrounding atmosphere, for between 25 and 60 minutes.

Fire drill. For the purposes of this drill (required to be carried out weekly in passenger ships and fortnightly in cargo ships) an outbreak of fire should be assumed to have occurred in a part of the ship (not the engine-room) selected by the officer in charge of the drill and a mock attack on the supposed fire should be made. On receipt of the signal or other warning in the engine-room the fire pumps should be prepared for operation. The members of the crew forming the fire party or parties should be sent to the seat of the assumed fire. The hoses in that neighbourhood should be laid out and the fire extinguishers

COMPRESSED-AIR BREATHING APPARATUS
(*Reproduced by courtesy of Siebe Gorman & Co., Ltd, Chessington, Surrey*)

unshipped, and occasionally one of the extinguishers should be discharged. Water should be played through a proportion of the fire hoses selected by the officer in charge of the drill. In addition the hydrants should be tested under pressure. Men should be exercised in the closing of doors, ventilating shafts and other openings in the vicinity of the space affected by the supposed fire so as to reduce the supply of air to the fire and isolate it as far as practicable from other parts of the ship, especially stairways and lift shafts. The fire party should be exercised in the use of smoke helmets or any other breathing apparatus carried on the ship and should also be instructed in the use of all other descriptions of fire-fighting appliances on the ship. The fire appliances in other parts of the ship, including the engine-room and machinery spaces, should be examined so as to ensure that they are in good order and readily available for use in an emergency, and fire alarms and fire-detecting apparatus, where fitted, should, so far as possible, be inspected to see that they are in sufficient working order. If this is not done on the occasion of each successive fire drill arrangements should be made to ensure that it shall be carried out within the same intervals, i.e. weekly in passenger ships and fortnightly in cargo ships.

Drill in closing of doors, side scuttles, etc. In passenger ships drills for practising the closing of watertight and fire-resisting doors, side scuttles, ash-shoots, rubbish-shoots, lavatory and bath discharges, and other similar valves giving access to the sea must be so arranged as to secure compliance with the relevant requirements of the Merchant Shipping Act. Under this enactment the opening and closing of

  (i) all watertight doors in main transverse bulkheads,

 (ii) side scuttles in certain positions,

(iii) the covers and valves of all ash-shoots, rubbish-shoots or other similar contrivances having their inboard openings below the margin line, and

(iv) the closing mechanism of all scuppers having their inboard openings below the margin line,

must be practised once a week, and also before the ship proceeds to sea on any voyage which is likely to last more than a week; and every valve, the closing of which is necessary to make any compartment watertight, and every watertight door in the main transverse bulkheads and the mechanism and indicators connected therewith are to be inspected at least once a week.

The practices held at sea do not include those doors which the Schedule requires to be closed before the ship proceeds to sea and to be kept closed at sea.

Oil tankers. On this type of ship an efficient and highly trained fire-fighting organization must exist. Every crew member joining this type of vessel must quickly ascertain the whereabouts of each item of fire-fighting equipment and become proficient in both use and as an active member of each fire drill. If the fire occurs while the vessel is at the loading/discharging berth, sound the alarm immediately, shut the pumps and then the manifold valves. Close tank openings and pumproom doors. Do not throw any burning material overboard. A burning wad of waste, thrown overboard, would set any oil on the surrounding water alight.

Chapter 16

LINE-THROWING APPLIANCES

Every ship is required to carry a line-throwing appliance capable of throwing a line of 12½mm (½ in.) circumference a minimum distance of 228½m (250 yards) in such a manner that the lateral deflection of the line does not exceed 10 per cent of the length of flight of the rocket. The apparatus includes four lines of 12½mm (½ in.) circumference each having not less than 228½m (250 yards) in length and having a breaking strain of not less than 113k (250 lb.) and four rockets. Rockets and lines, together with a copy of directions for use of the appliance, should be stowed in a case which is sufficiently weather- and watertight to keep the rockets available for immediate use. Rockets must not be more than two years old, and out-of-date rockets should not be used for testing or practice purposes. The most popular of all line-throwing appliances is the Schermuly Pistol Rocket apparatus. To operate the Nos. 2 and 3 sets:

SEALING
TAPES

Open the watertight line box by tearing off the sealing tapes (fig. 1).

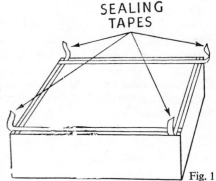

Fig. 1

Make fast a length of rope to the bowline end of the line so that in the event of the rocket exceeding its estimated range the end of the line will not be lost (fig. 2). NOTE.—Do not disturb the lay of the line in the box while doing this.

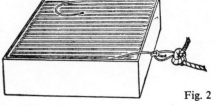

Fig. 2

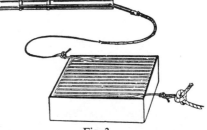

Take out a rocket and make fast the free end of the line in the line box to the loop at the end of the wire rocket tail (fig. 3).

Fig. 3

Take out the pistol. Pull back with the thumb the breech-locking device and load the pistol with one of the cartridges from the round tin (fig. 4).
Close the breech of the pistol but *do not cock the trigger*.

Fig. 4

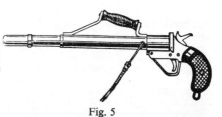

Insert the rocket as far as it will go into the muzzle of the pistol with the direction bridle on the underside (fig. 5).

Fig. 5

Stand behind, or on the left-hand side of the line box, cock the trigger, aim, and fire. NOTE.—Before firing make certain that there are no obstructions to prevent the free running of the line.

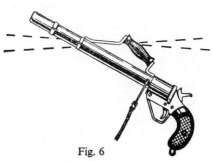

Aiming. Maximum distance depends on having the muzzle of the pistol raised to the correct elevation. This can be gauged by ensuring that the front bar of the hand-grip is very slightly above the horizontal (fig. 6).

Point of Aim. While the rocket itself is very little affected in its flight by a heavy cross-wind the line will form a bight to leeward of the rocket's flight. This must be allowed for when aiming.

Fig. 6

General rules for aiming:

(A) In calm weather, or in a
heavy wind blowing directly
from target to firer *aim
directly at the target* (fig. 7).

(B) In a moderate to heavy cross-
wind *aim at a point a few
yards to windward of target
to allow for the bight of the
line* (fig. 7).

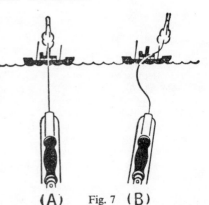

(A)   Fig. 7   (B)

NOTE.—In the event of a misjudged aim when it appears that the bight of the
line will fall to leeward of the target, it is possible to reduce the bight by waiting
until the rocket is near the end of its flight and then loosely grasping the outgoing
line in the hand. This gives a braking effect.

*Always clean and oil the pistol after use and replace used lines, rockets and signals
with spare ones.*

SIGNALS USED IN CONNECTION WITH THE LIFESAVING SERVICES ON THE COASTS OF GREAT BRITAIN AND NORTHERN IRELAND

SIGNAL	SIGNIFICATION
a) Signals to Vessels in Distress:	
Rocket throwing **white** stars, or **white** flare.	Distress signal or plight observed—assistance summoned.
One explosive sound signal showing bright **white** star on bursting.	Distress signal or plight observed—lifesaving apparatus called out.
Two explosive sound signals, showing bright **green** stars on bursting.	Distress signal or plight observed—lifeboat called out.
Three explosive sound signals, the first showing **white** star on bursting and the second and third **green** stars.	Distress signal or plight observed—lifesaving apparatus and lifeboat called out.

NOTE 1.—By day a **red** flag (rectangular or swallow-tailed) will be flown when
the lifesaving apparatus is called out, and a **red** flag (triangular) when the lifeboat
is called out.

NOTE 2.—Certain pyrotechnic signals consisting of either **white** flares or three
or more rockets throwing **white** stars on bursting or a **green** flare turning to
white are used on occasions for communication between the shore and a lifeboat—
or between a lighthouse or light-vessel and a lifeboat. A lifeboat when out on
service may make any of the following signals: A **white** flare to indicate that she
is approaching a wreck. **Red** flares to indicate to the shore that more aid is
required; and a **green** or **green** turning to **white** flare to notify to those ashore
that she is returning.

(*b*) Landing Signals:

By day—flag held upright overhead.
By night—**white** flare held steady or
stuck in ground.   } You may attempt to land here.

By day—flag waved from side to side.
By night—**white** flare waved from side
to side.   } Landing is extremely dangerous. You are advised to lay off until lifeboat arrives.

SIGNAL	SIGNIFICATION
By day—flag waved to right or left and then pointed in direction. By night—**white** flare held steady and carried along shore to right or left.	The best landing will be found in the direction in which flag is pointed or light carried.
By day—two flags held upright overhead, the men holding them being about 45m (50 yards) apart in line of approach. By night—two **white** flares held or stuck in ground or two bonfires placed as above.	You should attempt to land and by this line of approach.

(c) Standing into danger signals:

The International Code Signal JD. The letter U (· · —) flashed by lamp or made by foghorn, or whistle, etc.	You are standing into danger.

NOTE.—If it should prove necessary the attention of the vessel is called to these signals by a **white** flare, a rocket showing **white** stars on bursting, or an explosive sound signal.

DIRECTIONS FOR USE OF THE ROCKET LIFESAVING APPARATUS

1. If lives are in danger and your vessel is in a position where rescue by the rocket lifesaving apparatus is possible, a rocket with a line attached will be fired across your vessel. Get hold of this line as soon as you can. When you have got hold of it signal to the shore as follows:

By day, one of the crew—if possible separated from the rest—should wave his hand, or handkerchief, or hat or a flag. By night, a flare should be burnt, or a light should be waved. If the visibility is poor, one short blast on the whistle can be made, in place of the above signals, by day or by night.

Alternatively, if your ship has a line-throwing appliance and this is first used to fire a line ashore the line will not be of sufficient strength to haul out the whip, and those ashore will secure it to a stouter line. When they have done this they will wave a red flag (at night—a red light). On seeing this signal, haul in on the line until the stouter line is on board. Then make signal as indicated above, after which the procedure laid down in paragraph 2 onwards will be followed.

2. When you see a red flag (at night—a red light) waved on shore, haul upon the rocket line until you get a tail block with an endless fall rove through it (called the 'whip').

3. Make the block fast, close up, to a convenient position, bearing in mind that the fall should be kept clear from chafing any part of the vessel, and that space must be left above the block for the hawser (see paragraph 5). Unbend the rocket

line from the whip. When the tail block has been made fast, and the rocket line unbent from the whip, signal to the shore again, as in paragraph 1 (page 171).

4. As soon as this signal is seen ashore a hawser will be bent to the whip and will be hauled off to the ship by those on shore. Except when there are rocks, piles or other obstructions between the ship and the shore, a bowline will have been made with the end of the hawser round the hauling part of the whip.

5. When the hawser has been hauled aboard the bowline should be cast off. Then, having seen that the end of the hawser is clear of the whip the end should be brought up between the two parts of the whip and made fast to the same part of the ship as the tail block, *but just above it and with the tally board close up to the position to which the end of the hawser is secured* (this will allow the breeches buoy to come right out and will facilitate entry to the buoy).

6. When the hawser has been made fast on board, unbend the whip from the hawser, see that the bight of the whip has not been hitched to any part of the vessel and that it runs free in the block. Then signal to the shore, as in paragraph 1.

7. The men on shore will then set the hawser taut, and by means of the whip will haul off to the ship the breeches buoy into which the person to be hauled ashore is to get. He should sit well down in the breeches, and when he is secure signal again to the shore, as in paragraph 1, and the men on shore will haul the person in the breeches buoy to the shore. When he is landed the empty breeches buoy will be hauled back to the ship. This operation will be repeated until all persons are landed.

8. It may sometimes happen that the state of the weather and the condition of the ship will not admit of a hawser being set up; in such cases a breeches buoy will be hauled off by the whip which will be used without the hawser.

The system of signalling must be strictly adhered to. It should be noted, however, that while the signals referred to in paragraph 1 are made only when the crew have got hold of the rocket line; when the tail block has been made fast; when the hawser has been made fast; and when a person is in the breeches buoy ready to be hauled ashore, the rescue operations as a whole will, as a rule, be greatly facilitated if signal communication (by semaphore or flashing lamp) is established between the ship and the shore (or lifeboat). The majority of livesaving companies and lifeboats have trained signalmen.

All women, children, passengers and helpless persons should be landed before the crew of the ship. Masters and crews of stranded vessels should bear in mind that success in landing them by the lifesaving apparatus depends, in a great measure, upon their own coolness and attention to the instructions laid down.

Tankers—Use of rocket line-throwing apparatus. Attention is called to the danger of attempting to establish communication by means of a rocket line-throwing apparatus with an oil tanker if she is carrying petrol, spirit or other highly inflammable liquid, and be leaking. In such case the *assisting vessel should lie to windward of the tanker* and the communication should be established from the ship requiring assistance. *Therefore before firing a rocket to such a vessel it should be ascertained whether it is safe to do so.* When a vessel in distress is carrying petrol spirit or other highly inflammable liquid and is leaking, the following signals should be exhibited to show that it is dangerous to fire a line-carrying rocket by reason of the risk of ignition:

By day—flag B of the International Code of Signals hoisted at the masthead.

By night—a red light hoisted at the masthead.

When visibility is bad the above signals should be supplemented by the use of the following International Code signal made in sound:

MQF (— — — —·— ·—·) 'It is not safe to fire a rocket'.

NOTE.—Attention is also called to the International Code signal:

MQH (— — — —·— ···) 'Is it safe to fire a rocket?'

Chapter 17

LOAD LINE AND DRAUGHT

Load line provisions are contained in Part II of the Merchant Shipping (Safety and Load Line Conventions) Act, 1932, which gives effect to the International Load Line Rules, 1959 (see note at end of chapter), and first of all exempts:

(a) Sailing ships under 80 tons register engaged solely in the coasting trade.

(b) Ships exempted by the D.T.I. (These may include (1) any ship plying on international or other voyages between near neighbouring ports, and (2) any class of steamers under 80 tons register engaged solely in the coasting trade, not carrying cargo.)

(c) Ships solely engaged in fishing.

(d) Pleasure yachts.

Ships not exempt are 'load line ships' and are classified as follows:

(a) **International load line ships**—those of 150 gross tonnage or upwards which carry cargo or passengers;

(b) **Local load line ships**—those of 150 gross tonnage or upwards which do not carry cargo or passengers and those of less than that tonnage.

The master of every British sea-going ship which is not a 'load line ship' must, upon proceeding to sea, record the draught of water and extent of freeboard in the official log (if any) and produce the record to any chief officer of Customs.

Marking of load lines. No British load line ship registered in the United Kingdom shall proceed to sea unless the ship: (a) Has been surveyed in accordance with the load line; (b) complies with the conditions of assignment; (c) is marked on each side with a deck line (uppermost complete deck) and load lines.

The load line rules. Under these rules application for the issue or renewal of a load line certificate is to be made to an assigning authority, i.e. the D.T.I., Lloyd's Register, etc. The authority will assign freeboards to a ship after being satisfied by the report of a surveyor that it complies with the provisions of the rules, including the conditions of assignment set out in Part V of the rules. These relate to openings in

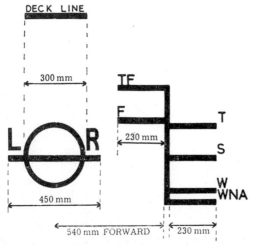

ALL LINES ARE 25 mm IN THICKNESS

freeboard and superstructure decks and in sides of ships and to freeing ports in well decks, etc.

On receiving from the assigning authority particulars as to the deck line and load lines the owner is to cause them to be marked on each side of the ship. The deck line is a horizontal line marked amidships. Below it is the load line disc intersected by a horizontal line passing through the centre. This is the summer load line. Forward of the disc are, on a steamer, horizontal lines indicating the maximum depth to which the ship may be loaded in different circumstances and different seasons as follows:

T.F.	Tropical Fresh Water Load Line.
F.	Fresh Water Load Line.
T.	Tropical Load Line.
S.	Summer Load Line.
W.	Winter Load Line.
W.N.A.	Winter North Atlantic Load Line.

A sailing ship is to be marked with deck line, load line disc and F. and W.N.A. lines.

Steamers to which timber load lines are assigned are to be marked with an additional set of horizontal lines abaft the load line disc indicating the maximum timber load lines in different circumstances and in different seasons. The lettering is the same as on the other lines except that an 'L' is prefixed to each, e.g. 'L.T.F.', 'L.F.', and so on.

A detailed schedule of zones and seasonal areas is set out in the Load Line Rules and on a coloured chart of the world attached to them. The general scheme is that the tropical zone is a belt covering the equatorial regions; north and south of this are summer zones. On the border lines between the permanent tropical and summer zones are various seasonal areas which are tropical during part of the year and summer during rest of year. North of northern summer zone are seasonal areas and a seasonal winter zone. South of southern summer zone is another seasonal winter zone.

On being satisfied that a ship has been marked as required and the prescribed fee has been paid, the assigning authority delivers to the applicant a load line certificate.

Submersion of the load line. A British load line ship registered in the United Kingdom shall not be so loaded as to submerge in salt water the appropriate load line. A master who takes (or other person who is a party to sending) a ship to sea in contravention of this section is now, by the Merchant Shipping Act, liable to imprisonment for such contravention.

Load line certificates. The certificate is: (*a*) In the case of an international load line ship a Load Line Convention certificate; and (*b*) in the case of a local load line ship a United Kingdom Load Line Certificate. No ship may proceed to sea without certificate and a clearance or transire will not be granted by Customs until certificate is produced.

Publication of certificate and entry of particulars. Certificate is to be framed and posted up on board and the master is to enter in the official log particulars as to position of deck line and load lines specified in the certificate. Before leaving any dock, wharf or harbour to proceed to sea the master is to (1) enter in the official log further particulars prescribed by regulations; and (2) post up the particulars in some conspicuous place on board.

By D.T.I. regulations home trade ships are exempted from the last-mentioned obligation (2) to post up particulars. Further particulars to be entered in the official log are the actual draught as shown on stem and stern post when the ship is loaded and ready to leave port together with actual freeboard amidships and mean freeboard. If the load line is submerged entry must also be made of the density of the water in which the ship is lying, and also of allowances, if any, to be made in order to arrive at the mean freeboard the ship will have when she first reaches salt water. The particulars to be posted up on the official form are those specified in the certificate with particulars of actual draught and freeboard.

Agreements with crew. Before any agreement with the crew is signed by any member of the crew the master is to insert in the agreement particulars relating to deck line and load lines specified in the certificate.

Metric amidships loadline and draught marks.
Assigning authority is the Norske Veritas.

READING THE DRAUGHT

The draught is read at bow and stern. The numerals are accurately cut and painted on both sides of stem and stern post. The bases of the numerals are on the even foot, and inches have to be estimated by eye. This is a simple matter because both the numerals and the vertical distance between them are 152½mm (6 in.) depth.

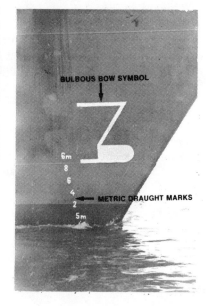

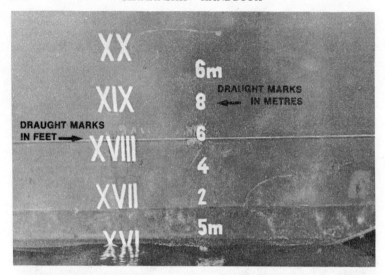

At the 1966 International Load Line Convention new measures were put forward to allow vessels equipped with watertight steel hatchcovers to load to a deeper draught than vessels fitted with the more vulnerable wooden covers and tarpaulins. Tankers also benefit under the new regulations. Changes were also proposed for alterations to the boundaries of existing loading zones.

These new regulations have now been agreed to by the requisite number of Maritime Nations and the proposed changes will take effect during June, 1968.

With the spread of metrication, vessels are increasingly having load lines and draught marks cut into the ship's side in metric measurement (see also 'reading the draught'). This practice will sooner or later take over. At present load lines and draughts may be found marked in feet or metres or in both. The photograph (page 177) also shows the 'bulbous bow symbol'.
Note:
Certain other countries also have assigning societies. The metric illustrations are of the Norwegian Society 'Norske Veritas'.

Chapter 18

SHIP'S MAINTENANCE AND DECK STORES

SHIP'S MAINTENANCE

Washing. All previously painted surfaces, except the hull should be washed with soda to remove all dirt and grease, and any paint blisters should be scraped off. Equipment required for this work will consist of buckets, turks heads, paint scrubbers, wads and flat scrapers for blisters. If Sugi, a solution of special soap powder, is used, the washing-down gang will work from the weather to the lee side and start from the top and work downwards to avoid runs. Soft soap is supplied in $6\frac{1}{2}$ or $12\frac{1}{2}$K (14 or 28 lb.) drums and is used for washing down. Hard soap is supplied in bars and is used for deck or alleyway scrubbing. When using hoses, one of the hydrants on the deck line should be opened, when the hose is not turned on, in order to relieve the pressure on the deck line. After use, hoses should be hung up to dry and, for stowing away, the hose should be laid on the deck and the coupling end brought back to lie against the nozzle. The bight is then rolled up so that the final coil has both hose and coupling ends ready for quick use when required.

Cleaning. Glass windows and ports can be washed and polished with chamois leather, but a useful cleaner is a window scrim cloth. This cloth is boiled before use and, when almost dry, can also be used for polishing the glass. Brass is cleaned with metal polish and polished with a dry cloth, and if a mixture of bathbrick and oil is used, the polished surface is less liable to tarnish from the effects of sea spray.

Chipping and scaling. Plates covered in rust should be chipped, scraped and wire brushed. Two coats of metal primer are then applied before the top coat is put on. The area chipped should be wiped over with a wad soaked in boiled linseed oil before knocking off. Chipping hammers should be soaked in a bucket of water before use to tighten the heads, and goggles should always be worn to protect the eyes.

Wood-sheathed decks. These can be cleaned with caustic or any of the special chemical preparations such as Atlas or Climax. When washing off with the hose, care must be taken not to get splashed in the eyes, and seaboots and oilskins should be worn to protect the clothes. Holystones are also used particularly for removing 'dead' wood from the surface.

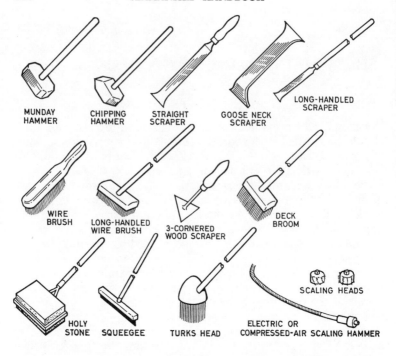

After hosing down, the surplus water is cleared to the scuppers by using a squeegee. In the tropics, wood-sheathed decks should be hosed down each day to prevent the seams from opening.

Fresh-water tanks. Open the manhole and, as the tank is draining, swill the water round to ensure that all rusty water is drained away. Wash out thoroughly with fresh water, then cement wash. Leave for twenty-four hours to dry before filling. This is a job which is best carried out in hot weather as the tank will dry more rapidly. If possible, a second coat of cement wash should always be applied.

Bilges. Lift off the limber boards and stow them on the margin plate gussets. Each 'bay' should then be thoroughly cleaned out and all dirt, etc., put into a bucket. Work along, bay by bay, towards the strum box. The strum box is the suction end of the bilge pipelines and will be found at the after end of the forward holds and at the fore end of the after holds. When clean and all bilge water has been drawn off, bilges should, when dry, be painted with bitumastic paint.

Double-bottom tanks. Before attempting to open any double-bottom manhole make sure that the tank is empty as, if pressed up, both injury and flooding may result when you loosen the nuts. The tank must be thoroughly ventilated to ensure that the air is fresh before men enter the tank. Portable lights will be required and buckets for holding any scale, etc., which is brushed up. A hand should always be stationed at the manhole in case anyone gets into difficulties in the tank and also for handling the buckets as they are passed up for emptying. Double-bottom tanks are either painted with bitumastic paint or cement washed. A special grease paint is also available for use in double-bottom or peak tanks and provides a very good preservative coating.

Paints. Paints are stowed in the paint locker which is usually sited under the fo'c'sle head. Drums are stowed on dunnage and are periodically turned upside down to allow the contents to mix thoroughly. Damaged stock and old drums should be used first. Very few, if any, shipping companies mix their own paint nowadays and the paint supplied on board is ready to use as required. The most common kinds of paint found on board are:

Metal primers. Red lead, red oxide and yellow chromate are the main priming coats which are applied to a bare surface to give protection against rust and to act as a key for the next coat to be applied.

Undercoats. White lead, white zinc and titanium white are used over the primer before the top coat.

Finishing coats. Colours will depend on those used by the shipping company. Paints in this range are the least porous of all paints and provide a hard cover to the underlying paint.

Signal red. Used for the port side-light and for lifebuoys and fire appliances.

Green. Used for starboard side-light.

Funnel paints. Heat-resisting paints which will be in colours required by the shipping company.

Silverine. A heat-resistant paint for radiators, pipes, etc.

Bitumastic paints. Used where a good finish is not required, e.g. for tanks, bilges, deck machinery, etc.

Hull paints. A sufficient quantity of paint is always carried on board to paint the hull as shown in the diagram. Topside paint is supplied in company colours, usually black or grey, and is

TOPSIDE PAINT
BOOT TOPPING
ANTI-CORROSIVE AND ANTI-FOULING

applied either in port or in dry dock. Boot-topping paint, usually red or green, is either applied in dry dock or when the ship is light. Anti-fouling and anti-corrosive paint contains arsenic to kill weeds and marine growth, and is applied in dry dock. Within twelve hours the dock is filled, while the paint is still wet.

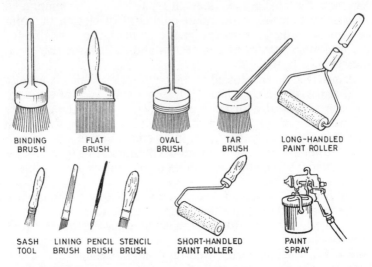

Paint brushes. New brushes should be soaked in water before use to swell the butt and tighten the bristles. New brushes should be broken in by using on light paints to start with and then turning to darker colours and primer paints as the brushes get older. The following brushes are those used most frequently on board:

Binding brush: a round brush bound with rope yarn to reduce the length of the bristle. Most brushes are now supplied with a metal binding.

Flat brush: may vary in size from $12\frac{1}{2}$mm to $101\frac{1}{2}$mm ($\frac{1}{2}$ in. to 4 in.) and is the most popular brush for general painting.

Oval brush: may vary in size and is used for rough painting where a good finish is not required.

Tar brush: may be either short or long handled.

Sash tool: a small brush used for painting corners or areas where a flat brush would be too large.

Lining brush: used for painting lines such as draught figures or load lines where a clearly defined edge has to be painted.

Pencil brush: used for small lettering such as on fire extinguishers, etc.

Stencil brush: a short-handled brush with short hard bristles, used on the metal stencils for painting S.W.L. marks on derricks, etc.

Rollers, both long and short handled, are now in common use on board ship, particularly for overside work.

Sprays are in common use on board ship and, as there are different types and means of operation, one should familiarize oneself with operating procedure. In all cases, air is forced into the container and this, in turn, forces the paint out through fine jets in the nozzle in the form of a spray of small globules. Spray painting should never be attempted during windy conditions.

When painting, always brush on evenly and avoid runs by applying the paint thinly. Avoid 'holidays', i.e. leaving small areas unpainted. Before 'knocking off' for a meal hour or for the day, square off any plate or section which you are painting, i.e. do not leave an irregularly finished area. Always complete the plate or section that you are working on. When painting overside always see that deck scuppers are plugged until paint is dry and that toilet doors are either locked or have notices pinned to them.

Varnishing. The wood surface must first of all be properly prepared by washing down thoroughly with caustic and all old varnish removed by scraping with a triangular scraper. Any holes and tears in the wood should be filled with putty or wood solution. The surface must then be sandpapered smooth and wiped over to remove all dust. When applying the varnish, it must be thoroughly worked into the wood, using the brush vigorously—not stroked on as is the case when applying paint. Before varnishing the wood can be darkened, if thought necessary, by the application of raw linseed oil, applied with a wad.

Oils. Various oils, either natural or synthetic, must be used when preparing for painting. The following are found on all ships:

Turpentine: used to thin paint which is too thick for application. It is more suitable for thinning white than boiled oil, but too much will damage the gloss finish of the paint.

Boiled linseed oil: also used for thinning paint but should not be used for white gloss.

Terebine: a drier which can be added to the paint so that it dries more quickly. If too much is used it will have the effect of reducing the quality of the paint.

Raw linseed oil: used to treat woodwork and also to protect the buoyancy tanks in the lifeboats. Applied with a wad.

Colza oil: used for oil in the binnacle lamps and for mixing with bathbrick for brass cleaning.

Fish oil: used for treating steel decks and for running wires. Applied with a wad.

N.B. Some shipping companies paint their steel decks with a special deck paint, usually green or reddish in colour.

Paraffin: used for cleaning paint brushes and for general cleaning. Its primary purpose is for use in the navigation lights.

Although they are not oils, the following are included in this section as they are used in the general 'brightening-up' of the ship:

White lead: used with tallow for standing rigging and applied with a wad.

Stockholm tar: also used on the lower part of the rigging and applied with a round or tar brush.

Cotton waste: used extensively on board for cleaning and supplied in either half or hundredweight bags. All wads used in cleaning and painting are of cotton waste.

Emery paper: supplied in various grades and used for cleaning metal-work.

Sand paper: supplied in various grades and used for rubbing down woodwork, particularly before varnishing.

Pumice stone: used for smoothing or polishing rough surfaces.

DECK STORES

The following list of deck stores is basic equipment on every cargo vessel:

Messenger. A coil of 76mm (3 in.) rope used for hauling out a hawser or wire to a buoy or, on a long lead, along the deck. It is warped on the windlass or winch drum end.

Heaving lines. Usually made of 18-thread tarred three-strand ratline, in lengths of 15 fathoms. A monkey's fist, double wall and crown, or heaving line knot is bent on to one end to give weight to the line for distance throwing. It is used for sending mooring wires and ropes ashore, lowering and raising pilot's baggage and has a hundred and one other uses.

Gantline. A 63½mm (2½ in.) rope which, when married to the dummy gantline, can be rove through the topmast sheave. It is used for sending men aloft, riding the stays, etc.

Dummy gantline. A rope, slightly lighter than an ordinary gantline, which is permanently kept rove through the masthead block. When married to the gantline, it is hauled down and carries the gantline up through the block and back to the deck, thus cutting out the work of sending a man aloft with the gant-line to reeve it through the sheave of the block and bring it back to deck level.

Boat rope. A 76mm (3 in.) rope secured on the foredeck and passed outboard and aft and finally secured on the afterdeck. The long outboard bight hangs down by the gangway or pilot ladder so that launches and boats can secure to it.

Guest warp. Bights of 76mm (3 in.) rope secured along both sides of the ship to which barges can tie up. Barges should never be allowed to tie up to ships' rails as this can both damage and bend them, particularly in tideways and when several are moored alongside.

Pilot ladders. The diagram shows a pilot ladder which must

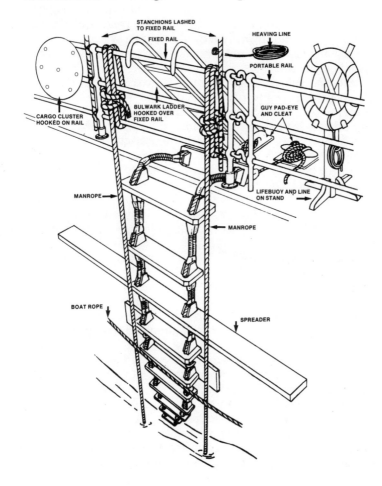

be long enough to reach the edge of the water when the ship is at her lightest draught. Gear required for use with the pilot ladder will be a heaving line, two manropes, arc light and lifebuoy. If the pilot is expected during the hours of darkness, all this equipment should be got ready and placed on top of the hatch during daylight, so that it can be easily carried to and secured on whichever side the pilot is to board.

Several different types of mechanically operated pilot hoists are now being manufactured and, if your ship is so equipped, the operating of this equipment should be thoroughly learnt.

Handy billy. A very useful light tackle which consists of a double block with a tail and a single hook block. Also called a Jigger.

Tail block. A single sheave block with a tail. Normally used with a gantline and bosun's chair. These three items of equipment should always be on the fo'c'sle when anchoring in case a hand has to be put over the side to clear a foul anchor when heaving in cable.

Lead and snatch blocks. Single-sheave metal swivel blocks which are nearly always required when heaving on mooring springs to give a direct lead to the drum end when warping. The wire bight is led to the snatch block which is opened, the wire is placed over the sheave and the block closed and the pin replaced. A snatch block saves the time of having to reeve the end of the wire through the block, as has to be done in the case of a lead block.

Shackles. These vary in size and are usually hung from the deckhead in the storeroom. All shackles used for cargo work and rigging have their safe working load, in tons, stamped on the shackle.

Chain and rope stoppers. These are required for stopping-off ropes and wire when berthing, etc. The correct methods of applying these stoppers are illustrated in the chapter on mooring.

Seizing wire. A seven-ply wire consisting of six wires round a central wire heart, it is used for binding and seizing, particularly the pins of shackles.

Bottle screw. A bottle screw is used for tightening wires and chains such as devil's claws, rigging, etc. Bottle screws on standing rigging, which have only to be loosened when the rigging is released, have to be protected from the effects of sea and weather. The exposed screws are coated with tallow and then served with rope yarn to give a smooth surface. A collar of canvas is then sewn over the screw. Bottle screw preventers are fitted to standing rigging and these are held in place by a

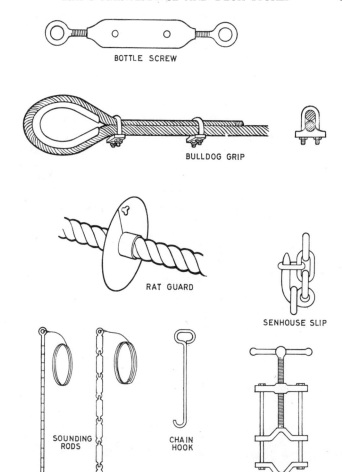

BOTTLE SCREW

BULLDOG GRIP

RAT GUARD

SENHOUSE SLIP

SOUNDING RODS

CHAIN HOOK

RIGGING SCREW

bolt which passes through the hole normally used for the insertion of the spike or podger when turning the screw for tightening or release.

Rigging screws. Used to bend a wire to the shape of a thimble for splicing.

Senhouse slip. A quick release apparatus used on chains. It is used on all boat gripes.

Wire or bulldog grip. Used instead of splicing for holding a wire.

Chain hooks. Used for manhandling anchor cable either in the chain locker or on the fo'c'sle head when hanging off an anchor.

Rat guard. Used on a mooring rope or wire in port to prevent rats leaving or coming on board via the moorings. When placed on the rope or wire it must be sufficiently far out from the fairlead to prevent the rats jumping from rope to deck or v.v.

Oakum. Tarred rope yarns used for caulking the seams in wooden decks. Pitch or marine glue is then poured into the seam to make it watertight.

Fenders. Both cane and cork fenders are carried on board for use when docking and for fending off barges, etc.

Cold sets. Used for cutting heavy wire and the ends of strands after splicing.

Buckets for washing, etc. They are usually of galvanized metal and of two-gallon capacity.

Funnels in different sizes for filling cans, etc.

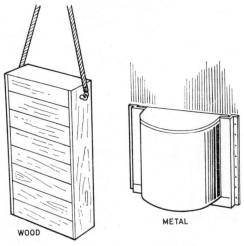

WOOD   METAL

OVERSIDE DISCHARGE COVERS

Discharge covers for covering overside discharges when barges are working underneath or the men are painting overside.

Burlap. Coarse canvas used on board for covering steel, etc.

Sounding rods. Used by the carpenter for sounding tanks, bilges and double bottoms. These are supplied either as a metal rod or a sectional rod. Rubbed with chalk, they are lowered down the sounding pipe until the end strikes the bottom. On pulling up, the length where the chalk has been washed off denotes the depth of water. With the sectional rods, used where there are bends in the sounding pipe, care must be taken that the rod just touches the bottom; otherwise a false reading will be obtained. If too many sections were to be lowered into the tank clear of the pipe end, there is always the chance that the joins of this type of rod will foul the pipe end, thus jamming the sounding rod.

Putty. Usually supplied ready made in drums.

Sand. Used for cementing, covering oil spillage, etc.

Cement. Supplied in bags which must be kept dry. Used for cementing spurling boxes and making cement boxes, i.e. temporary repairs to leaking plates, rivets, etc. in the hull.

Ventilator plugs and covers. For plugging and covering the ventilator trunk when the cowl has been removed. Circular covers are also part of the equipment for covering the actual mouth of the cowl.

Rope yarns are usually fathom strands cut from old mooring ropes and used for seizings.

Serving boards and mallets for serving wire.

Spikes for splicing, tightening and releasing shackle pins, etc.

Marline. Two-strand tarred hemp supplied in hanks.

Spun yarn. Strands soaked in tar and used mainly for 'serving'. Supplied either in balls or coils.

Thimbles, either round or heart-shaped, for fitting into the eyes of the splice in rope or wire.

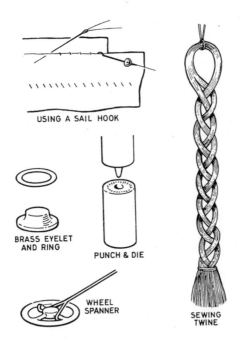

USING A SAIL HOOK

BRASS EYELET
AND RING

PUNCH & DIE

WHEEL
SPANNER

SEWING
TWINE

Fids. Tapered hard-wood spikes used for splicing mooring ropes.

Palms and needles. Palms are supplied both right and left handed and sewing needles in various sizes from 0 to 16.

Sail twine. Supplied in hanks. It has to be made up into skeins for use and a strand is pulled from the skein as required.

Bees wax. Used for rubbing down sewing twine before use. It smooths down the surface of the twine and makes it waterproof.

Sail hooks. Used for 'holding' the canvas while sewing.

Eyelets. Supplied in small cartons and used for eyes in canvas work. Made of brass, they are closed by means of a 'punch and die'.

Spanners in different sizes, for opening manholes, overhauling cargo gear, etc.

Wheel spanners for turning valve wheels.

Grease and grease gun for servicing cargo gear, davits, etc.

Lubricating oil and oil can for rollers, hinges, locks, etc.

Packing for manhole covers, etc.

Port holes. Armour glass and rubber packing for repair of damaged port holes; in various sizes to fit all on board.

LIGHTS AND SHAPES

Emergency navigation lights. In the event of an electric failure on board duplicate navigation lights must always be available, filled with oil and trimmed ready for use.

Anchor lights, visible all round the horizon, one to be hoisted forward and one aft when at anchor. Power points are sited under the fo'c'sle and aft, and the cables must be long enough to reach these when the lights are hoisted.

Anchor ball. Ball or shape, 609½mm (2 ft.) in diameter, hoisted in place of the lights from sunrise to sunset.

Not under command lights. When the vessel is unable to manoeuvre as required by the Rules through engine breakdown or faulty steering, two all-round red lights, 1m 829mm (6 ft.) apart, must be exhibited where they can best be seen. The masthead lights are switched off and, until the vessel loses her way through the water, the side lights are kept burning. The best position for all-round visibility is from the signal mast or triatic stay above the bridge and most ships, if they are not fitted with fixed lights, hoist an electric cable to which are connected up to four electric sockets with glass covers and brass protective shields. The glass can be either red, green or clear so that ordinary bulbs are used.

Not under command balls or shapes. From sunrise to sunset, two shapes or balls, not less than 609½mm (2ft.) in diameter and 1m 829mm (6 ft.) apart, are shown in place of the two red lights. These are usually kept bent on to the gantline on the monkey island ready for hoisting quickly if required.

Note. 'Not under Command' is an emergency which must be quickly signalled to other ships particularly in busy pilotage waters. It is essential to see that lights are in working order and always ready, and that the shapes or balls are clear and ready for instant hoisting.

Portable cargo clusters or arch lights. Used for cargo work, gangway illumination, pilot ladder, etc. When not in use, they are stowed either under the fo'c'sle or in the lamp room.

Chapter 19

SAFETY ABOARD

Accident Prevention. *The following is a lecture on Safety by Second Officer J. H. Lewis of the National Sea Training School, Gravesend:*

Accidents are costing Shipowners vast sums of money, but the cost to some unfortunate injured seamen and their dependants in lifelong misery and suffering cannot be measured in terms of money.

On you, depends not only your safety, but also the safety of your shipmates. The constant development and introduction of new equipment means that new skills have to be learnt, and much thought is given to ways and means of making life at sea as safe as possible; so why do accidents happen? They happen because someone didn't think; because someone took a chance or a short cut, or ignored instructions. If you follow advice given, you will have gone a long way to reducing the risk of injury not only to yourself, but to others. Remember that an accident, which may result in serious injury or death, is not always something which happens to the other person. IT COULD HAPPEN TO YOU. Remember also that accidents don't just happen; there is always a cause—and if you see a shipmate doing a job in an unsafe way TELL him at once, for his own safety and for the protection of others. Most accidents can be avoided. This has been proved by investigation which has shown that the same circumstances repeatedly lead to the same type of accident. Don't let yourself be influenced by any foolhardy members of your crew, who cannot control themselves; you will see what fools they make of themselves and what a danger they are to themselves and to you. Imagine, for instance, putting up a derrick while intoxicated. You have to top and lower derricks while you are undergoing your training and you know that you cannot take any chances with safety. Whilst on the subject of alcohol, remember that in some countries their laws deal quickly and heavily with drunks—and then think, too, of the ways in which you could come to grief returning at night to your ship. On many docks there are railways, and being run down by a train is not good for the health. Ships are tied up alongside and you could trip or fall over a mooring line or wire. You may fall between the ship and the quay and, if the dock water has a swell running,

you could be squashed to death between the ship and the quay.
You may trip over something approaching the gangway,
although gangways should be made safer by the introduction
of the safety net which is set underneath the gangway in order
to catch someone accidentally falling off.   ALWAYS USE
THE GANGWAY: never step from the dockside on to the
ship's rail, or climb on to the ship's rail to get ashore.   There
may be some grease or ice on the rail and you might land
up in the water.

Once on board the ship you must take care where you walk;
watch you don't trip over wires, cleats, ring bolts, bollards and
cargo gear, dunnagewood, etc. If you rush around not looking
where you are going, you may trip over a mooring rope or
hose pipe. Watch out, too, for cargo wire. Keep away from
open hatches and don't get into the habit of walking across
hatches; one night some hatch boards may not be in place and
IF you wake up, you will have one heck of a headache, or a
broken limb.   When opening or closing all types of hatches
take care to follow the instructions carefully; don't get on top
of a MacGregor type hatch when opening or closing it and,
if a lever is being used to lift the lid, don't let it slip.   Never
swing on overhead pipes. They make look strong but the inside
may be rusted and your weight may cause them to break.
When in the tropics don't do too much sun-bathing to start
with and never lie beneath lifeboats; you may roll over the side
if you fall asleep. A good knife is part of your trade; keep it
sharp and wear it only when you are working; never play games
with it or throw it at anything—it may kill someone.

Always obey NO SMOKING notices; there are heavy fines
on tankers and in oil ports large fines and imprisonment. You
may even be carrying an explosive or dangerous cargo, so
think before you light that cigarette—it may be your last.

Fire is one of your greatest dangers at sea. One way in
which a fire can be started is by a person falling asleep after
lighting up a cigarette. Fire can spread quickly through the
accommodation and many lives can be lost; you may fail to
stub out a cigarette properly in the ash tray and, if the ship rolls
heavily, the ash tray can fall on the deck and you have started
a fire.

A booklet issued by the Shipping Federation and the Em-
ployers' Association of the Port of Liverpool is a very useful
guide and is illustrated to show you some of the accidents
which are constantly occurring and ways in which they can be
prevented. There are illustrations, for instance, of the correct
way in which to make fast a pilot ladder. This is of great

importance. If you use a ladder at sea to paint a derrick always make sure it is lashed or you may fall off. If you are a night-watchman in port always look after the gangway and see that it is correctly positioned and that man ropes are not too slack or too tight.

Always use a safety harness or line when working aloft or over the side; find out the correct way in which to make fast a bosun's chair with a shackle, and, when heaving a mooring line, stand so that you pass the rope in front of you, not behind, and that the rope is coiled down. Don't stand in a bight: you may take your foot off. Eye injuries can be painful and some-times serious, many being caused by fragments of metal, rust, or paint, entering the eye when someone is chipping or using a powered tool to scale the decks. WEAR CHIPPING GOG-GLES.

It would be impossible to itemize every type of accident in the space we have in this book, so every time you have a chance to read an accident analysis, or report, do so and learn, if necessary, from someone else's bitter experience. Do not disregard the advice of older and more experienced crew members who can help to keep you out of trouble. Follow safety rules, think 'safety', and reduce the accident rate.

The following sections offer additional advice and, in some cases, underline the importance of what has been said.

Rope ladders. Always make sure that the rope ladder is in a good and safe condition before it is put out. Check that there are no broken or faulty steps; that the treading surfaces are not slippery; make sure that the ladder is fully extended and of sufficient length.

Make fast the ladder so that it cannot carry away. Never use the main deck rail or rail stanchion, unless it can bear the weight of a man and the ladder. Other safer alternatives are usually available—pad-eyes, cleats, davits.

Hand ladders. Don't over-reach to adjust valves, regulators and lights, or to paint that 'little extra'. In every case the proper means should be used to reach the object instead of risking getting off balance and inviting a fall. Great care should be taken when using ladders on board ship. Because of the motion of the vessel they must never be used unless they are properly and safely lashed.

Gangways and accommodation ladders. The practice of rigging ships' gangways on ships' rails is dangerous, and should never be used unless the rail is reinforced. When the accom-modation ladder is in use, and especially in tidal waters, attention should be paid to the manropes. The accommodation ladder should have constant attention and the manropes kept taut. With the rise and fall of the tide care should be taken to ensure that the distance between the platform and the quay is not too great. Frequently accidents occur through not using the proper means of getting on or off the ship. Never jump from the ship to the quay.

Staging. Accidents frequently occur on staging. Make sure that the gantlines are not faulty and that they are properly made fast at the horns on the staging. Staging planks stowed in warm places deteriorate rapidly and become unsafe for use.

Safety belts or lines. When working overside or aloft, especially when attending to blocks, etc., a safety belt or line should be used. Special care and attention should be given to safety belts. To avoid damage never store them tightly coiled or near chemicals, such as caustic soda. If they become soiled with grease, oil, paint, etc., scrub them briskly with a mild soap solution—never use a harsh detergent.

Bosun's chair. Make sure that the bosun's chair is properly made fast, and that the bow and not the pin of the shackle is on the stay, otherwise you are inviting a fatal accident.

Holds. Falls into holds are often fatal and care should always be taken when working near an open hatchway. Special care must be taken when working with your back to an open hold. Always make sure, whether at sea or in harbour, that hatchways at which work has ceased are fenced or securely covered. If trimming or other hatchways in the 'tween decks have to be opened at sea, the opening must be fenced, and well lighted. Never walk on a hatchway unless the hatchway beams and covers are properly secured.

Wooden hatch covers. When wooden hatch covers are removed they should be stacked to allow free passage alongside the hatch coaming. When closing hatches, beams and hatch boards must be replaced in their correct position.

MacGregor hatch covers. Always look before you get on to a hatch cover. Never stand on cover top when more than two wheels are in the raised position. Never climb on to the stowed covers unless securing chains are in place. Keep fingers well clear of lower edge of cover side plate when lowering the panels. Keep 'out of line' when eccentric wheels are being lifted or lowered by lever.

Chipping. Eye injuries are serious and always painful. Many are caused by fragments of metal or paint. Always wear goggles for your protection when chipping, scaling, using a lathe, a cold chisel or grinding tools, etc.

Engine-room plates and hand rails. When a floor plate or handrail is removed, always fence the opening.

Gauge glass covers. If gauge glass covers are removed and not immediately replaced when the boiler is under pressure, serious eye injuries and scalding can occur by the bursting of a gauge glass. If the gauge glass cover is removed to renew the gauge glass, always make sure that the cover is replaced.

Blowbacks. Blowbacks are usually, if not always, due to carelessness, by not flashing boilers in the proper way. Make sure that you know the correct lighting up procedure and carry it out:

Before lighting up:

(1) Blow through with air,
(2) Check fuel temperature, and
(3) Stand clear when lighting.

Tools and loose parts. Have a thought for those below. Never leave tools and small loose parts lying on stagings, gratings, etc. They should always be placed in a box, bucket or bag, or lashed to prevent them being accidentally kicked or, through the motion of the ship, falling and injuring persons passing or standing below.

Tools dropped from a height can often cause serious injury. The safest method of lowering is by using a piece of pointline or gantline and making fast the part or tool with the line.

When using an eye-bolt to lift heavy machinery parts, make sure that the eye-bolt collar is firmly down, otherwise you may trap your fingers.

Hand tools. Never risk injury by using defective tools. Always check that handles are securely fitted to hammers screwdrivers and files. Before using a spanner or wrench, see that the jaws are not worn and that the spanner or wrench fits squarely on the nut. Barbs must be ground off cold chisels before use. When using a cold chisel see that you hold it in the right way, i.e. grasped firmly in the hand with the cutting edge extending out beyond first finger and thumb.

Cargo. Cargo can fall or break adrift from slings. When cargo is being worked, never run the risk of it falling on you.

Chapter 2

HEAVY WEATHER

When heavy weather is expected it is important to take early action to see that all deck equipment and any deck cargo is securely lashed and that all necessary precautions are taken to make the holds and 'tween decks weathertight.

The following are some of the more important precautions which must always be carried out:

Fo'c'sle head. Clear the deck of anything that is likely to be washed away or take charge when seas come on board. Check the anchor brakes and compressors, hawse- and spurling-pipe plates. Bowse anchor cables together. If on a coastal passage, and mooring ropes have been left on deck, stow them away under the fo'c'sle.

Fore deck. If hatches are equipped with wooden covers and tarpaulins, see that locking bars are fitted, and tighten wedges and cross lashings. Many ships flake a mooring rope on top of the tarpaulin at the fore end of No. 1 hatch; cover this with a cargo net and then cross lashings to break the force of seas coming down over the fo'c'sle and damaging the tarpaulins. See that derrick heads are properly secured and lashed in the crutches, and rig North Atlantic lashings to prevent movement and vibration. A North Atlantic lashing is made by securing a gantline to a ring bolt on the coaming, taking a round turn round each derrick and securing to the ring bolt on the opposite coaming. The lashing must be hove as taut as possible. Lash down and tom-off where possible all paint drums, barrels and gear liable to move in the for'ard storerooms.

Unship all cowl-type ventilators and fit plugs and covers. Stow cowls under the fo'c'sle or lash securely on deck. See that all stays are tight and that lanyards and halyards have clear leads and are separated to prevent fraying.

Fit lifelines port and starboard, and see that scuppers are clear and freeing ports well oiled and working properly. See that all ports and deadlights (if fitted) are secure and that fo'c'sle head doors are properly locked.

After deck. See that hatches are properly secured, locking bars fitted, and wedges and cross lashings tight. Derricks should be properly lashed, cowl-type ventilators removed, and plugs and covers placed and lashed. Rig lifelines port and starboard, and see that scuppers and freeing ports are clear and in efficient working order. If towing a log line and rotator see that it is streamed on the lee side.

Cabin and saloon fittings. See that crockery and all loose gear is either properly stowed or secured, and that doors in wardrobes and drawers are either locked or secure against rolling or pitching. When going on watch do not leave your cabin door to bang to and fro. Either close it or put it on the latch provided for this purpose.

Look-out. If the look-out is stationed on either the fo'c'sle head or crow's nest, bring him aft to either bridge wing or monkey island.

GLOSSARY

Aback. When the wind presses on sails so that the forward motion of the ship is impeded, or she is forced to make sternway, the sails are said to be aback.

Abaft. Aft of. Towards the stern. Opposite to forward of. Abaft the mast means on the after side of it. Abaft the beam means aft of a horizontal line drawn through a ship at right angles to the keel at the mid length.

Abeam. On a line which forms a right angle with the keel at the mid length. In a direction 90 deg. from the ship's head.

Aboard. In a ship. On board.

Abreast. Side by side. On a line with the beam.

Adrift. Floating at random. In a drifting condition. Not secured by moorings of any kind.

Affirmative flag. Letter 'C' of the International Code, meaning 'Yes'.

Afloat. Waterborne. In a floating condition.

Aft. At, near, or towards the stern.

After breast rope. A rope leading from the poop or after mooring deck in a direction at, or nearly at, right angles to the ship's fore and aft line.

Afterguard. A term sometimes used by seamen berthed in the forecastle to describe the master and officers berthed amidships or aft.

Afternoon watch. The watch from noon to 4 p.m.

After spring. The wire hawser, with or without a rope pennant, leading forward from the after deck to a bollard on shore to check sternway.

Ahead. Forward of, or before, the bow.

Allotment note. Amount which a crew member can allocate from his wages to be sent to a relative or bank, either fortnightly or monthly, during his period on articles.

Aloft. On a part of the ship high above deck or superstructure level.

Amidships. The middle portion of a vessel. The point of intersection of two lines, one drawn from stem to stern on the centre-line and the other athwartships or across the beam (or widest part) at the middle length is the actual midships.

Anchor (to). To let go, to come to, to lie at, or to ride at, anchor.

Anchorage. Where a ship anchors or may anchor. An area established for vessels anchored in a harbour clear of the fairway where harbour traffic is not interfered with, the sea bottom provides good holding ground, where there is maximum shelter from wind and sea, sufficient water at low tide, and ample room for ships to swing.

Anchor buoy. A small buoy made fast by a line to the anchor and used to mark its position in case it has to be slipped.

Anchor stations. Predetermined positions of crew members when a ship is going to anchor, or when the anchor is about to be hove up. In a merchant ship the carpenter's anchor station is always at the windlass.

Anchor watch. Men kept on duty when a ship is at anchor ready to perform any duty that may be required. The number of men in an anchor watch is invariably less than the number in a sea watch, but there should always be one deck officer and at least one able seaman on watch when a ship is anchored.

Answer. When a vessel alters course in response to a helm alteration, she is said to be answering her helm.

Answering pennant. A pennant (striped red and white vertically) of the International Code which is flown when answering a signal.

Apeak. In a vertical position or nearly so. The anchor is apeak, and a ship hove apeak, when cable has been hove in, and the ship ahead so that the cable is perpendicular to the anchor without breaking it from the ground.

Arm. The elbow, terminating at the flukes, at the lower end of the shank of an anchor.

Ash bucket. A steel bucket used in coal burners for hoisting ashes from the stokehold to the upper deck where they are dumped in the ash chute. In all but the smallest and oldest ships the operation of dumping ashes is carried out mechanically.

Ash chute. A steel chute either portable or fixed by which ashes are dumped overboard from a coal-burning vessel.

Astay. In line with a stay. The anchor is astay when, in heaving in, the direction of the cable forms an acute angle with the water's edge.

Astern. In a vessel's wake. Behind a vessel.

Athwart. Across. Thus the oarsmen's seats in an open boat are called thwarts.

Athwartships. Across a ship from side to side, or in that direction.

Auto-alarm signal. A radio signal permitting automatic reception of a distress call at times when the radio room is not manned. When the wireless operator of a ship carrying only one goes off watch he switches on the auto-alarm so that he will be immediately summoned by the ringing of a bell in the event of a distress call being received.

Automatic steering. A mechanical device for steering ships and dispensing with the helmsman. The gyro-pilot is the only device used for the automatic teering of merchant ships. Colloquially termed the 'I.M.'

Avast. An order to stop or pause in any operation or exercise.

Awash. The condition of anything that is alternately exposed to and covered by the sea, such as a wreck or rock. A ship's decks are said to be awash when seas are being shipped and the decks are more or less continually flooded.

Aweather. Towards the weather or windward side. The converse of alee.

Awning. A canvas covering spread as a protection from the sun. Awnings are named according to their locations—forecastle awning, bridge awning, boat deck awning, poop awning, etc.

Back and fill. To work a sailing vessel to windward when there is insufficient seaway for tacking, by alternately backing and filling the sails. A steamer is said to be backing and filling when she is manoeuvring in constricted waters by means of the helm and engines, the latter being alternately put ahead and astern.

Back around. In the Northern Hemisphere when the wind changes direction in a counter-clockwise direction it is said to back. In the Southern Hemisphere the wind backs around when it shifts in a clockwise direction. A backing wind is the converse of a veering wind.

Backstays. Wires forming the standing rigging. They extend from mast-heads (except with lower masts) and tend aft, supporting the masts against forward pull, and are named according to the mast they serve.

Backwater. To backwater means to direct a boat astern by pushing on the oars instead of pulling on them. Alternatively oarsmen on one side of the boat might be ordered to backwater so that the craft can be manoeuvred without headway being made.

Baggage master. A petty officer in charge of passengers' luggage stowed in the hold or baggage room.

Baggage pass. Pass issued on board to enable you to take your gear or personal baggage ashore.

Barnacle. A small, marine animal with calcareous shell, which lives attached to foreign objects, such as a ship's bottom. Immersion in fresh water for 48 hours or so will kill it, but its shell will remain attached to the bottom until removed by scraping.

Barometer. An instrument for measuring atmospheric pressure. There are two kinds for shipboard use, the aneroid and the mercurial.

Barque. A three-, four-, or five-masted sailing vessel with fore-and-aft rig on the aftermost mast, the other masts being square rigged.

Barquentine. A three-masted sailing vessel square-rigged on the foremast and fore-and-aft rigged on the main and mizzen.

Beam. The greatest width of a ship. The maximum breadth.

Beam-ends. A ship is said to be 'on her beam-ends' when she is heeled or listed to an angle where her beams are almost vertical and the power to right herself is insufficient to return her to the upright.

Beam wind. A wind blowing in a direction at right angles to the keel.

Bear away. To put up the helm, i.e. towards the wind, and run to leeward. To turn a ship's head away from the wind.

Bear down. In a boat under sail, to put the helm down and turn towards the wind. To approach from windward a ship or any other object.

Bearing. The direction by compass, or relative to the ship's head, of any object.

Bear off. To fend off from a wharf or the ship's side. To shove off. Also, to steer away from.

Beat. To make progress against the wind by steering a zigzag course with the wind first on one bow and then on the other.

Becalmed. Said of a sailing vessel unable to make progress owing to the absence of wind. In the Doldrums, where there is normally little wind and much rain, sailing ships were sometimes becalmed for weeks.

Becket.
1. A short piece of rope with a knot at one end and an eye at the other, or an eye at both ends.
2. A rope grommet or metal eye at the base of a block for making fast the standing part of a fall.
3. A becket, as applied to lifebuoys, is the length of line secured around them in the form of four loops.

Before the mast. An expression once used in sailing ships to describe seamen berthed in the forecastle, as distinct from officers, who were berthed amidships or aft. It is still used to describe the status of a member of the deck department other than an officer, petty officer, apprentice or cadet.

Before the wind. Said of a ship, sail or steam, running with the wind right aft.

Belay. To make fast a rope around a cleat or belaying pin by means of turns.

WOODEN BELAYING PIN

Belaying pin. A short bar of metal or wood employed for making-fast flag and signal halyards, etc.

Bell rope. The rope attached to the clapper of a bell.

Belly. The part of a sail that bulges out under the pressure of wind. An awning or tarpaulin is said to 'belly out' when the wind gets underneath it and extends its middle.

Bend (to). To secure with a bend or knot. To bend on a sail is to make it fast to its yard, gaff, or stay preparatory to setting it.

Berth.
1. Bed or bunk allotted to a passenger or member of the crew as a sleeping place. Thus a cabin with two beds or bunks is said to be a two-berth cabin.
2. Distance, whether for safety or convenience, between one vessel and another, or others, or the shore. The expression to 'give a wide berth' means giving ample clearance.
3. A place allocated to a vessel in port whether in an anchorage or alongside a pier, quay, or wharf.

Berthage. Space alongside a wharf or quay for the reception of shipping. Also, berthing dues or charges, payable to port authorities by ships utilizing berths for loading, discharging or repairs, or when laid up.

Between wind and water. The section of a ship's side between the light and load water-lines.

Binnacle. The structure on which the compass bowl is supported and in which it is slung in gimbals. The base is usually built of teak and contains the thwartship, fore and aft, and vertical compensating magnets.

Binnacle cover. The dome-shaped brass helmet or hood that fits over the top of the binnacle, protecting the compass and housing the oil lamps.

Blink. A glow caused by the reflection of light from floating ice. It is sometimes referred to as ice blink.

Blue Ensign. A flag worn by ships belonging to Colonial Services by vessels under Government charter, by Fleet auxiliaries, and by merchant ships having a master—the number is varied by the Admiralty from time to time—who is a Commodore or Captain in the R.N.R.

Blue light. A pyrotechnic light used for night signalling, usually by ships requiring a pilot.

Blue Peter. Letter P of the International Code. It is a blue, square flag with a white square in the centre, hoisted on the foremast by merchant ships to indicate that the vessel is about to proceed to sea.

Boat cover. A protective canvas cover spread over a ship's lifeboat. Supported longitudinally by a wooden 'strongback' and transversely by wooden stays from strongback to gunwale, the usual method of securing the sides is by means of lacing (boat lacing) around studs below the rubber.

Boat Drill. Exercise in swinging out, lowering and handling ship's lifeboats, carried out by the crew at regular intervals.

Boathook. An iron hook with a straight prong or spike secured at the end of a long pole. It is used for heaving the boat alongside, or fending her off, also for holding on to a gangway, quay, buoy, etc.

Boat plug. A small tapered plug made usually of cork for wood boats. It is used for stopping up the drain hole in the boat's bottom. Metal boats are equipped with a brass screw plug.

Boat stations. The station allotted to each person on board in the event of an emergency. When the boat drill or emergency signal is sounded, everyone should proceed to the station which appears opposite their names on the muster list.

Boatswain. The petty officer in charge of all deck hands. Usually a first-class seaman, the bo's'un is the chief officer's right-hand man. In large ships, particularly passenger liners, he is assisted by one or more boatswain's mates.

Boatswain's chair. A wood plank about 19mm (¾ in.) thick and 457mm (18 in.) long into which four holes are bored, one near each corner. A length of line is passed through the holes in such a manner that two large loops are formed, the ends of the line being short-spliced on the underside. It is used for sending a man aloft, or over the side, being hove up or lowered by means of a gantline.

Boatswain's mate. A petty officer assisting the boatswain.

Bold hawse. When her hawse holes are high above the surface of the water a ship is said to have a bold hawse.

Bollard. Cast steel or wooden posts secured to a quay or pier for mooring purposes.

Boltrope. Manila or wire rope secured at the edges of sails for strengthening purposes. Each boltrope derives its name from its position on the sail, thus luff rope, leech rope, foot rope. Sometimes called roping.

Bonded stores. Ship's stores delivered under special arrangements with the Customs authorities from a bonded warehouse without payment of duties.

Boom. The name given to any projecting spar or pole that provides an outreach, thus log boom, sounding boom, boat boom, etc. Ship's derricks are frequently referred to as booms which, of course, they are—cargo booms—though strictly speaking the term should only be used in connection with spars extending outboard.

Bore. A tidal wave or series of waves of unusual height which moves with considerable rapidity in some narrowing estuaries, the Severn for instance.

Boss. Centrepiece of a compass card, supported by the pivot. In dry card compasses it is usually made of aluminium in the form of a cone fitted at the apex with a polished stone, sapphire or agate usually. In liquid compasses it is the float which gives buoyancy to the card.

Bottle screw. A turnbuckle with a single screw and a swivel at the end opposite to the screw, or a double screw each having a forged eye, the screw being enclosed in a tube. It is used for connecting rigging to the ship's structure, and for many other purposes where it is necessary to have stays really taut.

Bottom log. A term used to describe various types—the Chernikeeff, for instance—of patent logs which are fitted to the ship's bottom plating. Bottom logs are supplied mainly to high-speed merchant and naval ships for which the towing log is unsuitable.

Bound. A term indicating a ship's destination.

Bow. Fore part or head of a ship, beginning where the sides tend inward and terminating where they unite in the stem.

Bower anchor. One of the anchors carried on each bow. Bower anchors are the anchors by which a ship rides. Two are always ready for immediate use on entering or leaving port, one being shackled to the port anchor cable and the other to the starboard. A spare bower anchor is always carried in addition to the working bowers.

Bowline. A knot made by an involution of the end and a bight upon a rope's standing part. A most useful knot which will not slip or jam and which can be readily let go as the rope slackens.

Bowman. Member of a boat's crew who mans the foremost oar and handles the boat hook when coming alongside or leaving ship or berth.

Bow rope. A mooring rope led forward through a bow chock and making a small angle with the ship's fore and aft line.

Bowse. To haul taut, with a line or tackle. Hence to 'bowse in', or 'bowse down'.

Bow wave. Wave created by the bows of a vessel moving through the water.

Box gunwale. Upper part of the sides in an open boat when a capping is worked over the top edge of the planking.

Box hook. Sharp pointed steel hook with short shank and thick wooden handle which is used by stevedores for handling bales, slings, etc.

Brackish. When fresh water has been mixed with sea water it is said to be brackish.

Break.
1. The point at which a deck or superstructure member is discontinued; thus, break of the forecastle, break of the poop.
2. To break out the anchor is to haul it out of the ground. To break a flag is to unfurl it at the masthead, gaff or flagstaff after it has been hoisted into position, rolled in a bundle and lightly secured by means of a slippery hitch. It is unfurled by giving a sharp jerk on the downhaul.

Breakage.
1. Space lost unavoidably in stowing general cargo; in other words, broken stowage.
2. An allowance for loss owing to destruction of goods.
3. A term in Bills of Lading referring only to breakage of goods caused by unavoidable circumstances.

Break bulk. To take part of a ship's cargo out of the hold by opening up hatches and commencing to discharge.

Break out. Releasing the anchor from the sea or river bed.

Breast off. To haul a vessel some distance away from her berth to allow lighters to work between ship and quay, or for any similar reason, such as placing a heavy fender in position.

Breast rope. A mooring line leading out at an angle in the region of 90 deg. to the fore-and-aft line.

Bring to. To cause a ship to come to a standstill. To 'bring to an anchor' means making her stationary by means of the anchor. When she is stationary she is said to be 'brought up'.

Broach to. A term used mainly in connection with a sailing ship running with the wind on the quarter when the ship's head comes quickly into the wind due to bad steering or a sea striking the quarter.

Broken back. A ship is said to have a broken back when, due to defective construction or from stranding, her structure is distorted, causing both ends to rise or sag, and the centre girder to sheer.

Broom at the masthead. A traditional method to indicate a ship was for sale was to lash a broom to the masthead.

Bull rope. A rope used when goods or gear have to be dragged from the ends or wings of a hold to the square of the hatch so as to prevent the cargo runner chafing on the underside of the hatch coaming, and to secure a more direct lift.

Bumboat. A small pulling or sailing boat used by traders in overseas ports, in which vessels customarily anchor, for transporting their wares for selling to ships' passengers or crews.

Bung. A large stopper, usually wooden, for the hole in the bilge of a cask through which the cask is filled.

Bunk board. A portable board fitted along the open side(s) of a bunk to prevent the occupant from being thrown out when, in bad weather, a ship is rolling heavily.

Bunting. Fabric made of coarse English wool in an open and plain weave, With a two-ply warp and a single weft, it is mainly used for making and repairing flags.

Buoy. A floating object used as an aid to navigation in narrow channels and fairways, also to mark sunken dangers, rocks, mined or torpedo grounds, telegraph cables, etc. A mooring buoy is used for making a ship fast instead of anchoring. In some ports vessels let go their anchors, and moor aft to a buoy.

Buoyancy. Resultant of upward forces exerted by a liquid upon a floating body.

Buoyant apparatus. A term used in connection with deck seats, life rafts, lifefloats, and other similar equipment supplied to passenger ships. The buoyancy of the equipment is ascertained by dividing by 32 the number of pounds of iron that it is capable of supporting in fresh water. The result gives the number of persons it is capable of supporting. The buoyant apparatus must have a line becketed around the outside, and must be of such size, strength, and weight as to be handled without mechanical appliances and thrown overboard, without damage, from the deck where it is stowed.

Bureau Veritas. French classification society and register of shipping established in 1828.

Burgee. A swallow-tailed flag. There are two burgees in the International Code, the letters A and B.

Burlap. Sacking made from jute and used for making bags, separation cloth, etc.

Bush. The centrepiece of a block fitted in the centre of the sheave and forming the bearing for the pin.

By the head. The condition of trim of a ship drawing more water forward than aft.

By the run. To let go a rope when lowering instead of slacking away slowly. Also, with a run.

By the stern. A ship's condition of trim when she draws more water aft than forward.

By the wind. Sailing as close to the wind as the ship will lie with her sails full. Also, on the wind, on a wind.

Cable.
1. A term usually employed to indicate the means by which a ship is connected to her anchor. Formerly cables were made of hemp, but nowadays cables are exclusively chain.
2. A unit of nautical measure: one-tenth of a nautical mile, roughly 183m (600 ft.).

Cable-laid rope. A rope consisting of nine strands, made by laying three hawser-laid ropes left-handed. Also known as water-laid rope.

Can hooks. An arrangement for slinging casks, by the ends of the staves, or drums. Also called chine hooks.

Canvas. A double-warp, single weft material made of hemp, flax, or cotton fibres. It is used for making sails, awnings, covers of various kinds, tarpaulins, etc. Canvas is classified by number according to its strength, the numbers varying according to the material employed. Canvas is supplied in bolts, which have different measurements in each country. In Britain a bolt is $38\frac{1}{2}$m (42 yards). Canvas is also classified by weight.

Cap. The centrepiece in a compass card which is supported by the pivot.

Cape Stiff. A colloquialism by which sailing-ship crews denoted Cape Horn.

Capsize. To turn over; to upset.

Cargo. The goods, merchandise, commodities, or anything conveyed by merchant ships for payment of freight.

Cargo block. Any single- or multiple-sheaved metal block used for cargo working purposes. This includes topping lift, derrick-head, heel or lead blocks. Cargo blocks are subject to statutory requirements in most maritime countries. Sheaves are made of cast metal and are provided with means for ready lubrication. Hooks, eyes, beckets, shackles are made of wrought iron or mild steel, and side plates and cheeks of mild or cast steel, wrought iron or malleable cast iron. With every block a test certificate is supplied by the manufacturers, the safe working load in tons being stamped on it.

Cargo fall. Manila or wire rope rove through the head and heel blocks of a derrick and leading to the winch drum. It is used for cargo-working operations. Also termed cargo runner, cargo whip.

Cargo hook. The hook shackled to the end of a fall for loading and discharging cargo.

Cargo liner. A ship carrying cargo and possibly up to twelve passengers and operating with sister ships over a fixed route on regular schedules.

Cargo mat. A mat made of rushes or other fibrous material and used as an extra protection for some kinds of cargo over dunnage wood.

Cargo net. A square net of varying size but usually about $2\frac{3}{4}$m $\times$ $2\frac{3}{4}$m (9 ft. $\times$ 9 ft.) made of manila or wire rope, and used for slinging some kinds of cargo, such as case goods and small packages.

Cargo plan. Plan detailing the quantities, description, disposition, and destination of the various items comprising a ship's cargo. Also called stowage plan. Its purpose is to provide information enabling the owners' agents to make arrangements in advance for the expeditious discharge of the cargo. The plan also provides information valuable to ships' officers for trim and stability purposes.

Carpenter's mate. A petty officer who assists the ship's carpenter in large liners.

Carry away. To give way, break, or part.

Cast. Taking a sounding by means of the hand, deep-sea or patent lead.

Cast off. To throw off, or let go, as when unmooring ship.

Catch a crab. Failure to extricate an oar from the water at the end of a stroke, or to insert it properly at the beginning, or catching the water with the reverse side of the blade.

Cat's paw.
1. The ruffled surface of the water during light airs.
2. Twisting the bight of a rope in such a way that two eyes are formed.

Caulking.
1. Burring or driving up the edges of iron or steel plates and sections along riveted seams to make them watertight.
2. Forcing a quantity of oakum into the seams of the planks in a ship's decks or sides to make them watertight. After the oakum has been driven in, hot melted pitch or marine glue is poured into the groove to ensure water-tightness of the seams. Caulking cotton and cotton wick are used in place of oakum for thin planking.

Caulking edge. Edge accessible for caulking. In shell and deck plating it is the outside (or sight) edge.

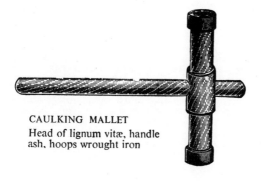

CAULKING MALLET
Head of lignum vitæ, handle
ash, hoops wrought iron

Caulking iron. A general term for the various implements (chisels) used in caulking wooden plank seams.

Caulking mallet. A mallet for driving in caulking irons.

Cement wash. A wash made of two-thirds cement and one-third fire-clay mixed with fresh water and used for protecting steel work against corrosion in double bottoms, peaks, fresh-water tanks. Nowadays these compartments are more often than not coated with bituminous compositions which provide better and more lasting protection.

Centrifugal pump. A pump consisting of a shaft to which vanes are attached and which rotates in a circular casing. Water is sucked into the casing near the centre of rotating shaft and is impelled outward along the vanes by centrifugal force, escaping through a discharge pipe at the circumference of the casing.

Certificate of discharge. A written testimonial given to a seaman at his request at the termination of a voyage when he is paid off.

Chain hook. A long steel hook used for handling and stowing the anchor cable in the chain locker when heaving in the anchor, or shortening cable.

Chain sling. A length of chain used for working cargo. It is usually fitted with a ring at one end and a hook at the other.

Chamfer. To bevel the edge of a plank or plate.

Channel money. An advance on wages paid to crew members to tide them over until they pay off. It is only granted at the final port when the articles of agreement are to be terminated.

Charter party. A contract between a shipowner and a merchant or other person, for the carriage of goods or the hire of a ship. It binds the owner to transport them to a particular place, for a sum of money which the merchant contracts to pay them as freight.

Check helm. Helm applied to prevent a ship going beyond her proper course and to stop the swing as the ship's head approaches the course. Also to reduce the rate at which a ship is swinging.

Chief engineer. The head of the engine-room department aboard ship. He is responsible for the working and maintenance of the ship's main and auxiliary machinery, and also for the engagement, conduct and discipline of all engineer officers and engine-room ratings.

Chief officer. The officer ranking next to the master. As command of the ship would devolve upon him in the event of the death or serious disability of the master, the chief officer usually possesses, in deep-sea ships, a master's certificate of competency. In ships carrying three navigating officers the chief officer, or mate, invariably keeps the 4-8 watch a.m. and p.m. In large passenger liners an additional watch-keeping officer is carried in order that the chief officer may be relieved of his watch-keeping duties. He is responsible for the every-day work of the ship.

Chief steward. The head of the catering department, in charge of food supplies and responsible for the discipline of all catering officers and ratings, and in liners for the comfort of, and services to, passengers.

Chilled cargo. A term applied to cargo chilled by means of a mild process of refrigeration whereby only a thin outside layer of the product is cooled.

Chipping hammer. Small hammer with sharp peen and face set at right angles to each other, used for chipping and scaling steelwork.

Chips. Colloquial name given to a ship's carpenter.

Clap on. Put on. To clap on a stopper or a tackle means to put on a stopper or a tackle. To clap on canvas means to put on more canvas; to make more sail.

Class. This term means the character assigned to a vessel by a classification society, depending on her design, quality of the materials employed in her construction, the scantlings of the various structural members, and the outfit and equipment, all of which must be at least up to the standards specified by the society's rules. To maintain their class, ships are periodically surveyed by surveyors of the society concerned.

Cleading. Lining of boards covering boiler-room bulkheads to prevent cargo from being damaged by the heat. The term may be applied to other wooden coverings fitted for protective purposes. The cleading in a lifeboat, for instance, is fitted to protect the buoyancy tanks from damage.

Clean full. When sails are kept drawing steadily they are said to be clean full

Clear (to).

1. Observance of Customs' formalities by the master when his ship is about to sail. A document called a clearance label is issued by the Customs after all legal charges have been paid.
2. To free anything—a rope, tackle, or cable, for instance—which has become foul.

Clear view screen. A device fitted on a port or window on the navigating bridge which provides navigators with a 'clear view' ahead when it is raining or snowing, or the ship is taking over spray. It consists of a glass disc which, driven by an electric motor, rotates at high speed and prevents rain, snow or spray from settling on it.

Clinker built. Said of a ship or boat constructed with clinker planking.

Clinker plating. A system of hull plating in which the edges overlap and the ends abut.

Close-hauled. The trim of a vessel's sails when she is sailing as close to the wind as possible under the prevailing weather conditions.

Close-link chain. Chain in which the links are so short relative to their width that it is not possible or practicable to fit studs.

Close up. A flag or hoist of flags is said to be close up when hoisted as far as it can be on ensign staff, jack staff, gaff, stay or mast.

Clump block. A small block with a solid rounded shell, wide sheaves and swallows. Clump blocks are rarely used in merchant ships nowadays.

Coaster. A ship specially designed, built, equipped and manned for employment in the home trade. North-East Coast colliers, the small ships operated by Coast Lines Ltd., and various types of craft trading between the Elbe and Brest, i.e. within Home Trade Limits, are all considered to be coasters, a term which includes tramps and liners.

Code flag. A pennant striped, red and white vertically, of the International Code. It is also called the answering pennant, q.v.

Coil. A quantity of rope made up into a series of rings one above the other.

Coil (to). To lay or make up a rope in a series of rings, or circular turns. With right-handed rope it is coiled clockwise and vice versa if the rope is left-handed. One ring or circle of rope is known as a fake. The hollow space in the centre of the coil is called the tier.

Colours. The distinguishing flag worn by a ship at the ensign staff or gaff to show her nationality.

Come to. To turn towards the wind. To luff to bring the ship's head into the wind.

Come up.

1. To slacken a rope.
2. To 'come up' with another vessel is to overtake her.

Commodore. A courtesy title given to the senior master of a line or company of merchant ships.

Common link. The standard link in an anchor cable of which the chain is made. It has a length six times the diameter of the steel from which it is made.

Compass adjuster. A specially trained and usually certificated person specialising in the adjustment of magnetic compasses.

Compass bearing. A bearing given in the form of a compass direction and expressed either in points or in degrees.

Compass bowl. A hemispherical receptacle, made of non-magnetic material and covered by a glass plate, in which the compass card is mounted.

Compass card. The graduated, circular card made of rice paper, in the case of a dry compass, and non-magnetic and non-corrosive metal in the case of a liquid compass, which is attached to the needles of a magnetic compass.

Compass course. The course by magnetic compass steered by the ship.

Compass pivot. The pointed, iridium-tipped, pivot in the centre of the bowl of a magnetic compass on which bears the boss of the card.

Continuous discharge book. A book issued by the Registrar-General of Shipping and Seamen, or the superintendent of a Mercantile Marine Office. It contains a description of its owner—height, colour of hair and eyes, tattoo marks, etc.—and records the ships in which he has sailed, length of time spent in them, and remarks as to his conduct and ability. Seamen hand in their books to the master when they sign articles, and they are returned to them when articles are closed or the seaman leaves the ship.

Cork fender. A net made of rope yarns and filled with cork shavings. It is used as its name implies, for 'fending off' purposes, e.g. when a ship is coming or lying alongside a quay.

Corporation of Trinity House. The Corporation is the General Lighthouse Authority for England and Wales. The Corporation is also the Principal Pilotage Authority in the U.K. with authority for forty-one districts which include the Thames, Solent and Plymouth.

Cotton canvas. Sailcloth made up from the raw fibres of cotton. Also known as duck canvas.

Course. The direction in which a ship is steered by magnetic or gyro compass. The ship's track.

Coxswain. The person who is in charge of and steers a boat.

Crew. A ship's company. Strictly, it includes officers and men comprising her complement, but the term is loosely applied to 'other ranks' only.

Crew list. A list containing the name and nationality of every member of the crew, his rank or rating, and his rate of pay.

Cross bearings. Bearings of two or more objects which intersect at the position of the observer; they are employed for fixing a ship's position when coasting.

Dangerous cargo. A general term embracing all goods liable to cause damage to the ship or to endanger human life, as well as those which are a source of danger to other cargo.

Day's run. Distance sailed or steamed by a ship from noon one day to noon the next.

Deck cargo. Goods carried on the open decks. Typical deck cargoes are timber and esparto grass.

Deck log. A record of a ship's voyage, written up and signed by each officer at the end of his watch, the main entries being courses steered, distance run, compass variation and deviation allowed, estimated leeway, set and drift of the current, conditions of sea, weather, sky, readings of the barometer and thermometer, etc. A deck or scrap log is a very important document on which courts of inquiry place a great deal of reliance, as do insurance interests in the event of damage to ship or cargo. Usually a 'fair copy' is made of the deck log, and this is signed by the master and chief officer, and forwarded to owners for record purposes at the end of each voyage.

Deck officer. A term which applies to all navigating officers, as distinct from engineers, pursers, stewards, wireless operators, etc.

Deck paint. A hard- and quick-drying paint used on steel decks.

Deck seamanship. Practical seamanship at which able seamen may reasonably be expected to be adept—knots and splices, reeving tackles, steering, heaving the lead, keeping a lookout, etc.

Deck steward. A member of a passenger liner's catering department who attends to, and fetches and carries for, passengers while they are on deck.

Deck stores. Expendable stores supplied by owners for the cleanliness, maintenance and working of the ship, and the handling of her cargo. Ropes, paint, tarpaulins, blocks, flags, oils, fenders, marline spikes, chipping hammers—these and numerous other items come under the the heading of deck stores.

Departure. Distance made good east or west, expressed in nautical miles.

Deratisation. An operation periodically carried out aboard ships in port to destroy rats; cyanide and sulphur dioxide being the most popular material used at the present time. When ships have been successfully fumigated or inspected, if found free of rats, they are issued with a deratisation certificate.

Dimensions. Measurements defining the hull, length overall, length between perpendiculars, moulded breadth, moulded depth, registered length, registered breadth, and registered depth.

Dip (to). To dip an ensign is to lower it and hoist it again. It is a form of salute made by a merchant ship when passing an H.M. ship, a foreign naval craft, or another ship belonging to the same owners.

Dipping lug. A type of lugsail formerly more or less standard in ships' lifeboats. The traveller was hooked to the mast strop about two-fifths of the length of the yard measured from forward. When going about, the yard had to be 'dipped' each time to the new lee side of the mast. This type of rig has been superseded in lifeboats by the standing lug.

Dirty ship. An expression used to denote a tanker which carries dirty oils, as distinct from those which carry lubricating oils, petrol and paraffin.

Discharge book. Contains a continuous record of sea service with dates of signing on and paying off. Conduct and ability is also recorded in the discharge book and this is usually either V.G. or D.R. (Decline to Report).

Distressed British Seaman (D.B.S.). A shipwrecked seaman or a seaman found otherwise such as through illness, ship sale, etc. at any port outside the U.K. A deserter is not a D.B.S.

Dock or Port Dues. Dues paid on the n.r.t. of the vessel for port upkeep.

Dock pass.
1. A document issued by the dock authorities before a vessel leaves the dock certifying that dock dues have been paid.
2. A pass given to seamen, transport drivers and others who may be carrying goods. It is handed in at the dock gates as they leave, and serves as an authority for the bearer to take goods out of dock premises.

Dog watch. One of the two two-hour watches between 4 and 8 p.m. Working dog watches in the days of 'watch and watch' (four hours on duty and four off) ensured that the same men would not have the same watch every night. The first 'dog' is from 4-6 p.m., the second from 6-8 p.m.

Donkeyman. A senior engine-room rating or petty officer in charge of a ship's donkey boiler in port.

Double-banked. When two opposite oars are pulled by oarsmen seated on the same thwart, the oars are said to be double-banked.

Double luff tackle. A purchase comprising two double blocks.

Double whip. A purchase comprising two single blocks, one movable and the other fixed, the standing part being made fast to the former. It is also called a gun tackle.

Down to her marks. A vessel loaded right down to the area load line.

Drag (to). To drag anchor is to draw it along the sea or river bed, either deliberately or accidentally—when there is bad holding ground or sufficient cable has not been paid out.

Draught marks. Marks cut into and painted on each side of a merchant ship's stem and sternpost or near her sternpost for indicating the draught. The height of the figures or letters and the vertical distance between them is 152·4mm (6 in), and they are painted a colour which contrasts with the colour of the hull.

Dress ship. To decorate a ship with flags to mark a special occasion.

Drop (to). To drop astern; to shift or move astern.

D.T.I. The Department of Trade and Industry is the Government department concerned with marine affairs.

Dunnage. Timber of various sizes, or other material, used to separate cargo in the hold or to keep it clear of steelwork, and the ceiling.

Earing. A short length of rope spliced to a cringle (a loop or eye) for hauling out the sail to its yard, gaff or boom.

Ease. To ease the helm means to reduce the amount of helm a ship is temporarily carrying. To ease a line means to slacken it steadily and reduce the tension on it.

Electric log. A term for patent logs fitted with an electrical arrangement for transmitting the reading to a register in the chartroom and/or wheelhouse.

Emergency steering gear. Independent hand- or power-operated gear provided for use in the event of a breakdown of the main steering gear.

Even keel. A ship is said to be on an even keel when she lies evenly in a fore and aft direction; when her draught is the same forward and aft.

Fair in place. A term used in ship repairing meaning to set or restore to its original form any damaged part of the structure without removing it; to repair in position. Also to fair on.

Fair wind. A favourable wind; one which assists the ship to make progress through the water; one which is abaft the beam.

Fall. All the rope in a purchase.

Fall astern (to). To be out-distanced by another vessel. Also to drop astern.

Fall off. To fall away from the wind and make leeway.

Farmer. When a four-hour watch is comprised of three men, two take a two-hour trick at the wheel each, and the third, the farmer, keeps the first and last hours as a stand-by man, and the middle two as a lookout man.

Fathom. A nautical measurement equal to 1m 828·8mm (6 ft.).

Feather (to). Turning the oar by wrist action at the end of a stroke so that the blade momentarily becomes parallel to the surface of the water before the next stroke is commenced, the object being to reduce wind resistance on the blade and also to lessen the chances of inadvertently catching the water.

Fire detector. An apparatus provided for the purpose of locating and reporting automatically by visible and audible means to the officer on watch an abnormal rise in temperature or the presence of smoke in any compartment of the ship. Probably the best-known fire-detection arrangement in the British Merchant Navy is the Lux-Rich system.

Fire drill. An exercise carried out by the crew periodically in order to ensure that every man is familiar with his station and his duties in the event of fire and also so that the ship's fire-fighting equipment is maintained in good working order.

First dog. The watch from 4-6 p.m.

Flood. The inflow or rising of the tide.

Flood (to). Broadly, to fill or partly fill a compartment with water admitted from the sea. Strictly, to fill completely a compartment below the waterline.

Flying light. Said of a vessel in ballast.

Fogbound. A vessel unable to berth at or leave a port due to fog.

Fog gun. A fog signal consisting of a gun on shore fired at regular intervals.

Following sea. One running with the ship, i.e. in a direction which is the same, or practically the same, as the ship's course.

Fore and aft. In the direction of a line drawn from stem to stern. Placed or directed parallel to the keel.

Foreign-going vessel. One employed in foreign trade, i.e. outside home trade limits.

Forenoon watch. The watch from 8 a.m. till noon.

Forward spring. A mooring line, usually a wire, with or without a rope pennant leading from forward in the ship to a point ashore about abreast of amidships to check a ship's forward motion when berthing. Also known as the forward back spring.

Foul ground. An area where the sea bed does not afford good holding for the anchors.

Foul hawse. If a ship's cables are entangled, in other words, if they have turns in them, she is said to have a foul hawse.

Fourfold block. A block having four sheaves.

Fourfold purchase. A purchase consisting of two blocks with four sheaves in each.

Frap (to). To bind or draw together tightly by passing ropes around. Bracing together the parts of a tackle or other ropes to increase tension.

Freeboard. The vertical distance measured on the ship's side amidships from the waterline to the uppper side of the freeboard deck.

Free surface. A mass of liquid in a tank the surface of which is free to remain horizontal when the ship rolls and pitches is said to have a free surface. Also called slack water.

Freight. Money paid to a shipowner for the carriage of goods by sea.

Fresh breeze. A wind of force 5 on the Beaufort scale, i.e. one having a velocity of 17 to 21 nautical miles per hour.

Full and by. Broadly, sailing with the wind before the beam. Strictly, when all sails are drawing full and the course steered is as close to the wind as possible.

Funnel marks. Distinctive symbols, letters or marks painted or affixed to a ship's funnel(s) to indicate her ownership.

Furl. To roll up a sail or awning to its yard, boom, mast or stay, and secure it with a gasket.

Galley wireless. Source of gossip on board.

Gangway. A narrow, portable platform used as a passage by persons entering or leaving a ship berthed alongside.

General cargo. Cargo consisting of miscellaneous goods carried in small quantities and varying in weight, dimensions, nature, class and condition.

Gentle breeze. A wind of force 3 on the Beaufort scale, i.e. one having a velocity of 7 to 10 nautical miles per hour.

Gimbals. A system of rings moving one within the other and arranged to enable a suspended object to maintain a horizontal position irrespective of the ship's trim or motion in a seaway. Compasses, mercurial barometers, and chronometers are items of bridge equipment slung in gimballs aboard ship.

Gin block. A metal cargo block with a single, large sheave fitted in skeleton framework.

Glory hole. The stewards' accommodation in a liner, and the firemen's quarters in a coal-burning steamer.

Grain. According to the British maritime law the term grain is used to denote corn, rice, paddy, pulse, peas, beans, seeds, and other species of plants, such as oats, nuts or nut kernels; in Canada it includes corn, wheat, rye, barley, peas and other grain except oats; in Australia, wheat, barley, oats, peas, and cargoes of like nature are all considered to be grain.

Grip (to). To hold. An anchor is said to grip when its flukes embed themselves in the ground.

Gripe (to). A ship's tendency to come up into the wind when sailing close-hauled.

Grommet. A ring of rope or wire made from a single strand by laying it up three times around its own part.

Ground swell. A swell remaining after or preceding a gale.

Ground tackle. A general term for all gear and equipment used in anchor work—anchors, cables, etc.

Guard rail. The uppermost of a series of rails fitted around an upper deck for safety purposes.

Guest rope. A grabline leading from forward and hanging overside in a bight to assist boats coming to the gangway.

Hail. A ship is said to hail from the port at which she is registered.

Hail (to). To call out; to address.

Hailing station. A post established in some ports for hailing inward ships to ascertain their last port of call, and outward ships their destination.

Half mast. A flag is considered to be half-mast when it is hoisted below maximum height, not necessarily half way, between the deck and mast truck or peak of a gaff. It is a sign of mourning.

Halo. A large luminous ring coloured or uncoloured, around the sun or moon.

Halyard. A rope rove through a block or pulley aloft for hoisting or lowering yards, spars, sails, flags, anchor lights, etc.

Hand rail. A rail fitted along the sides or above the steps of a ladder, and, in passenger ships mainly, on bulkheads below decks and on deck.

Handsomely. The opposite to hastily; gradually, moderately or carefully, as when lowering an object or easing a rope.

Hand steering gear. Steering gear in which the rudder is controlled and operated by a hand-driven steering wheel directly connected to the rudderhead or indirectly through steering chains.

Hank.
1. A ring of wood or metal, or a catch-hook by which sails are made to run on stays with their luff close to it.
2. A coil of small cordage, signal halyards, twine, for example.

Hard. To the maximum extent. Thus to put the helm hard over is to put it over as far as it will go to port or starboard. The brake of a windlass is said to be 'hard up' when it has been screwed up as far as possible, thereby securing the gypsy or cable-holder.

Hard and fast. Said of a vessel when firmly aground. Fixed or immovable.

Hard lay. In cordage, an angle of lay greater than the standard lay. Although hard-laid rope is not as strong or as flexible as a soft-laid one of the same size, it is more compact and better resists wear and moisture.

Hatch batten. A flat steel bar used to secure the edges of the tarpaulin against the hatch coamings.

Hatch beam. A portable transverse beam placed across a cargo hatchway, and acting as a bearer supporting the hatch covers. The ends fit into sockets riveted to the inside face of hatch coamings.

Hatch cleat. One of the clips, at least 63mm (2½ in.) wide, welded or riveted to the outside of the hatch coamings for holding hatch battens and securing tarpaulins.

Hatch cover. The wooden cover fitted between beams in a hatchway.

Hatch end protections. Compulsory fittings of galvanized protections to the ends of wooden hatch covers. These protections are either of the open-end band or closed-end shoe types.

Hatch wedge. A piece of hardwood of triangular shape employed for securing hatch battens and tarpaulins against the coaming. Wedges are made of wood possessing good swelling properties when wet. English elm, for instance.

Haul. To pull on a single rope.

Hauling part. The free end of a fall, as opposed to the standing part which is secured.

Haul off. To alter course so as to clear an object.

Haul taut. To tighten.

Head on. Two ships are said to be head on when they are end on, stem to stem, and therefore on directly opposite courses. Thus a head-on collision involving two ships is one in which they meet, stem to stem.

Head sea. One which runs in a direction directly or nearly directly opposite to the ship's course. The opposite to a following sea.

Headway. A ship's forward progress through the water.

Heart. The soft-laid core, usually of hemp, running through shroud-laid and wire ropes.

Heave short. To pick up the slack of an anchor cable until the ship is nearly over her anchor or there is just sufficient cable out to hold the ship in position pending leaving an anchorage.

Heave the lead. To ascertain the depth of water by means of the hand lead.

Heave to. To bring a sailing ship head to wind by putting the helm down or hauling in the weather braces or both, so that the wind acts on the fore surface of the sails; to dispose the sails so that they counteract each other and check her headway. In the case of a power-driven ship heaving to is considered to be reducing speed so that the ship makes no headway, and bringing the wind either right ahead or fine on either bow, so that the ship lies comfortably and does not ship much water.

Heel. Transverse inclination due to the action of the wind and sea, or an uneven disposition of the weight on board. When the heel is of a more or less permanent character it is referred to as a list. To heel is to careen or lay her over for one reason or another.

Helm. Broadly, the entire steering-gear wheel, engine telemotor, etc. Strictly, it is the tiller alone.

Helm down. A sailing order to push the tiller to leeward.

Helm orders. Orders given by the master, officers or a pilot to the helmsman or quartermaster. At an international conference in London it was agreed:

1. That the order given to the man at the wheel should indicate the direction in which the ship's head should turn.
2. That this practice should be uniform throughout the world.
3. That the words port and starboard or their ordinary national equivalents should no longer be used in giving helm orders.
4. That the words left and right or their ordinary equivalents should be adopted.

However, the words port and starboard are still used in the British Merchant Navy, and it is improbable that they will be superseded by left and right respectively in the foreseeable future.

Helm up. A sailing order to push the tiller to windward.

High seas. In international law all navigable water lying outside the territorial waters, and therefore the jurisdiction, of the various countries. The open sea.

Hitch. Twists made with rope to form knots which can be readily let go. The half-hitch, two half-hitches, clove hitch, timber hitch and Blackwall hitch are the principal hitches.

Holystone. A soft porous stone used in conjunction with sand for cleaning ships' wooden decks and other woodwork such as teak, which it is usual to oil or varnish but not to paint.

Home trade. In Britain all trade carried on within the following limits: All ports of the United Kingdom and Eire, the Isle of Man, the Channel Islands, and ports on the Continent between the River Elbe and Brest, inclusive.

Homeward bound. A term meaning the return of a ship to her country of origin or port of register.

House flag. The private flag of a company or line operating one or more ships. Except in the Brocklebank and probably one or two other lines, house flags are hoisted at the mainmast.

Hull. The body of a ship exclusive of masts, yards, sails, rigging, etc. In other words, the shell of a vessel.

Hull down. When a ship is so far from an observer in another ship or on shore that, due to the convexity of the earth's surface, only the masts and/or funnel(s) can be seen, and the hull remains below the horizon.

Ice blink. The glow on the horizon caused by the reflection of light from floating ice or from land covered with snow.

Icebound. When a vessel is prevented by ice from proceeding on her voyage.

Icebox. An insulated box packed with ice in which food is preserved.

Icebreaker. A specially constructed and very strong vessel used for creating and maintaining a navigable passage through ice.

Ice patrol. The International Ice Patrol created and operated by the United States Government and subscribed to by various countries, to patrol north of the Atlantic liner routes and issue warnings by radio of the whereabouts of ice during the spring and summer months when icebergs are carried southward from Arctic waters by the Labrador current.

Idler. A day-worker aboard ship. One who does not keep a watch.

Inboard. Within a ship, in contradistinction to outboard.

Inflammable cargo. Any type of cargo which is liable to spontaneous combustion, and volatile liquids emitting inflammable vapours.

In oars. A boating order to lay the oars along the thwarts. Also termed boat oars.

Inside cabin. A cabin without direct access to an outside deck, or one separated from the ship's side by other cabins or compartments.

In stays. The position of a sailing craft when head to wind during a tacking operation.

Intermediate vessels. A term rather loosely applied to ships inferior to first-class mail liners and scheduled to perform a given voyage in a longer time.

International Code of Signals. The code adopted by all maritime nations assigning meanings to different flags and arrangements of flags, also morse and semaphore.

International load line certificate. A certificate issued by a Government department or classification society, on which is stated the minimum freeboard and the position of the loadline disc on the ship's side. A loadline certificate is issued to every ship of 150 gross tons or over engaged in international trading, other than to yachts, fishing craft, ships carrying neither cargo nor passengers, H.M. ships and pilot boats.

Irish pennants. Superfluous rope yarns or any odds and ends of rope which hang untidily from the rigging and detract from the neat and orderly appearance of a vessel.

Jack staff. A small flagstaff at the stemhead on which, in port, merchant vessels hoist the Pilot Jack, their owners' house flag or other insignia, and warships, the Union Jack.

Jetsam. Cargo which sinks after being jettisoned, or sacrificed, for the safety of the ship. Cargo which floats after being jettisoned or after a shipwreck is called flotsam.

Jettison. The act of sacrificing goods by throwing them overboard to lighten the ship when done for safety purposes.

Jibe. To shift suddenly and with force from one side to the other. Said of fore-and-aft sails when the wind, when aft or on the quarter, catches the mainsail on the lee side, causing it to crash across to the other. Also gybe.

Jigger mast. The aftermost mast of a four- or five-masted barque; the fourth mast on a ship having four or more masts.

Jolly boat. A small boat carried in merchant ships for the convenience of the crew when the ship is anchored off a port, and for many other purposes of a similar nature.

Jumper stay. The wire stay extending from the funnel to the foremast, to which blocks are secured and halyards rove through them for signalling purposes.

Jump ship. To desert; to leave a ship unlawfully.

Jury rig. Any temporary fitting or rig used in an emergency; a substitute.

Kapok. A cottony fibre covering the seeds of a tropical tree. It is very light and buoyant and is used in the manufacture of lifejackets and other lifesaving appliances in preference to cork.

Kedge anchor. A small light anchor now rarely carried by merchant ships for warping purposes.

Kedging. Warping a ship from one point to another by means of the kedge anchor and a hawser.

Kentledge. Scrap metal used as ballast.

Ketch. A trading vessel with two masts, main and mizzen, both fore-and-aft rigged, the mizzen with or without a topsail.

King spoke. Upper spoke of a hand steering wheel which is vertical when the rudder is amidships. It is usually brass-tipped or has some other special mark.

Knot.
1. A unit of speed equivalent to one nautical mile in an hour.
2. An interlacing of ends or sections of a rope by twisting and drawing taut for the purpose of fastening them together or to another object or to prevent slipping.

Lacing. Small cordage used for a variety of shipboard purposes such as securing boat covers, and awnings, also for lashing the head of a lifeboat's mainsail to the yard.

Lamp room. A small compartment in which oil lights and lanterns which all ships are legally obliged to carry are stored. Also called lamp locker. In passenger liners it is the responsibility of the lamp trimmer, but in others the bosun usually has charge of the locker and its contents.

Lamp trimmer. A petty officer responsible for all oil lamps on board, and keeping them trimmed ready for immediate use in the event of failure of the ship's electrical power.

Landfall. Land first sighted at the end of a sea passage.

Lash (to). To bind, make fast, or secure with rope.

Lashing. Rope securing any movable object.

Lead. A leaden weight secured at the end of a line and used for ascertaining the depth of water beneath a vessel and also the nature of the sea bed. Sounding leads are of different weights and sizes according to whether they are for use in shallow or deep water, though nowadays machines are used universally for soundings in excess of 20 fathoms.

Lead block. A name given to any block used to guide a rope, or alter the direction of a pull.

Leading marks. Navigational aids erected on shore and comprising two conspicuous objects which, if kept in transit (i.e. in line) will lead a vessel away from known dangers.

Leading part. Hauling part of a fall, led through a snatch block.

Leadsman. The hand deputed to take or assist in taking soundings.

Leadsman's platform. A small platform or grating projecting over the ship's side forward of the bridge and used when a cast of the lead is being taken. It is hinged to the side so that it can be lashed at sea, and at other times when it is not likely to be used. Also called the chains.

Lee. The lee side of a ship is the side opposite to that upon which the wind blows; the side sheltered from the weather. A lee shore is one upon which the wind blows, in other words, the shore lying under a vessel's lee.

Leech. The sides of a square sail, or the after edge of a fore-and-aft sail.

Lee helm. A sailing craft is said to carry lee helm when the helm has to be kept a'lee in order to counteract a tendency to run away from the wind.

Leeward. On the lee side; away from the wind.

Leeway. The lateral movement of a ship to leeward of her course; the distance or difference between the course steered and the course made when this deviation is caused by action of the wind and sea.

Liberty boat. The boat which conveys crew ashore and back.

Lifeboat. A wood or metal boat specially built, designed and equipped for lifesaving purposes.

Lifebuoy. A buoyant object of circular shape and equipped with a grabline becketed to it for throwing to a person who has fallen overboard.

Lifebuoy light. A device on a lifebuoy for automatically producing a bright light when the buoy is thrown overboard.

Lifeline.
1. A line stretched fore and aft along an open deck in heavy weather to assist members of the crew who may have to traverse the deck.
2. One of the two lines secured to and hanging from the wire span between davit heads for the use of the crew when lowering or hoisting a lifeboat.
3. A 60mm (2 in.) line secured around a lifeboat (below the rubber) or other buoyant apparatus and hanging in bights for persons in the water to grab and hang on to. Also called grabline.

Lifejacket. A device for supporting the body in the water. Lifejackets may be made of any of a number of officially approved materials, and are of various types.

Liferaft. A raft-like construction designed to save, and equipped to sustain life in the event of a shipwreck. During the war all seagoing ships were required to carry a certain number of liferafts. They were equipped with lifelines, oars, etc., as well as with food and water. Liferafts should not be confused with other types of buoyancy apparatus required to be carried by passenger ships in peacetime.

Lifting tackle. One used for lifting and lowering derricks.

Light-airs. A light variable wind barely enabling sailing craft to maintain steerage way. Force 1 on the Beaufort scale.

Light breeze. A wind of force 2 on the Beaufort scale having a velocity of 4-6 nautical miles per hour.

Light draught. A ship's draught when she is floating fully equipped for sea with water in boilers but having no crew, fuel, cargo, stores or fresh water on board; her draught at light displacement.

Light dues. Money collected for the upkeep of lighthouses, buoys, light vessels, etc.

Lighten (to). Transferring cargo, ballast, stores, etc., ashore or into lighters to reduce displacement and draught.

Light loadline. Line of immersion at which a vessel floats in light condition.

Limey. American term for a Briton. Nautical origin since British ships' crews were issued with lime juice to prevent scurvy.

Line of soundings. Soundings taken at regular and frequent intervals whilst the ship maintains a steady course. When corrected for chart datum and plotted on the chart the line of soundings gives a line of position.

Liner. A merchant ship, trading on one route and maintaining an advertised schedule.

Line-throwing pistol. A pistol designed to shoot a projectile with a light line attached to it for establishing connection between ship and shore or ship and ship.

Lizard. A short length of rope with a thimble or bull's-eye spliced into one end and used as a lead for rigging or a whip.

Lloyd's. An old-established London institution incorporated by Act of Parliament in which most forms of insurance can be effected. It does not subscribe policies, the risks being accepted by underwriting members, each of whom has to deposit securities for a large amount—depending upon his commitments—before he can be elected.

Lloyd's Register of Shipping. A British classification society, established in 1834, and united with the Underwriters' Registry for Iron Ships in 1885, and with the British Corporation Register in 1949. Lloyd's Register is governed by a committee representing shipping, shipbuilding, marine engine-building and underwriting interests. Lloyd's Register should not be confused with Lloyd's underwriting organization.

Load Displacement. The weight of water displaced by a vessel when floating at her loaded draught.

Loaded draught. Draught at load displacement.

Loadline disc. A disc 305mm (12 in.) in diameter marked amidships below the deck line and intersected by a horizontal line 457mm (18 in.) long and 25½mm (1 in.) wide, the upper edge of which passes through the centre of the disc. The letters on each side of the disc indicate the assigning authority—B.T., the British Government through the D.T.I.; L.R., Lloyd's Register; A.B., American Bureau of Shipping; N.V., Det Norske Veritas; B.V., Bureau Veritas; D.L., Danish Ministry of Shipping and Fisheries, and others.

Log (to).
1. To enter in the Official Log any unusual occurrence, or the name of a seaman, with the date, nature and particulars of any offence he may have committed and the penalty attached to it.
2. To record by means of a patent log distance run through the water.

Logbook. A book supplied by the D.T.I. to every merchant ship and kept by the master. It contains a tabulated summary of happenings on board and is regarded as legal evidence on matters which the master is required to enter in it. All entries are signed by the master and by the chief officer or another member of the crew. The official log should not be confused with the mate's, scrap, or deck log.

Log governor. A steadying device in the form of a wheel fitted to the line of a towing log and the taffrail register.

Log line. Braided line used for towing the rotator through the water. Its length varies according to the speed of the vessel.

Log register. Registering mechanism of a towing log which records the rotator's revolutions and converts them into nautical miles and fractions of a mile. Commonly referred to as the log clock.

Lookout. The able seaman, E.D.H., or ordinary seaman stationed on the forecastle head, in the crow's nest or on the bridge to watch for and report any objects in or near the ship's track. Whilst it is not laid down by any British maritime law that merchant ships must carry a lookout either by day or night, it is stated in the Rule of the Road that nothing in the rules shall exonerate any vessel owner, master or crew from the consequences of any neglect to keep a proper lookout.

Loom.
1. The glow of a light which is visible over the horizon before the light itself can be seen.
2. An object is said to 'loom up', when, under some atmospheric conditions such as in fog, it suddenly appears larger and nearer than was at first assumed.
3. That part of an oar extending from the leather or fulcrum to the grip or handle.

Loose water. Water in tanks, holds, peaks or other compartments which has a free surface and is free to move in any direction with the motion of the ship. Also slack water.

Lower. To let down. To slack away or ease a rope in a downward direction.

Lubber line. The vertical line painted or otherwise marked on the forward inner side of the compass bowl. That point of the compass which is immediately opposite to the Lubber Line indicates a ship's heading and therefore the course steered.

Luff. Fore edge of a fore-and-aft sail.

Luff (to). To bring a sailing craft's head closer to the wind. To luff up or luff round is to throw her head right into the wind.

Luffing. The vertical movement of a crane or derrick. One specially equipped for immediate movement in a vertical direction under the control of the crane or winch driver is termed a luffing crane or derrick.

Luff tackle. One consisting of a double and a single block.

Lugsail. A four-sided sail with head shorter than foot and luff shorter than leech which is bent to a yard and slung to the mast in a fore-and-aft position. Common types of lugsail are the standing or working lug, dipping lug, balance lug and Clyde lug.

Lurch. A heavy movement to one side which is half roll, half pitch.

Magnetic course. The course steered by magnetic compass with reference to the magnetic meridian; the angle between magnetic North or South and the fore-and-aft line of the ship. Thus N. 85° E. S. 85° W.

Mail flag. The white pennant with red crown in the centre between the words 'Royal' and 'Mail', also in red, flown by ships carrying mail when they are entering or leaving port. In other countries, of course, the mail flag takes different forms.

Manifest. A list of the ship's cargo which has to be shown at the Custom House.

Manrope. The name given to some ropes used for purposes of safety. Manropes, for instance, are hung over the side within easy reach of men working on stages for grabbing in an emergency.

Marine superintendent. One responsible to the directorate of a shipping company for the care, upkeep and repair of ships, manning the deck department, docking and undocking, expeditious loading and discharging of cargo, and numerous other jobs. In many companies the marine superintendent is one of the senior masters; in others he may not ever have attained command but has some special aptitude or qualification for the work.

Marks. Division used in marking the hand leadline at the second, third, fifth, seventh, tenth, thirteenth, fifteenth, seventeenth and twentieth fathoms. Intermediate fathoms, which may be marked or unmarked, are known as deeps.

Married gear. Two cargo falls shackled together or to the same hook. Also known as a union purchase.

Marry. To join or unite. Thus two ropes are married by reeving through a block by placing them end to end and whipping them temporarily. The unlaid strands of two ropes' ends are married by placing them together preparatory to joining them permanently by splicing.

Mast. A spar of round timber or tubular iron or steel set upright in a vessel to sustain yards, booms, derricks, sails, etc., and for mounting navigation lights.

Master. The commanding officer, whether professionally qualified or not, of a merchant ship; any person other than a pilot who is in command of a merchant ship.

Master-at-arms. A member of the crew of a passenger liner who is in charge of police duties, and has charge of a small number of patrolmen. In some liner companies the master-at-arms is also the baggage master.

Master compass. The instrument in which the gyroscope is installed in the gyro room. Movements of steering and bearing repeaters are instigated by the master compass, or, as it is often called, the master gyro.

Master's certificate. A professional certificate of competency issued by the Board of Trade to navigating officers who have qualified by examination and sea service to take command of a vessel. There are five kinds, viz. the Home Trade, the Foreign-Going, the Yacht Masters', the Square-Rigged, or ordinary, and the Extra Masters'.

Mean draught. Average of the draughts forward and aft.

Meet her. An order given to the helmsman to use the helm so as to check the swing of the ship's head.

Mess boy. Member of a ship's crew who sets tables, serves food, and waits on the tables of the crew's messroom, clears away and washes dishes after meals, and keeps clean eating utensils and mess equipment generally as well as the messroom.

Messenger. A line used to lead heavier ropes.

Middle watch. The watch from midnight to 4 a.m. Colloquially known as the graveyard watch.

Midshipman. A cadet or an apprentice in a merchant ship.

Midships. The same as amidships

Miss stays. A sailing craft is said to miss stays when she fails to come about when tacking and begins to fall off on the same tack. If she cannot be cast one way or the other, she is said to be in irons or 'hung up in the wind'.

Mizzenmast.

1. The aftermost mast of a full-rigged ship, barque, barquentine and three-masted schooner.

2. The third mast from forward of a vessel having more than three masts.

3. The after mast in a ketch or yawl.

Moderate breeze. A wind of force 4 on the Beaufort scale, i.e. one having a velocity of 11-16 nautical miles per hour.

Moderate gale. A continuous wind of force 7 on the Beaufort scale, i.e. one having a velocity of 28-33 nautical miles per hour.

Moderate sea. A comparatively light sea.

Moor.

1. To secure a ship by means of chains or ropes which are made fast to the shore, to anchors, or to mooring buoys.

2. To ride with both anchors widely apart, one leading ahead and the other astern, with the ship's head midway between them.

Mooring line. A hawser used to secure a ship in her berth.

Morning watch. The watch from 4-8 a.m.

Moulded breadth. The greatest breadth of the hull measured to the outside of frames, i.e. inside of the shell plating.

Moulded depth. Vertical distance measured amidships from the top of the keel (or intersection of the outside of the frame with the centre-line) to the top of the upper deck beam at gunwale (or of the second deck in a shelter- or awning-deck vessel).

Muster. Assembling of a ship's crew and/or passengers for inspection or drill.

Mutiny. Unlawful resistance to a superior officer. Persistent refusal to obey a lawful command.

National Maritime Board. An organization created in 1919 to establish minimum rates of pay and conditions of employment generally, for all British merchant seamen. Shipowners and seafarers are represented equally on the board and the various panels or sections concerned with the different ranks, ratings and shipboard departments. There are the masters', navigating officers', engineer officers', radio officers', sailors' and firemen's, and catering department panels, each having its own joint secretariat.

Nautical mile. Standard unit of measurement for marine navigation equivalent to one-sixtieth of a degree of latitude. For all practical purposes it is assumed to be 1853m (6,080 ft.).

Navigator. An officer whose main duty at sea is the navigation of the ship, care of navigational aids and instruments, correction of charts, etc., In deep-sea ships carrying three watchkeeping deck officers the second mate is usually the navigator, but in large transatlantic liners the first officer frequently performs this work.

Negative flag. Letter N of the International Code, meaning 'No'.

Night order book. A book in which the master leaves written directives to watchkeeping officers before he 'goes below'. The night order book is read and signed by each officer before he takes over the watch.

Nip.

1. The point at which a rope bends sharply.

2. To nip a cable or rope is to secure it with a seizing.

No higher. An order given to the helmsman of a sailing craft to keep the vessel from getting any closer to the wind.

Non-toppling block. A block weighted at its base so that it will maintain a vertical position.

Not under command. A ship which is unable to manoeuvre; a disabled ship.

Not-under-command lights. Regulation lights for a vessel not under command, consisting of two red lights, placed in a vertical line one over the other not less than 1·828m (6 ft.) apart and visible all around the horizon at a distance of not less than 3·219km (2 miles).

Number. A hoist of four alphabetical flags denoting a ship's identity. A ship's signal letters.

Numeral pennant. One of the ten International Code pennants used for signalling numbers.

Oar blade. Flat part of an oar, scull or sweep.

Oars. An order to a boat's crew to cease pulling and to keep the oars parallel with the surface of the water and the blades feathered.

Oil burner.
1. Colloquialism for a steamer burning fuel oil.
2. A device fitted at the mouth of a boiler furnace to atomize the fuel oil

Oil tanker. A ship specially designed for the sea transport in bulk of oils and spirits.

Only mate. The only deck officer other than the master in small craft.

Ordinary seaman. A deck hand with some sea service who is subordinate to an able seaman but superior to a deck boy.

Outside cabin. One having a port hole or window in the ship's side, or the superstructure.

Overboard. Over the side of a ship; 'board', in nautical terminology means the ship's side, thus inboard, outboard.

Overhaul (to).
1. To open out or extend the fall and blocks of a tackle after they have been brought close up.
2. To inspect or examine.
3. To catch up with, or overtake.

Overtake. To gain in speed on or overhaul another vessel. An overtaking vessel the Rule of the Road states is one which comes up with another from any direction more than two points abaft her beam.

Palm.
1. The flattened side of the flukes of an anchor.
2. A contrivance fitting the ball of the thumb and palm of the hand—used by seamen and sailmakers for canvas work.

Parcel (to). Winding greased or tarred strips of burlap or canvas around a rope and with the lay after worming but before serving to protect the rope. Splices in wire are parcelled and served but not wormed.

Passage. A journey by sea from one port to another. A voyage consists of at least two passages one outward one homeward.

Pay. To fill the seams of a deck with hot pitch or marine glue after caulking.

Pay off.
1. To allow a ship's head to fall a'lee i.e. to fall off from the wind. Some-times in tacking a lifeboat's head will not pay off and she becomes 'hung up in the wind'.
2. To pay the wages due to and discharge a crew at the termination of a voyage.

Pay out. To slacken out from inboard, e.g. a mooring line or anchor cable.

Peggy. A junior deck rating who keeps the crew accommodation clean and tidy, fetches the food from the galley, etc.

Pennant. A long, pointed flag; one with the fly usually much longer than the hoist and tapering to a point. Sometimes called pendant.

Pilot flag. Flag hoisted by a ship requiring a pilot, either letter G of the International Code, or a Union Jack with a white border (the Pilot Jack). The two-flag hoist PT may also be flown to summon a pilot.

Pilot ladder. A rope ladder in which each rung is made of a flat piece of wood pierced by four holes, two at each end, through which four side ropes are rove. Seizings are put on just above and below each rung at both sides binding the two side ropes together and making the rungs more firm.

Pin.
1. The metal axle of a block upon which the sheave rotates.
2. A form of threaded bolt employed for connecting a shackle.

Pitch. The residuum of boiled tar used for paying deck seams.

Pitch (to). A ship is said to pitch when she plunges with the bow and stern rising and falling alternately.

Pitting. Tiny cavities formed on the surface of propeller blades, steel plates, etc., by electrolytic corrosive action.

Plimsoll line. A popular name for the freeboard mark and loadline painted on a ship's sides which will always be linked with the name of Samuel Plimsoll, a British agitator, propagandist and reformer of the nineteenth century. Also called Plimsoll mark.

Point (to). To taper the end of a rope by unlaying the strands, removing some of them and weaving the remainder in a particular manner.

Pole mast. A mast all in one spar, i.e. one without a separate topmast.

Pound and pint. Colloquialism for the D.T.I. minimum victualling scale for ships' crews. Members of the crew are said to be on their pound and pint when they get what they are entitled to by law and no more.

Powder flag. Popular name for the red burgee B of the International Code which, when flown singly, signifies that the vessel flying it is taking in or discharging explosives.

Pratique. Permission given by port medical authorities for a vessel arriving from overseas to communicate with the shore. It is given on the master's assurance that his ship is free of infectious disease, after he has produced a clean bill of health from the last port, and/or after the ship has been inspected by the port medical authorities.

Prevailing wind. The mean wind in a particular area. Thus the prevailing winds in the northern North Atlantic are the westerlies.

Preventer. Any rope set up temporarily to give additional support to masts or derricks. Preventer backstays were set up in sailing ships from the masthead to the ship's side when a heavy press of canvas was being carried in strong winds. Preventer guys are set up on derricks when the normal guys are to bear an abnormal stress.

Pricker. A small pointed tool used by sailmakers for making eyelet holes in canvas.

Prolonged blast. A blast on whistle or siren of 4-6 seconds' duration.

Public room. A communal room in passenger ships used by passengers in the same class; the smoke-room, library, observation lounge, etc., are public rooms.

Pull (to). To row. To propel a boat by oars.

Pumpman. The petty officer in tankers who is in charge of the pumps used for discharging liquid cargoes.

Purser. A liner's accountant and paymaster. An officer in passenger ships who has charge of the clerical staff and who is responsible to the master for official papers and documents, as well as attending to the ship's disbursements, crew wages, and in some cases berthing passengers.

Put about. To tack. To turn a sailing craft's head so that the wind takes her on the other side.

Put back. To return to the port of departure.

Put into port. To deviate on passage by entering a port due to stress of weather; to land a sick seaman or passenger; to replenish bunkers in an emergency; or because of any untoward happening.

Put to sea. To leave port at the commencement of a voyage.

Quadrant davit. A straight steel davit in which the lower end forms a semi-circular arc cogged on its circumference. As the boat is swung outboard the cogs on the arc or quadrant work in a flat rack secured to the deck.

Quarantine signal. Any of the three flag signals, Q, QQ, or QL, flown by a vessel on entering port to indicate her state of health to the port medical authorities; also, the night signal—a red light over a white light not more than 1·828mm (6 ft.) apart—signifying that the ship has not been visited by the port health authorities and requests free pratique.

Quarter. Strictly, one quarter of a ship, but for all practical purposes the quarters are those areas of a ship's sides from 45 deg. abaft the beam to the stern.

Quartermaster. A senior deck rating carried only by liners, whose main task is steering the ship for four hours in every twenty-four. Other duties are to keep the bridge clean, read the log, take the sea and air temperatures, and generally perform any work on or around the bridge as required by the O.O.W. In port he usually stands a gangway watch, especially when passengers are embarking and disembarking.

Quarter rope. A mooring line run out from the quarter.

Racking turns. Turns taken in figure-of-eight style when making a racking seizing.

Radar. The Radio Aid to Direction And Range on which echoes of other vessels, land, etc., show up on a screen similar to that of a T.V. set.

Radial davit. A type of davit consisting of a vertical pillar of round section with the upper portion bent and having sufficient outreach so that the boat should clear the ship's side when the vessel heels at an angle of 15 deg. It is usually stepped in a socket attached to the ship's side or on the first deck below the one where the boats are stowed, near the side.

Ratguard. A circular or conical metal disc with a hole in the centre and split from the centre to the circumference, which is fitted over mooring lines to prevent rats from entering the ship by way of the line.

Ready about. The order given by the coxswain of a boat under sail to prepare for tacking.

Reef (to). To diminish the sail area by rolling up part of it and securing it by reef points, or lacing.

Reef band. A strip of canvas running across a sail and perforated at intervals with holes or eyes to receive reef points, or lacing.

Reef cringle. An eye or loop worked in the boltrope on the leech or luff of a sail through which the earing is rove.

Reef point. One of a series of short pieces of rope which confine the reefed portion of a sail.

Reeve (to). To pass a rope through any hole in a block, thimble, cleat, ringbolt, etc. To reeve a tackle is to pass a rope over its sheaves.

Registered breadth. The breadth measured to the outside of the shell plating at the greatest breadth.

Registered depth. Depth measured amidships, from the top of the double bottom or from the top of the floor, if there is no double bottom, or from a point not exceeding 76mm (3 ins.) above these points where ceiling planking is fitted, to the top of the tonnage deck beam at the centre-line.

Registered length. Length measured from the foreside of the stem on the line of the forecastle deck, to the after side of the head of the stern post or to the centre of the rudder stock where there is no sternpost.

Registered tonnage. The official tonnage, gross or net, as determined by the legal method of measurement, as shown on the tonnage certificate.

Regulation light. Any of the lights prescribed by the International Regulations for Preventing Collisions at Sea, which have to be carried by vessels under way, at anchor, not under command, aground, towing or being towed, or in any other circumstances.

Relative bearing. A port or starboard bearing in points or degrees expressed as a direction relative to the line of the ship's keel.

Relieving tackle. Temporary tackles fitted to relieve strain on a ship's steering gear in heavy weather.

Ride.

1. To lie at anchor.

2. A rope on a capstan winch or windlass is said to ride when one of the round turns, or the hauling part, is jammed over another.

3. To ride out a gale is to lie at anchor or remain hove to through it.

Ridge rope. A wire rove through holes in the top ends of awning stanchions, and to which the awning is secured.

Riding light. The regulation light or lights which a vessel must carry when at anchor. Also called anchor light.

Riggers. Shore gang who relieve the crew in port.

Rigging. A general term for all ropes, chains and gear used for supporting and operating masts, yards, booms, gaffs and sails. Rigging is classified as standing (fixed) or running (movable).

Rise and fall. The vertical movement of the tide caused by combined action of the sun and moon on the waters of the earth.

Rope clip. A mechanical contrivance used to secure a wire rope around a thimble instead of making a splice. Also called bulldog clip.

Round sennit. Sennit formed by plaiting an even number of strands in twos around a heart.

Round to. To bring a vessel head to wind.

Round turn. To pass a rope once around a bitt, cleat, winch drum, etc.

Rule of the Road. International rules governing the action of ships when approaching each other so as to involve risk of collision. The International Rules and Regulations for Preventing Collisions at Sea.

Run (to).

1. To navigate with the wind aft or nearly aft in heavy weather.
2. To sail before the wind.

Runners. Crew engaged on a running agreement.

Running agreement. An agreement used for deep-sea ships. It may be valid for two or more voyages when the average length of the voyage is less than six months. Under ordinary Articles of Agreement for deep-sea ships crews are paid off on the first arrival at or before leaving the U.K. after a round voyage has been made no matter how short that voyage may have been. Under a running agreement this is not necessary, no matter how many times the ship may visit U.K. ports whilst the articles are in force.

Rust. The scale caused by the combined corrosive action of carbon dioxide, moisture and oxygen on the surface of iron and steel.

Safety certificate. A Government certificate issued to passenger vessels complying with international requirements as regards watertight sub-division, lifesaving appliances, W/T apparatus, fire-fighting equipment, etc.

Safety hook. A cargo hook with a lip hinged to swing down and lock over the point.

Sailing vessel. One provided with sufficient sail to navigate under sail alone, whether or not she has auxiliary machinery. According to the Rules and Regulations for Preventing Collisions at Sea, 'every steam vessel which is under sail and not under steam is to be considered a sailing vessel'.

Scanner. The rotating aerial for the radar set.

Scarph (to). Joining wood or metal parts by sloping off the ends of each and maintaining the same cross-section throughout the joint.

Schooner. A fore-and-aft rigged vessel having originally two masts, fore and main, but now three or more.

Scope. The length of cable to which a ship is riding; it is measured from the hawsepipe to the anchor.

Score. The groove on the shell of a wooden block for taking the strop.

Scud (to). To run before the wind with sufficient canvas to keep the vessel ahead of the sea, i.e. to prevent her being pooped.

Scull. One of a pair of fairly short oars (sculls) used by one oarsman, for propelling a boat.

Scull (to). To work an oar over the stern of a boat by describing a figure of eight with the blade in the water and propelling the boat forward.

Scuttle (to). Deliberately to sink a ship by opening sea cocks or by cutting holes in her shell below the waterline.

Sea kindly. A ship is said to be sea kindly when she characteristically possesses the ability to withstand heavy weather without violent rolling or pitching. A sea kindly ship has an easy motion in a seaway, but this does not necessarily make her safer or less safe than a ship which is not sea kindly. It does, however, make it more comfortable for those on board.

Seamanship.

1. A term applying to the art of handling ships in all conditions of weather.
2. The practical aspect of working a ship.

Searchlight. A powerful electric light with large reflector, visible over a long distance. When fitted with a shutter, it may be used for signalling. Searchlights are compulsory for vessels passing through the Suez Canal at night.

Seaward. Towards the sea or offing.

Seaworthiness certificate. A certificate issued by a surveyor of a classification society enabling a ship to proceed on her voyage after she has been involved in an accident, and, though not necessarily, which has been repaired temporarily or otherwise.

Seize. To bind, lash or otherwise secure one rope to another, to a spar, etc., using small stuff, or, in the case of wire, seizing wire.

Seizing wire. Galvanized annealed steel wire used for serving, and making seizings on, wire rope.

Selvedge. The finished edge of sail cloth or of any woven material. Also called selvage.

Senhouse slip. A short length of chain with a slip hook at one end, its purpose being to allow the end of the cable or boat gripes to be easily slipped in case of emergency.

Serve. Tightly, evenly, and neatly to bind a rope with spun yarn or marline.

Serving mallet. A cylindrical piece of ash or lignum vitae wood fitted with a handle and having a groove on one side to fit the convexity of a rope and used in serving ropes.

Set sail. To commence a voyage.

Set up. To tighten up rigging.

Sheer off. To move, or bear, away from.

Sheet. A rope or chain attached to one or both of the lower corners of a sail, and used to extend it or to change its direction. Sheets take their name from the sails they work, thus the main sheet works the mainsail, and the jib sheets the jib.

Sheets. Spaces in the extreme forward (bow sheets) and after (stern sheets) end of an open boat.

Shell. The outer casing of a wooden block. Side plates form the shell of metal blocks.

Shift. To change or move. To shift ship in port is to move her to another berth. A shift of wind is a particular change in the wind's direction—i.e. clockwise in the northern hemisphere, anti-clockwise in the southern.

Shifting boards. A fore-and-aft bulkhead made of loose planking, temporarily erected in the centre-line of a ship's lower hold to prevent grain, and in some cases solid ballast, from shifting.

Ship.
1. To put an object (rudder, for instance, in the case of an open boat) into its proper working position.
2. To bring on board, e.g. to ship stores, to ship a crew.

Shipping office. An office maintained by the D.T.I. in which crews are engaged and disengaged under the supervision of a Government-appointed marine superintendent. Also called Mercantile Marine Office.

Shipshape Neat and tidy; everything in its proper place.

Ship's number.
1. Four letters of the International Code assigned to every registered vessel by the national government to which she belongs. Also called signal letters.
2. A ship's Official Number is that allocated to a ship by the Registrar of Shipping, at the port at which she is to be registered, after she has been measured for tonnage by marine surveyors.

Short blast. A blast of about one second's duration on a whistle or siren.

Shorten sail. To reduce the amount of sail by reefing or furling.

Short-handed. Deficient in personnel; inadequately manned; without the correct complement.

Side lights. The red (port) and green (starboard) lights carried by vessels when under way.

Signal halyards. Light lines running through sheaves at the gaff end, masthead, jumper stay, etc., for hoisting flags, night signals, not-under-command and anchor shapes.

Signing off. Discharging the crew at the termination of a voyage, and paying wages due.

Signing on. Signing the Articles of Agreement by individual members of the crew preparatory to the commencement of a voyage. This formality must in Britain, except in unusual circumstances, take place before the superintendent of a Mercantile Marine Office; abroad a consular officer superintends.

Single-banked. When one oarsman sits on each pulling thwart a boat is said to be single-banked.

Single up. Strictly, to take in all bights of mooring lines preparatory to leaving a berth, but generally to reduce the number of mooring lines before casting off altogether.

Sister-ships. Ships built to the same general plans and specifications. In the marine insurance world ships belonging to the same owners are considered to be sister-ships.

Skipper. The official title of a certificated person in command of a fishing vessel.

Slack away. To pay out without losing control of the rope being handled.

Sling. Rope or chain straps used for securing any object for raising, lowering or shifting.

Slip (to). To let go suddenly and entirely. To slip the anchor is to let it go from the ship in an emergency.

Slip rope. A mooring line arranged so that it can be readily released from the ship.

Snotter. A length of manila rope or wire rope with an eye spliced in each end. It is used for slinging and other shipboard purposes.

Sounding rod. A graduated rod used to ascertain the depth of liquid in bilges, wells, peaks, tanks, etc.

Spar. A general term for a piece of timber of round section and of great length in proportion to its diameter. Booms, yards and gaffs are all spars.

Spirit compass. A form of mariner's compass in which the card floats in liquid, originally alcohol and distilled water.

Splice (to). To unite or join together by interweaving the end strands, two ropes or parts of the same rope.

Splicing fid. A tapered hardwood pin. It is used for opening up the strands of a rope.

Squeegee. An implement with a rubber or leather edge used for scraping water from wooden decks.

Standard compass. A magnetic compass used primarily as an azimuth compass, to which other magnetic compasses and all courses are referred and by which the ship is navigated when a gyro is not fitted. It is placed as remote as possible from magnetic influences and is adjusted with great care. There must be two magnetic compasses aboard all ships.

Stand by. To be in readiness. To be prepared to execute an order.

Stand clear. To keep out of the way.

Stand in. To come in towards.

Stand on. To continue on the same course. To maintain course and speed.

Statutory deck line. A horizontal line 305mm (12 in.) in length and 25½mm (1 in.) in breadth marked amidships on each side of the ship and from which freeboard is measured. Its upper edge passes through the point where the continuation outward of the upper surface of the freeboard deck intersects the outer surface of the shell plating.

Steer. To guide a vessel by means of a wheel, yoke-line or tiller.

Steering. The act of directing a ship on her course.

Steering compass. The magnetic compass placed near to the steering wheel, by which the course is steered.

Stem (to). To meet head on. To stem the tide is to head in a direction contrary to that of the tide.

Stern light. A white light carried at the stern as nearly as practicable on the same level as the side lights. It is visible for a distance of at least 1 mile.

Stern pipe. A hawsepipe fitted aft on the centre-line in some ships for housing a stockless stream anchor.

Stern rope. A mooring line leading aft and making an angle of less than 45 deg. with the fore-and-aft line of the ship.

Stop (to). To tie anything temporarily. To stop a sail is to tie it preparatory to setting it.

Stopper (to). To check or hold fast any rope or cable by means of a rope or chain stopper.

Stow. To take in or furl a sail, awning, etc. To stow cargo is to arrange it so that it will not shift. To stow away is to put in a safe place for future use.

Strop.

1. A ring of rope put round a block for suspending it or shackling it in place.
2. A length of rope with both ends spliced together which is used for attaching a tackle to anything for slinging a weight.

Substitute flag. An International Code flag used in a hoist to repeat one which precedes it.

Sweat. Condensation on metal surfaces below decks due to differences between the temperature of cargo or the compartment and the sea or air temperature.

Swinging. A ship's head is said to swing when its direction alters under the influence of helm, tide or wind.

Swinging the lead. A slang expression referring to the action of a seaman who will not 'pull his weight', in other words he 'dodges'; he swings the hand lead instead of heaving it—which calls for the expenditure of rather more energy. Hence a malingerer is referred to as a 'lead-swinger'.

Tab nab. Cake or bun served with afternoon tea.

Tabling. A strengthening border or hem around a sail, awning, weather-cloth, etc., to which the roping is sewn. It is made by turning over the edge of the canvas for an inch or so and sewing it down.

Tack (to). To alter the course of a vessel or boat under sail by bringing her head into the wind and then letting the wind fill her sails on the other side, the object being to make progress against the wind. Also called to go about, winding, staying.

Tally. Checking the record of another person with respect to the number of parcels, bags, bales, slings, etc., shipped on board. If both records agree they are said to tally. Loosely employed, the verb to tally is synonymous with to count.

Tanker. A vessel designed and constructed for the transportation of liquid cargoes in bulk. There are oil tankers, spirit tankers, molasses tankers, wine tankers, milk tankers and water tankers.

Thole pin. A wooden or steel peg fitting into a hole in a boat's gunwale to keep the oar in position when rowing. They may be fitted in pairs, in which case the loom of the oar lies between them, or singly when the oar is lightly held by a grommet fitted at the fulcrum and over the thole pin.

Thoroughfoot (to). To coil down a new rope against the lay, bringing the lower end up through the centre of the coil, and coiling down again with the lay, the object being to remove kinks and turns.

Throat.

1. The upper forward corner of a quadrilateral fore-and-aft sail where head and luff join.
2. That part of the shell of a block nearest the hook or eye.

Throat seizing. A round seizing made at the point where two ropes cross.

Thwart. An across, or athwart, bench in an open boat.

Timber loadline. A special loadline which may be prescribed for vessels carrying timber deck cargoes, on complying with certain rules. There are five timber loadlines, which vary according to the zones through which a timber-laden vessel passes, and the time of year or season at which she passes through them. They are:

1. Summer timber loadline marked L.S.
2. Winter timber loadline marked L.W.
3. Winter North Atlantic timber loadline marked L.W.N.A.
4. Tropical timber loadline marked L.T.
5. Fresh-water timber loadline marked L.F.

Tomming down. Holding down the top layer of cargo, such as case or baled goods in a ship's hold, by inserting a length of timber between a deck beam and the cargo and wedging it in place.

Topping lift bullrope. A flexible wire rope used for topping a cargo derrick. One end of the bullrope is shackled into a union plate which is shackled to the derrick span, and the hauling part is taken to the drum of the winch. When the derrick is in its topped position it is held by the span chain or the bullrope.

Topping lift tackle. The fall used as a lifting tackle for derricks either in conjunction with a span or as a combination of span and topping lift, obviating the necessity for a bullrope.

Toss. To throw oars into a perpendicular position, with blades fore and aft and grips resting on the bottom of the boat.

Tramp. A trading vessel—deep-sea or coastwise—which is not committed to any regular route but will go wherever shippers may order.

Trice. To draw up, shorten or tighten, a tricing line being used for this purpose.

Trim. The position at which a vessel floats with reference to the horizontal. To trim a boat is to balance her so that she lies on an even keel.

Trim by the head. A ship is said to trim or be down by the head when she draws more water forward than aft.

Trim by the stern. When a ship draws more water aft than forward, in other words when her forward draught is less than her after, she trims by, or is down by, the stern.

Turnbuckle. A contrivance for adjusting the length of shrouds, stays, and funnel guys. Better known, perhaps, as a rigging screw or bottle screw.

Two-blocks. A tackle is said to be two-blocks when one is hauled up close to the other and the power gained by the purchase is destroyed.

Twofold purchase. One made up of two double blocks with the standing and hauling parts at the same block. Also known as a double luff purchase.

Unfurl. To unroll or loosen from a furled condition, as in the case of a sail or a flag.

Unlash. To unfasten, or free something which has been lashed.

Unreeve. To withdraw ropes from sheaves or blocks.

Unseaworthy. A ship is said to be unseaworthy when it would be unsafe to send her to sea. She may be inadequately maintained, improperly loaded, or her equipment or personnel may be deficient in one way or another. It is the absolute duty of a shipowner in every contract of carriage and employment of persons to use 'due diligence' as far as making the ship seaworthy is concerned before she puts to sea.

Unship. To remove anything from its proper place. To unship the bowl of a compass is to lift it out of the gimbals. To unship the rudder of a lifeboat is to lift it clear of the gudgeons or rudder bar.

Up. The helm of a sailing vessel is up when her rudder is to leeward of the sternpost.

Up and down. An anchor cable is said to be up and down when the anchor is directly under the forefoot.

Vast. Same as avast, meaning to stop heaving.

Veer. To release or to pay out a greater length of cable or rope. To slack off and allow to run out.

Veer (to). The wind is said to veer when it changes direction with the sun, .e. from east through south to west; in other words a shift of wind in a clockwise direction. Veering is opposite to backing.

Wake. The track a vessel leaves astern of her on the surface of the water.

Walk back. To reverse the direction of a windlass drum, winch drum or capstan so as to ease up the rope around it.

Warp.
1. A rope by which something is dragged; a rope by which a vessel is shifted in port.
2. A lengthwise measurement of canvas.

Warp (to.) To shift ship from one berth to another by means of warps made fast ashore or to buoys or anchors.

Warping winch. A winch used for docking, mooring or warping purposes and usually located aft, its construction being similar to that of a cargo winch except that it may not have a centre barrel and the main shaft is extended and has a large drum at each end. Also called docking or mooring winch.

Watch aboard, watch ashore. A traditional system in North-East Coast colliers. The deck and engine-room departments are divided into two watches, one of which stays aboard and works the ship for the duration of her stay at loading or discharging ports—the watch aboard—while the other proceeds on leave as soon as she docks, and rejoins her shortly before sailing. It is frequently found aboard these ships, which ply between North-East England and the Thames, that one watch is comprised of northerners and the other of southerners, the latter being the watch aboard at loading ports and watch ashore at discharging ports, and vice versa.

Watch and watch. The system in which all or part of a ship's deck complement is divided into two watches and alternately each maintains a four-hour watch on deck followed by a four-hour watch below.

Watch below. The section of a ship's watchkeeping personnel who are off duty when sea or anchor watches are being maintained, those on duty being termed the watch on deck.

Waterborne. Supported by water; afloat.

Watertight. Impervious to the passage of water; thus compartments with watertight doors are effectively sealed against the entry of water when the doors are properly closed and secured.

Way. A vessel's motion through the water, headway being forward progress, sternway when she makes progress astern, leeway when she makes progress to leeward.

Way enough. A boating order denoting that the boat has sufficient way to reach her destination. The oarsmen take one more stroke then cease pulling after the order 'way enough' has been given.

Ways. The baulks of timber on which a ship is built or launched.

Wear (to.) The opposite to tacking. To put a sailing vessel or boat on another tack by putting the helm up and paying off her head before the wind.

Weather (to).
1. To lie in a storm. A ship is said to weather a storm when she has ridden safely through it.
2. To weather a vessel when sailing is to pass to windward of her.

Weather bound. Unable to leave port owing to adverse weather conditions.

Weather cloth. A canvas screen rigged to provide shelter for the lookout man on fo'c'sle head or crow's nest, or the officer on the bridge. Also called dodger.

Weather helm. A vessel is said to carry weather helm when the helm has to be kept over to the weather side to counteract her tendency to run up into the wind.

Weather shore. The land to windward, i.e. in the direction from which the wind is blowing.

Weather side. The side of the ship on which the wind is blowing. Opposite to lee side.

Weft. The width measurement of canvas.

Weigh (to). To lift the anchor from the ground.

Whelp.
1. One of a number of projecting ribs—usually there are four—on the barrel of a capstan and the warping drum of a windlass to provide a better grip for the mooring lines.
2. One of the sprockets on the gypsy of a windlass which engage the links of the cable.

Whip. A rope rove through a fixed single block for lifting light articles.

Whip (to).
1. To bind the end of a rope with twine to prevent it stranding and fraying.
2. To hoist by means of a whip.
3. To use the whipping barrel of a winch for discharging cargo.

Whipping twine. Small, two-thread flax cordage used for whipping purposes.

Wind rode. When the effect of the wind on a ship anchored in a tideway is greater than that of the tide, and the ship lies with the wind and against the tide, she is said to be wind rode.

Windsail. A long canvas funnel stiffened by loops or rings used to ventilate compartments below decks in fair-weather conditions. A windsail is fitted with two guys for trimming it into the wind, and keeping it in position.

Worm (to). Following the lay of a rope between strands with thin pieces of line to provide an even surface for the serving, or to prevent moisture from penetrating to the interior of a rope.

Yard. A tapered cylindrical spar suspended from a mast for supporting and extending a sail.

Yard boom. A derrick swung over the ship's side for loading or discharging cargo. When loading, the weight is lifted by the yard boom (or yard derrick, as it is sometimes called) until it is above bulwark or hatch coaming level, when the weight is transferred to the hatch boom and lowered into the hold. When discharging the weight is lifted by the hatch boom and lowered overside by the yard boom.

Yaw (to). To deviate from side to side of the course owing to bad steering.

INDEX

Anchors	108
Balls	191
Buoys	115
Cables	108
Chain	108
Foul Hawse	116
Hanging off	114
Ordinary or standing moor	116
Running moor	116
Securing	118
Shackles	110
Auxiliary steering gear	135
Azimuth mirror	123
Bells	27
Anchor	27
Fire	28
Fog	28
Lookout warning	29
Watch	27
Bends	42
Double sheet	42
Fisherman's	48
Heaving line	44
Reeving line	47
Sheet	42
Bilges	4
Blocks	71
Overhauling	71
Parts of wooden block	72
Snatch block	75
Steel block	75
Types of wooden blocks and fittings	73
Cable laid rope	34
Cargo spaces	96
Gear	79, 100
Holds	96
Stowage	96
Ventilation	98
Watching	99
Working	98
Chain	41
Breaking strain	41
Chernikeeff log	145
Clothing	31
Compass	119
Accessories	127
Auxiliaries	127
Boxing the	124
Division into degrees	125
Dry	119
Gyro	126
Liquid	122

Magnetic	119
Reflector	123
Course recorder	129
Deck Stores	179, 184
Bees wax	190
Boat rope	185
Bottle screws	186
Buckets	188
Bulldog grip	187
Burlap	188
Cement	189
Chain hook	187
Chain stopper	186
Cold set	188
Discharge covers	188
Dummy gantline	184
Emery Paper	184
Eyelets	190
Fenders	188
Fids	190
Funnels	188
Gantline	184
Grease	190
Grease gun	190
Guest warp	185
Heaving lines	185
Lead block	186
Marline	189
Messenger	184
Needles	190
Oakum	188
Packing	190
Palms	190
Pilot ladder	185
Port holes	190
Pumice stone	184
Punch and die	189
Putty	189
Rat guard	188
Rigging screws	187
Rope stopper	186
Rope yarns	189
Sail hook	190
Sail twine	190
Sand	189
Sand paper	184
Seizing wire	186
Senhouse slip	187
Serving board	189
Serving mallet	189
Shackles	186
Snatch block	186
Sounding rods	188
Spanners	190

Deck Stores—*cont.*
Spikes ... 189
Spun yarn ... 189
Stockholm tar ... 184
Tail block ... 186
Thimbles ... 189
Ventilator covers ... 189
Ventilator plugs ... 189
Waste ... 184
Wheel spanners ... 190
White lead ... 184
Wire grip ... 187
Derrick rigs ... 79
Hallen ... 84
Preparing and raising ... 80
Stuelcken ... 84
Swinging Derrick with
'deadman' ... 83
Union purchase ... 82
Direction finder repeater ... 128
Draught, reading the ... 177
Dunnage ... 96

Etiquette ... 31

Fire appliances ... 155
Directions for use of rocket
lifesaving apparatus ... 171
Drill in closing of doors, side
scuttles etc. ... 166
Extinguishers ... 161
General rules ... 158
alternative appliances ... 161
breathing apparatus 161, 165, 166
fire buckets ... 159
fire hoses ... 159
fire-smothering gas or steam ... 160
portable fire extinguishers ... 159
pumps ... 156, 158
safety lamps ... 161
water service pipes ... 159
Line-throwing appliances ... 168
Provision of ... 155
Smoke helmets ... 161, 165
Tankers—use of rocket line-
throwing apparatus ... 173
Fire drill ... 165, 167

Ground tackle ... 108
Anchor cables ... 108
Anchor chains ... 108
Anchor shackles ... 110
Windlass ... 111
Gyro compass ... 126
Equipment ... 127
Gyro pilot ... 129

Hatches ... 89
Covering ... 89
Handling of ... 90
Stripping ... 90
Hawser-laid-rope ... 33

Heavy weather ... 197
Hitches ... 42
Blackwall ... 49
Clove ... 44
Marline spike ... 47
Rolling ... 44
Round turn and two half ... 42
Timber ... 44
Two half ... 42
Holds ... 96
Cleaning ... 96
Ventilation ... 98
Hooks ... 76
Cargo ... 76

Knots ... 42
Blackwall hitch ... 49
Bowline ... 44
Bowline on a bight ... 46
Cat's paw ... 48
Clove hitch ... 44
Crown ... 48
Double sheet bend ... 42
Fisherman's bend ... 48
Heaving line bend ... 44
Marline spike hitch ... 47
Overhand ... 42
Reef ... 42
Rolling hitch ... 44
Round turn and two half
hitches ... 42
Running bowline ... 46
Sheepshank ... 44
Sheet bend ... 42
Timber hitch ... 44
Two half hitches ... 42

Leads ... 141
Hand ... 148
Soundings ... 149
Lifesaving services, signals for ... 170
Lights ... 190
Anchor ... 190
Emergency navigation ... 190
Not under command ... 190
Portable ... 191
Load line ... 174
Agreements with crew ... 177
Certificates ... 176
Marking of ... 174
Rules ... 174
Submersion of ... 176
Log ... 141
Chernikeeff ... 145
Electric ... 141
Register ... 141
Shoe ... 141
Towing ... 142
Lookout ... 27

Magnetic compass 119
Maintenance 179
  Bilges 180
  Chipping and scaling 179
  Cleaning 179
  Double bottom tanks 180
  Fresh water tanks 180
  Washing 179
  Wood sheathed decks 179
Manning 22–32
  Catering department 25
  Deck department 22
  Engine department 24
  Radio department 26
Mooring 152
Mousing, a hook 54
  A shackle 55

Nylon rope 36

Oil tankers 15, 100
  Axia fan 102
  Butterworth tank washing
    machine 101
  De-rusting 103
  Dip can 105
  Dobbie McInnes teledip tank
    gauging instrument 104
  Fire-fighting 165
  Flexible hoses 100
  Gas freeing 102
  Hose saddles 102
  Hydrometer 105
  Measuring jar 105
  Meco fan 102
  Mine Safety Appliance Com-
    pany's 'Explosimeter' 102
  Novita oxygen equipment 104
  Saftey lines 101
  Safety on board 107
  Scaling 103
  Suction valves 106
  Tank cleaning 100
  Tank lids 104
  Tank loading 104
  Tank wash apertures 100
  Temperatures and samples 106
  Thermometer 105
  Ullaging 104
  Use of rocket line-throwing
    apparatus 173
  Victor Pyrate tank washing
    machine 101
  Washing machines 100
  Whessoe tank gauge 104
  Windsail 102
Oils 183
  Boiled linseed 184
  Cans 190
  Colza 184
  Fish oil 184
  Lubricating 190

Paraffin 184
  Raw linseed 183
  Terebine 183
  Turpentine 183

Paint 181
  Anti-corrosive 182
  Anti-fouling 182
  Bitumastic 181
  Boot topping 182
  Finishing 181
  Funnel 181
  Green 181
  Hull 181
  Metal primer 181
  Signal red 181
  Silverine 181
  Topside 181
  Undercoat 181
  Varnish 183
Paint brushes 182
  Binding 182
  Flat 182
  Lining 182
  Oval 182
  Pencil 182
  Roller 183
  Sash 182
  Spray 183
  Stencil 183
  Tar 182
Painting signal yard 51
Parcelling 70
Pre-formed wire rope 39

Repeater 128
  Bearing 128
  Direction finder 128
  Steering 127
Rigging 50
  a bosun's chair 50
  a stage 49
  to ride a stay 51
Rope 33
  Breaking strain 41
  Care of 40
  Combined steel and fibre 40
  Fibre 33
  Lays of 33
  Manufacture of 33
  Measuring gauge 41
  Nylon 36
  Pre-formed wire 39
  Stoppering 154
  Strength of 41
  Wire 38
  Working load of 41

Safety 192
  Accommodation ladder 194
  Belts 195
  Blowbacks 196

Safety—*cont.*
Bosun's chair   50, 194
Cargo   196
Chipping   194
Decks   194
Engine room plates   196
Gangways   193
Gauge glass covers   196
Hand ladders   194
Hand rails   196
Hand tools   196
Hatch covers   195
Holds   195
Lines   195
Rope ladders   194
Staging   49, 195
Tools and loose parts   196
Seizing wire   40
Seizings   57
Flat   58
Racking   58
Round   58
Throat   58
Serving   70
Shackles, types of   76
Sheaves, types of   74
Shortening a strop   54
Shroud-laid rope   34
Signals, lifesaving services   170
Slinging   52
Soundings   149
Splicing   60
Rope   60
cut   63
dogging the ends   62
eye   60
short   63
tools for   60
Wire   64
making a fivetuck thimble
splice in a right hand ordinary lay six strand wire rope   68
splicing an eye   64
Steel hatch covers   92

Steering   137
Helm orders   139
Steering gear   131
Auxiliary   135
Telemotor   131
Wheel   131

Tackle   76
Double luff   77
Double whip   77
Ground   108
Handy billy   77, 186
Luff tackle   77
Reeving a threefold purchase   78
Single whip   77
Threefold purchase   77
Telemotor   131
Towing log   142
Types of vessels   79
Bulk carriers   79
Cargo liners   79
Container vessels   80
Side loaders   79
Tramps   79
Roll-on roll-off   80
Refrigerated   19

Ventilators   99

Watch duties at sea   28
In port   30
Watchkeeping   28
Whipping   55
Winch   85
Driving   86
Electric   86
Steam   86
Windlass   111
Heaving anchor   111
Letting go anchor   111
Maintenance and upkeep   113
Warping   113
Wire ropes   38
Boulevant or five tuck splice   68
Breaking strain of   41
Worming   70